STUDIA LITTERARUM UPSALIENSIA

Editores:

Victor Svanberg et Gunnar Tideström

SCANDINAVIAN UNIVERSITY BOOKS

J. W. Cappelens Forlag, Oslo / Gyldendalske Boghandel-Nordisk Forlag, København
Svenska Bokförlaget-P. A. Norstedt & Söner–Albert Bonnier, Stockholm
Akateeminen Kirjakauppa-Akademiska Bokhandeln, Helsingfors
William Heinemann Ltd., London, Melbourne, Toronto

STUDIA LITTERARUM UPSALIENSIA · I

Time and Eternity

A STUDY IN
THE STRUCTURE AND SYMBOLISM
OF

T. S. Eliot's Four Quartets

BY

STAFFAN BERGSTEN

SVENSKA BOKFÖRLAGET / *Bonniers* / *Stockholm*

J. W. CAPPELENS FORLAG / *Oslo*
GYLDENDALSKE BOGHANDEL / NORDISK FORLAG / *København*
AKATEEMINEN KIRJAKAUPPA / AKADEMISKA BOKHANDELN / *Helsingfors*
WILLIAM HEINEMANN LTD. / *London* / *Melbourne* / *Toronto*

Printed in Sweden

BERLINGSKA BOKTRYCKERIET
LUND 1960

To Gunilla

Preface

"Poetry", Eliot writes, "is a constant reminder of all the things that can only be said in one language, and are untranslatable". To this it might be added that poetry can be fully understood only by those who speak the same language as the poet. But Eliot also emphasizes the function of poetry as a means of "spiritual communication between people and people", and much of the critical literature on Eliot shows that his poetry fulfils this function. In this book I have concentrated on such aspects of Eliot's *Four Quartets* as seem most readily available to a foreigner and hence I have been chiefly concerned with intellectual understanding and with the tracing of a wider, international background.

From the very beginning of my study of Eliot, my work has been supervised and guided by my greatly respected teacher, Professor Gunnar Tideström. His advice and help has been as generous as it has been kindly and behind the discipline of the scholar I have always felt the encouragement and sympathy of the friend. I take this opportunity to express my deep gratitude.

I have also had the benefit of the wisdom of several scholars with a special knowledge of the various subjects I have treated, and I wish to express my gratitude to Professor H. W. Donner, Professor Carl-Martin Edsman, Professor Konrad Marc-Wogau and Professor Victor Svanberg.

I also wish to thank Dr. Gunnar Boklund, Dr. Olov Fryckstedt, Dr. Erik Frykman, Dr. Sven Linnér and Mr. Peter Malekin for valuable criticism, and Miss Tina Pierce for her help with the proofreading.

My thanks are also due to Mr. George Campbell for his many suggestions with regard to the style and arrangement of the work. Without his invaluable help this book would have been completed long ago.

Uppsala, March 22, 1960. *S. B.*

Contents

Introduction

Written between 1934 and 1942, T. S. Eliot's *Four Quartets* belong to a period in the poet's mature life when he had developed a poetic style and technique of his own. Though rooted in Eliot's personal experience, these poems also reflect his wide and varied reading and thought, and the emotional and the intellectual elements are integrated into a whole by means of a complex poetic structure.

The subject of the *Four Quartets* can be defined in various ways. From the very outset, however, the poet emphasizes one particular theme – the theme of time:

> Time present and time past
> Are both perhaps present in time future,
> And time future contained in time past.
> ("Burnt Norton" I)

This theme is gradually developed in "Burnt Norton" and the subsequent *Quartets*, and it is also contrasted and interrelated with another theme – that of timeless eternity. The antithesis of time and eternity may be regarded as a symbol of two different aspects of Eliot's experience as man and poet, a symbol which in its wider application comes to cover two in his view fundamental aspects of human life and history in general. It is also an antithesis which is basic to the very structure of the *Quartets*. It is the aim of the present study to analyse this antithesis both as a poetic theme and as a structural principle in the *Quartets* and, as a means to this end, to study the sources of the theme in the literary and philosophical tradition to which Eliot belongs.

It is thus the intellectual analysis of the *Four Quartets* that is the chief concern of this study. But analysis of this kind is not always enough. There are elements in the *Quartets* which seem to point beyond the poems themselves to the personal situation of the poet, to some special experiences he seems to have had. In pursuing such externals, the critic often has to resort to conjectures and suggestions which, though supported by probability, can seldom be based on absolute evidence. The relation between an author and his work and the process of artistic creation, are things of which very little can be known for certain and yet it is sometimes necessary to make suggestions concerning these things in order to solve problems of interpretation. A critic who set himself the task of making a thorough interpretation of poetry such as the *Four Quartets* without saying anything that could not be supported by undisputable evidence, would probably find himself with nothing but the obvious left to be said. However, since very little is known of Eliot's life and inner experience, any suggestion concerning their influence on the *Quartets* must be tentative. But as regards his cultural environment and tradition, a great deal may be affirmed with reasonable certainty. Of the outlining of this wider background something should be said here.

The interest devoted during the present century to the problem of time has gone to such lengths that certain critics have considered themselves justified in speaking of an "obsession" with the idea of time.[1] This obsession does not originate in poetry or fiction, however, but is prompted by the contemporary development in science, philosophy and psychology; the two best known representatives of this development are no doubt Einstein and Bergson. The literary effect of this interest in time is perhaps most noticeable in fiction – it is, for example, clearly distinguishable in the novels of Marcel Proust, Thomas Mann and Virginia Woolf – but it may be observed in poetry as well. In considering the theme of time in Eliot's *Four Quartets*, this background – scientific, philosophical and literary – should be taken into account, and though primarily concerned with the *Four Quartets* in themselves, the present study may perhaps also throw some light on a striking feature of contemporary literature in general.[2]

[1] See Mendilow, A. A., *Time and the Novel*, London, 1952, p. 3.

[2] The problem of time in contemporary literature has been instructively discussed by Hans Meyerhoff in his *Time in Literature*, Berkeley / Los Angeles, 1955.

Eliot is not wholly representative, however, of the majority of writers who have been influenced by the discussion of time during the beginning of this century. Though undoubtedly important factors in arousing Eliot's interest in the problem of time, the modern scientific and philosophical theories of time can hardly be said to have supplied him with the ideas that are to be found in his poetry. The effect of these theories seems rather to have been to direct Eliot's attention towards the theories of time in ancient philosophy, Eastern as well as Western. The authors of these theories are often mystics as much as they are philosophers, and they may be regarded as forming a kind of intellectual and spiritual tradition; this tradition is an important element in the background of the *Four Quartets*. Moreover, the idea of a timeless eternity, so significant in the *Quartets*, is to be found everywhere within this tradition, whereas it is often completely neglected, or abandoned altogether, by modern philosophers and scientists. As regards the excursions, for these reasons made in the present study, into the history of philosophy, one thing should be made clear. There is no intention here of giving an account of the various theories of time and eternity as they appear in the history of philosophy, but merely of emphasizing such aspects of these theories as seem to have influenced Eliot and of drawing attention to such images and metaphors as reappear in the *Four Quartets*. It is a question of trying to see the philosophic issues through the eye of the poet.

It is obvious, then, that in following various indications in the *Quartets* back to their sources in a literary and philosophical tradition, the critic must necessarily venture into domains beyond the frontiers of ordinary literary criticism. These ventures have in the present study been facilitated by the fact that others have gone before, and this debt must here be acknowledged.

Although the *Four Quartets* have been published for less than twenty years, they have already given rise to a comprehensive critical literature, frequently in the form of running commentaries on

The outline that follows later of the general discussion of the problem of time during the twentieth century, is based on a bibliography of the literature on time compiled by the present author and available at Litteraturhistoriska Institutionen, Univ. of Uppsala.

each poem. These commentaries range from inconsiderable reviews to elaborate studies, from trifling observations to searching analyses, sometimes separately conceived and sometimes integrated with a sustained study of Eliot's work as a whole. It is of course the duty of anyone writing on the *Quartets* to go through as much as he possibly can of this critical literature, comprising some two or three hundred books, theses, essays, articles and reviews, but it can hardly be considered his duty to comment upon them all, to give his reasons for citing some and neglecting others, or even to list them in an exhaustive bibliography. It should be sufficient here to mention a few of the most important studies on Eliot's more recent poetry; others are referred to in the course of this study.

F. O. Matthiessen's *The Achievement of T. S. Eliot*, first published in 1935, and in 1947 enlarged to include a study of the *Quartets*, is in many respects the basis of much subsequent criticism. As the first complete survey of the work, ideas and background of Eliot, it is still most valuable. Helen Gardner, perhaps more sensitive than Matthiessen to the spiritual qualities of the *Quartets*, made an important contribution to the understanding of these poems with *The Art of T. S. Eliot* (1949). Though characterized more by a devout enthusiasm than by critical discernment, Raymond Preston's *"Four Quartets" Rehearsed* (1946) is a very detailed and useful commentary. Of an altogether different kind is Kristian Smidt's *Poetry and Belief in the Work of T. S. Eliot* (1949), the first and still the only really systematic study of Eliot's work; the second chapter especially of the present study is greatly indebted to Smidt's book.

It is not altogether easy to estimate the collected achievement of Eliot's critics. At the very least it may be said that they have introduced the poet and his work to a wider public, outlined his intellectual and literary development, considered isolated points from a more scholarly aspect and supplied abundant commentaries on separate works. The majority of the books on Eliot are devoted to his work as a whole and analyses of particular aspects of his work have mainly been confined to shorter essays. The most useful contribution to the critical study of Eliot's poetry at the present moment therefore seems to be a detailed and thorough analysis of a limited part of his work on a particular aspect of major significance. Attempting such an analysis and selecting the theme of time and eternity as the major aspect of the *Four Quartets,* the present author has hoped to achieve something more than special elucidation of the poems. By considering the idea of time and eternity in the *Quartets,* not merely as a poetic motif, but as basic to the very structure of the poems, he has hoped to solve some of the fundamental problems involved in the interpretation of the *Quartets.*

The theme of time in Eliot's work has already been discussed by a number of critics and scholars, which is natural enough in view of the prominence of this theme in Eliot's work. In shorter essays this aspect has been studied by Lloyd Frankenberg, Hideo Funato, Lars Roar Langslet, Reid MacCallum and Morris Weitz, none of whom have gone far beyond introductory observations.[3] Of a different kind are the dissertations by Fritz Bohnsack and Ilse Strömsdörfer who, representing a different tradition of criticism and scholarship, tend rather to overstress the systematic approach by attempting to elicit a consistent philosophy of time and eternity from Eliot's poetic and dramatic work.[4] There also seems to be a tendency to consider the value of this supposed philosophy apart from its function within Eliot's work and thereby to go rather beyond the domain of literary criticism. There are, however, many observations and suggestions by these and other writers that have stimulated the author of this study.

In conclusion something should perhaps be said of the plan of the present work. In order to avoid distracting excursions into the literary, philosophical and religious background of the poems in the course of the continuous interpretation of the *Four Quartets,* such interpretation is withheld until the last chapters, which are based

[3] Frankenberg, L., "Time and Mr. Eliot", in *Pleasure Dome: On Reading Modern Poetry,* Cambridge (Mass.), 1949, pp. 39–117; Funato, H., "T. S. Eliot's Idea of Time", *Rikkyo Review* (Tokyo), No. 16, 1955, pp. 19–51; Langslet, L. R., "Tidsopplevelsen i Eliots 'Four Quartets'", *Kirke og Kultur* (Oslo), Vol. 61, 1956, pp. 609–614; MacCallum, R., "Time Lost and Regained", in the author's *Imitation and Design and Other Essays,* ed. by W. Blissett, Toronto, 1953, pp. 132–161; Weitz, M., "T. S. Eliot: Time as a Mode of Salvation", *Sewanee Review,* Vol. 60, 1952, pp. 48–64.

[4] Bohnsack, F., *Zeit und Ewigkeit im Spätwerk T. S. Eliots. Versuch einer Deutung,* unpublished diss., Hamburg, 1951; Strömsdörfer, I., *Der Begriff der Zeit bei T. S. Eliot,* unpublished diss., München, 1957.

on the results achieved in the previous chapters. This has inevitably meant leading the reader through a great deal of rather abstruse background material before arriving at the real subject of the study. This will, it is hoped, contribute to the unity of the last chapters.

CHAPTER I

The Theme of Time in Eliot's Early Work

I

"The sense of the past [. . .] You said it was the thing in life you desired most to arrive at, and that wherever you had found it – even where it was supposed to be most vivid and inspired – it had struck you as deplorably lacking intensity." [1]

These words are addressed to Ralph Pendrel in Henry James' unfinished novel, *The Sense of the Past*, published posthumously in 1917. The words themselves and the context of the novel form a not inappropriate introduction to a study of T. S. Eliot. The novel is a strange story, mingling acute psychological observation with a fantastic and bewildering plot; it is a wild construction and at the same time a personal document. Ralph Pendrel, a thirty-year-old New Englander of good family, well educated and with an attractive personality, is a perfectly normal young man but for one thing: his uncommonly keen sense of the past. His determination to develop this sense fully is frustrated by his New England background, which in spite of its superficial refinement seems to lack real tradition and history. His attempt to compensate for the deficiency of his environment by immersing himself in historical studies, stimulates him to write an "Essay in Aid of the Reading of History", with the result that his sense of loneliness and of estrangement from his compatriots is heightened. His sole hope of realizing his ambition lies in going to Europe where the past is still alive, manifestly coexisting with the present in the old and venerable cities. It then so happens that Ralph Pendrel inherits an old house in London. Immediately upon his arrival there he is thrown into a series of happenings which exceed

[1] James, H., *The Sense of the Past*, ed. by P. Lubbock, London, 1917, p. 32.

his wildest hopes and aspirations. He not only attains the full realization of his sense of the past, but finds himself carried in some strange way a hundred years back in time to the London of the early nineteenth century, where he becomes involved in a love affair with a society beauty. With subtle irony James makes this flowering beauty both more vital and less sensitive than Ralph, who cannot feel quite at home either in the present or the past. At this point James' story was left incomplete by his death. We are not told how Ralph manages to return again to the twentieth century.

The fragment as it stands is nevertheless quite sufficient to reveal that James was trying to express the effect of the shortcomings of the New World on a young and sensitive soul, and the needs these created – needs that would be met neither in the past nor present, but only in terms of something much more profound. The effect of the novel on its readers was intended to be something like the effect of *The Turn of the Screw*, according to James' own notes for the novel.[2] Ralph Pendrel's strange adventure is an extended metaphor of the inner reaction of a young man from the New World suddenly confronted with the historical memorials and living tradition of an old European city. Ralph is the last in a long line of heroes in James' novels who leave America to search for true refinement and a sense of tradition; to search for their own past, in fact, since they were, in many cases, the descendants of old English families. Ralph's ready adjustment to the past into which he is thrown, is in part explained by his natural connection with his new environment: he comes to London as the heir of the last member of the English branch of the Pendrel family, and had it not been for his forebears' emigrating to America, he would never have been cut off from the stem of European civilization.

Eliot read *The Sense of the Past* soon after its appearance and in 1918 he described it as marking the expression of the culmination of James' psychological insight, though by no means his best novel.[3] In Eliot's praise of James' psychological insight a feeling of recognition may well be surmised.

[2] Ibid., p. 300.

[3] "On Henry James", *The Question of Henry James*, ed. by F. W. Dupee, London, 1947, p. 132.

Very little is known of Eliot's private life at that time, but what is known suggests a certain affinity between him and Ralph Pendrel. The descendant of an old English family that emigrated to New England in the seventeenth century, Eliot left his native country after having assimilated the best it had to offer in the way of education, and at the age of about thirty he settled down in London, successfully striving to adjust himself to his new cultural environment and working on a literary program centred on the concept of tradition. Ralph Pendrel, James tells us, put down his thoughts on tradition and the sense of the past in his "Essay in Aid of the Reading of History", and in 1919 Eliot wrote his famous literary manifesto, "Tradition and the Individual Talent".

This parallel between Ralph Pendrel and Eliot is perhaps incidental, but Eliot's relation to Henry James, Pendrel's creator, is rather more essential. Like James, and the characters he created, Eliot left America in order to settle in Europe, seeming to prefer the sensibility and tradition of the Old World to the New. Eliot himself, in his essay on James (1918) significantly extends the parallel to Nathaniel Hawthorne and suggests that the tendency to turn from the New to the Old World is no new thing in American literature. Since nothing is known of Eliot's more personal motives for leaving America, the parallel to Ralph Pendrel and Henry James is here intended as a suggestion rather than as an explanation. But as an illustration of a tendency in American literature, it is of special interest.

An attempt to explain the nature and causes of this tendency as it is reflected in the lives and works of these three writers, has been made by F. O. Matthiessen in his *American Renaissance*. His idea is that a harsh Calvinist heritage in men of their intellectual temperament tended to increase their self-consciousness and feeling of loneliness. They thus felt themselves alienated from their less sensitive compatriots, and consequently turned to the Old World, the home of their ancestors. There they could lose their loneliness and individualism in a deeper tradition, and make up for the feeling of remoteness from the present by developing their sense of the past.[4] It is difficult to tell what motives were the dominant ones in Eliot's

[4] Matthiessen, F. O., *American Renaissance*, Oxford Univ. Press, 1941, pp. 292 ff., 351–368.

case, but there is much to suggest that a personal demand for intellectual and spiritual stability lies behind his attitude towards tradition. But although successfully acclimatized in Europe, Eliot seems never to have renounced his American heritage, and in his search for origins and meaning in the *Four Quartets* he also returns to the America of his childhood and youth.

The essay, "Tradition and the Individual Talent" (1919), seems primarily a literary manifesto proclaiming an anti-romantic, impersonal doctrine of literature, but it is also one of the very few works in which Eliot directly deals with the problems of tradition, history and time in discursive terms. In spite of his long academic study of philosophy he usually avoids approaching such complex matters from a purely theoretical point of view, and prefers to give an oblique, poetical rendering of his speculations on time. Tradition, for Eliot, rests on the historical sense, "and the historical sense involves a perception, not only of the pastness of the past, but of its presence".[5] In its more personal aspects this sense seems closely related to Ralph Pendrel's sense of the past, but in its particular application to literature it becomes a criterion of classicism in Eliot's sense of the word; the historical sense is set against the romantic doctrine of originality or divine inspiration. Thus Eliot's theory of tradition appears, at first sight, to be a matter of literary taste and sympathies, but he proceeds one step further, subtly shifting his ground from subjective predilections to the idea of an objective order:

> The existing monuments [of art] form an ideal order among themselves, which is modified by the introduction of the new (the really new) work of art among them. The existing order is complete before the new work arrives; for order to persist after the supervention of novelty, the *whole* existing order must be, if ever so slightly, altered; and so the relations, proportions, values of each work of art toward the whole are readjusted; and this is conformity between the old and the new. Whoever has approved this idea of order, of the form of European, of English literature will not find it preposterous that the past should be altered by the present as much as the present is directed by the past.[6]

[5] *Selected Essays*, 3rd ed., p. 14.
[6] Ibid., p. 15.

This passage may be interpreted in either of two ways. On a very simple and obvious level it can be taken to mean that in the mind of the poet or critic there is a constant interplay between past and present, that the critic's evaluation of the literary works of art of the past is modified by his reading of new books. Thus interpreted, the idea, far from being "preposterous", is almost a platitude. But Eliot speaks of an "ideal" order, not of a psychological pattern, and by ascribing an objective existence to this order he leaves the realm of literary criticism and approaches the frontier of metaphysics. A similar ambiguity is prevalent in Eliot's statement that "this historical sense, which is a sense of the timeless as well as of the temporal and of the timeless and the temporal together, is what makes a writer traditional".[7] It is not quite clear what is meant by the timeless in this context. Eliot may refer to the timelessness of permanent values, but he may also have had in mind a conception of the timeless belonging to the same realm of thought as the "ideal order". In the last paragraph of the essay on tradition Eliot affirms that "This essay proposes to halt at the frontier of metaphysics or mysticism, and confine itself to such practical conclusions as can be applied by the responsible person interested in poetry".[8] Whether he does halt at that frontier is doubtful, and in any case the very fact that he approaches it is sufficient to make his readers ask themselves what kind of metaphysics might have been expected, had he crossed his self-imposed frontier.

The search for a literary doctrine that may have influenced the ideas of time and the timeless in Eliot's essay on tradition, leads back to French Symbolism. It may be questionable whether that movement involved any coherent philosophy of art, but in their speculations on the nature of the literary symbol, the Symbolist poets, and even more their critics, became involved in metaphysical categories. This is in particular true of Arthur Symons' *The Symbolist Movement in Literature* (1899), to which work Eliot owes his first acquaintance with the French Symbolists.[9] Symons' definition of the literary symbol is contained in a quotation from Carlyle:

[7] Ibid., p. 14.

[8] Ibid., pp. 21 f.

[9] See Smidt, K., *Poetry and Belief in the Work of T. S. Eliot*, Oslo, 1949, p. 28.

> In the Symbol proper, what we can call a Symbol, there is ever, more or less distinctly and directly, some embodiment and revelation of the Infinite; the Infinite is made to blend itself with the Finite, to stand visible, and as it were, attainable there.[10]

Substituting time for the Finite, and eternity, or the timeless, for the Infinite, a vague relation to Eliot's theory of tradition may be discerned, but on the whole the above definition is too much coloured by what Eliot would call romanticism to be acceptable to him. And yet it points in the right direction: derived from Carlyle, Symons' notion of the symbol is indirectly related to German philosophy of the Romantic period, and Eliot's philosophical outlook shortly before 1920 seems to have been dominated by the English Idealist school, and in particular by F. H. Bradley who built on the foundations laid by German metaphysicians.

In the philosophical systems of Bradley, Royce, MacTaggart, Taylor and others of the same school, Eliot was confronted with a conception of time as an illusory deception of the sensuous world and of eternity as the essence of the semi-religious Absolute,[11] and Eliot's conception of an "ideal order" may perhaps owe something to the Idealist conception of the Absolute.[12] If this is the case, it is not difficult to understand why he preferred to halt at the frontier of metaphysics, since to go beyond it would have meant raising issues other than the "practical conclusions" with which Eliot here concerns himself. Fifteen years later, however, he did not shrink from giving much fuller expression to an Idealist doctrine of time and the timeless in his poetry.

So far, "Tradition and the Individual Talent" has been considered

[10] Symons, A., *The Symbolist Movement in Literature*, London, 1899, pp. 4 f.

[11] For a systematic treatment of the time philosophy of the Idealist school, see A. Gunn, *The Problem of Time*, London, 1929.

[12] Cf. Josiah Royce's conception of an "Eternal order": "I declare that this same temporal world is, when regarded in its wholeness, an Eternal order. And I mean by this assertion nothing whatever but that the whole real content of this temporal order, whether it is viewed from any one temporal instant as past or as present or as future, is *at once* known, *i.e.* is consciously experienced as a whole, by the Absolute." *The World and the Individual*, II, New York, 1901, p. 138. (Royce was one of Eliot's teachers of philosophy at Harvard; see Kristian Smidt, p. 31.)

against Eliot's background both as a philosopher with certain definite views and as an emigrant from the New World. In these senses, the essay is not only an affirmation of positive demands and beliefs, but a rejection of contrary opinions. It is manifestly opposed to purely subjective emotionalism in poetry and in life, and probably owes something to his former teacher at Harvard, Irving Babbitt. To some extent, too, these views may represent a reaction to Henri Bergson's view of time, which, at the time the essay was written, was attracting considerable attention in England. It is interesting to note that Babbitt, in 1919 in his *Rousseau and Romanticism*, characterized Bergson as a typical exponent of the disastrous heritage of Rousseau, the chief source of romantic subjectivism.[13]

Eliot's doctrine of tradition may be interpreted as a rejection of Bergson's doctrine of time. From his first work, *Les données immédiates de la conscience* (1889; the English translation, *Time and Free Will*, appeared in 1910), the concept of time is a central theme in Bergson's philosophy and a vital point in his doctrine of the "creative evolution". For Bergson time, or duration, is the very essence of life, and the only real thing is the present, which contains the past as a living recollection. Outside a given mind at a given moment the past does not exist. Time is thus, for Bergson, equal to the psychological experience of time, and nothing else. The concept of time employed in science is a false conception involving a "spatialization" of time. The picture of time as a straight line divided into past and future by a point called the present is an adaptation of spatial categories to time, brought about by the analytic intellect, which is the negative principle in Bergson's thought. Real time, the *durée réelle*, is psychic duration, and cannot be pictured or measured by the intellect. Now Eliot's "ideal order", involving a constant reorganization of the past and consequently assuming the objective existence of the past outside a given mind, is fundamentally opposed to the *durée réelle*, and Bergson would no doubt have classified Eliot's concept of tradition among the false, "spatializing" concepts of time.

This opposition to Bergson seems on Eliot's part to be deliberate and conscious. He was well acquainted with Bergson's philosophy, and had taken his stand against it. In 1911 he attended Bergson's

[13] Babbitt, I., *Rousseau and Romanticism*, Boston, 1919, p. 364.

lectures at the Sorbonne,[14] and "The Love Song of J. Alfred Prufrock", written at that very period in Eliot's life, seems to owe something to Bergson. Many years later Eliot significantly stated that his "only conversion, by the deliberate influence of any individual, was a temporary conversion to Bergsonism".[15] Thus Eliot may well have felt himself guilty of some kind of apostasy when writing "Tradition and the Individual Talent". Nevertheless the more positive influence of Bergson is noticeable in much of Eliot's later poetry as well, but for the moment only the negative influence will be considered.

There are two obvious reasons why Eliot may have disapproved of Bergson's philosophy. First, because of its subjective, anti-intellectual "romanticism", of which the particular time philosophy is but one aspect; and secondly, he may have disapproved of it on purely philosophical grounds. It may have been Bertrand Russell's severe criticism of Bergson's thought in 1912 that opened Eliot's eyes to its formal weakness, since Russell was one of his teachers of philosophy at Harvard,[16] but Eliot's specific rejection of Bergson's ideas in 1919 had other and more obvious reasons than the laying of a ghost of his own past. By then Bergsonism was established in England, and Eliot's affirmation of his own standards of criticism involved, of necessity, a censure of all that Bergson stood for. Bergson's more significant works had been translated into English before the first world war, and the scholarly interest in his philosophy, as reflected in the philosophical journals, reached its peak during the first years of the war.[17]

[14] Matthiessen, F. O., *The Achievement of T. S. Eliot*, 2nd ed., Oxford Univ. Press, 1947, p. 183.

[15] *A Sermon Preached in Magdalene College Chapel*, Cambridge, 1948, p. 5.

[16] See C. Bell, "How Pleasant to Know Mr Eliot", *T. S. Eliot. A Symposium from C. Aiken et al.*, ed. by R. March and Tambimuttu, London, 1948, p. 15. The major part of Russell's highly critical exposition of Bergson's philosophy in *History of Western Philosophy*, London, 1946, was published in *The Monist*, Vol. 22, 1912, pp. 321–347.

[17] Of the translations of Bergson, *Time and Free Will* appeared in 1910; *Creative evolution*, in 1911, new ed., 1919; *Matter and Memory*, 1911; *An Introduction to Metaphysics*, 1913. The estimation of the academic interest in Bergson is based on the frequency and length of the articles on his philosophy in *Mind* and *The Monist* 1900–1930, the former being one of the leading English philosophical journals, and the latter one to which Eliot has himself contributed and is likely to have studied.

The influence of Bergson went far beyond academic circles and in one way or another many of the literary movements of the early twentieth century are indebted to him. One such movement was a literary coterie Eliot frequented during the 1914–1918 war, which revolved around the figure of Ezra Pound. Here the most recent tendencies in literature and art were discussed. Inspired by an almost revolutionary fervour and enthusiasm for the newest "isms", Pound's circle must have been stimulating for an ambitious young poet.

Of the many literary "isms" in vogue at that time, Futurism is of special interest in the present context. The debt of Futurism to Bergson has not yet been fully investigated, but it seems quite clear that its rejoicing in the unbounded possibilities of the future owes something to Bergson's conception of an undetermined, creative evolution. Where and when Eliot first heard of Futurism is uncertain; very likely as early as 1911 in Paris, or perhaps not until his entering Pound's coterie; but in 1917 the movement was, as it were, officially introduced to the English public by Henry Newbolt in an essay entitled "Futurism and Form in Poetry", and as such it is of considerable interest, sharply emphasizing, as it does, Eliot's anti-Futurist doctrine of tradition. Thus, for instance, the following passage:

> Futurism is the revolt against the oppression of the present by the past. A more appropriate name for it would be that of Presentism, for it is the present, the moment of actual life, that it seeks to defend and express; but as its success is a matter of expectation rather than possession, it is content to claim the future only.[18]

Thus Futurism appears diametrically opposed to the ideas expressed by Eliot in "Tradition and the Individual Talent".

II

As a critic Eliot thus seems to have rejected Bergson's philosophy of time and evolution, but as a poet he has no doubt been influenced by

[18] Newbolt, H., *A New Study of English Poetry*, London, 1917, reprinted 1919, p. 244.

him. Eliot's heightened awareness of the inner perception of time, for example, noticeable in much of his poetry, may well owe something to the influence of Bergson. For although rejecting Bergson's philosophy as a whole, Eliot may nevertheless have adopted more isolated ideas and images from him.

The division between conceptual time and perceptual time, usually clear enough in modern scientific thought, also applies to time in literature. Novels, and occasionally also poems, may contain passages in which time is analysed as an intellectual concept, but in most cases it is treated in its perceptual aspect, *i.e.* as something immediately experienced by human beings. Both aspects are present in the *Four Quartets*, in which intellectual speculation is brought to bear on the immediate experience of time. In Eliot's earlier poetry, however, time appears mainly as a psychological phenomenon.

As his earliest extant poem clearly shows, the experience of time seems to have puzzled Eliot from the very beginning of his poetic career:

> If space and time, as sages say,
> Are things that cannot be,
> The fly that lives a single day
> Has lived as long as we.
> But let us live while yet we may,
> While love and life are free,
> For time is time and runs away,
> Though sages disagree.
>
> The flowers I sent thee when the dew
> Was trembling on the vine
> Were withered ere the wild bee flew
> To suck the eglantine.
> But let us haste to pluck anew
> Nor mourn to see them pine,
> And though the flowers of life be few
> Yet let them be divine.[19]

This little "Song" (in its first version dated 1905) bears out Eliot's statement that an element of conventional romanticism coloured the literary background of his youth. His romantic period lasted up to

[19] *Harvard Advocate*, June 3, 1907; cf. D. Gallup, *T. S. Eliot. A Bibliography*, London, 1952, p. 79.

his twenty-second year.[20] This "Song" hardly expresses a consistently romantic philosophy of life, which is natural enough since Eliot wrote it at the age of sixteen; and there is nothing to suggest that it was based on a personal experience. It appears primarily to express ideas and feelings derived from his reading, rather than a deeply emotional experience of life. The brevity of human life and the sadness of fading beauty and transient love are themes as old as lyric poetry, and Eliot's treatment of them hardly seems original. His general approach to these themes may owe something to Horace and to the Fitzgerald *Rubáiyát*, for example, for both of which he has confessed his admiration at that time,[21] but above all he seems to have been dependent upon his reading of English poetry. In fact the "Song" was written, Eliot says, "as an exercise for my English teacher and was an imitation of Ben Jonson".[22] In view of these facts it may be inappropriate to take the poem too seriously or attempt to read any profound ideas into it.

In sixteenth and seventeenth century poetry as well as in the poetry of the so-called Romantic movement, the experience of time is often suggested by the contrasting of mortal life and eternal values of some kind – aesthetic or vaguely religious. Keats, for example, contrasts the timeless perfection of the Grecian urn with the exuberant life decorating its surface. In the poem, "Time",

> Unfathomable Sea! whose waves are years,
>   Ocean of Time, whose waters of deep woe
> Are brackish with the salt of human tears!
>   Thou shoreless flood, which in thy ebb and flow
> Claspest the limits of mortality . . .[23]

Shelley contrasts the mortality of man with the eternal sea – as does Byron in the celebrated lines from the last Canto of *Childe Harold*. For Keats as well as for Shelley time and the timeless are not abstract concepts but categories of experience, often presented in cur-

[20] *The Use of Poetry and the Use of Criticism*, pp. 32 ff.

[21] Ibid., p. 33.

[22] Hall, D., "The Art of Poetry: T. S. Eliot" (an interview with Eliot), *The Paris Review*, No. 21, 1959, p. 49.

[23] *The Complete Poetical Works of Percy Bysshe Shelley*, ed. by Thomas Hutchinson, London, 1907, p. 631.

rent conventions. A similar formal conventionalism in Eliot's early poems makes it difficult to distinguish in his work between literary commonplaces on the one hand and, on the other, what has become almost personal experience, but the persistency of certain themes speaks in favour of a persistent attitude towards life. Thus the motif of flowers faded too soon, common in romantic poetry, recurs in a number of Eliot's early compositions and finally emerges in his later frequent use of the symbolism of the garden.

In "Before Morning" of 1908, for example, a personal overtone may be heard, animating the traditional theme:

> While the East was weaving red with grey,
> The flowers at the window turned toward dawn,
> Petal on petal, waiting for the day,
> Fresh flowers, withered flowers, flowers of dawn.
>
> This morning's flowers and flowers of yesterday
> Their fragrance drifts across the room at dawn,
> Fragrance of bloom and fragrance of decay,
> Fresh flowers, withered flowers, flowers of dawn.[24]

In the triad of the last line Eliot seems to give a summary of his adolescent experience of life; "Fresh flowers, withered flowers, flowers of dawn" – youth, frustration, new hopes. The romantic melancholy which pervaded the young Eliot's experience of time, was of short duration, and has left hardly any traces in his mature work.

The Epicurean doctrine of converting time into a maximum of pleasure, expressed in the "Song" of 1907, is not very remarkable in itself, but seen against Eliot's personal background it becomes more interesting. The elements of Puritanical asceticism present in his parental home appear to have left indelible marks on his personality and on his work. In so far as the "Song" is more than a stylistic exercise, it is probably an expression of adolescent revolt against the moralism of Eliot's environment. This was not a whole-hearted revolt, however, for soon the "Puritan" experience of time prevailed over the frivolous gospel of hedonism. To the Puritan mind time was not a thing to be wasted in idle, irresponsible enjoyment of life, but

[24] *Harvard Advocate*, Nov. 13, 1908.

a talent to be turned to account before God, the Eternal; or, as St. Paul put it, "Redeeming the time, because the days are evil"[25] – words that are echoed in "Ash-Wednesday". When quite young Eliot had dissociated himself from the spiritual and moral beliefs of his home, but speaking of himself in retrospection at the age of sixty-six, he claims to combine "a Catholic cast of mind, a Calvinistic heritage, and a Puritanical temperament".[26] His early hedonism, therefore, suggests something thought and observed, rather than directly experienced. It was a passing phase in his development, and soon gave way to a disillusioned melancholy – steps on the path to a renewed, positive contact with Christian morality.

The impact of traditional English poetry on the young Eliot's poetic exercises was thus temporary, and was to be followed by an influence of deep and more permanent effect, the influence of French Symbolism. After reading Symons' book on Symbolism in 1908,[27] Eliot wrote a poem, "Nocturne", in the very next year in a tone completely different from the early flower pieces.[28] The poem is clearly an imitation of Jules Laforgue, the Symbolist who seems to have fascinated Eliot most at that time. In 1910 he published a translation of a piece by Laforgue called "Humoresque",[29] and the typical Laforguian irony and cynicism are characteristic of many of Eliot's poems during the subsequent ten years. By the time he wrote "The Love Song of J. Alfred Prufrock" Eliot had assimilated the new impressions and had found his own style. Not published until 1917, in *Prufrock and Other Observations*, the poem had been written as early as 1910–1911. Begun before Eliot left Harvard, it was completed during his sojourn at the Sorbonne and at the time of his first acquaintance with the philosophy of Bergson.[30] The poem may in fact be interpreted as an illustration of the decadent impotence against which Bergson reacted in preaching his gospel of free-will.

[25] *Eph.*, v: 16.
[26] *On Poetry and Poets*, p. 209.
[27] See Kristian Smidt, p. 28.
[28] *Harvard Advocate*, Nov. 12, 1909.
[29] Ibid., Jan. 12, 1910.
[30] *American Literature*, Vol. 18, 1946–47, p. 319. (Letter from Eliot to J. C. Pope.)

The sense of time is, once again, the central theme of "Prufrock". Prufrock is a self-conscious, inhibited middle-aged man, tormenting himself with the idea of passionate self-surrender. Painfully aware of the brevity of life – "I grow old . . . I grow old . . ." – he yet tries to persuade himself that there will be time:

> And indeed there will be time
> For the yellow smoke that slides along the street
> Rubbing its back upon the window-panes;
> There will be time, there will be time
> To prepare a face to meet the faces that you meet;
> There will be time to murder and create,
> And time for all the works and days of hands
> That lift and drop a question on your plate;
> Time for you and time for me,
> And time yet for a hundred indecisions,
> And for a hundred visions and revisions,
> Before the taking of a toast and tea.

In fact there will be time for Prufrock to do everything except that which he feels he should do:

> To have squeezed the universe into a ball
> To roll it toward some overwhelming question

In this overt allusion to Marvell's "To his Coy Mistress", Eliot gives an ironic dimension to Prufrock's meditation on time. The aging man with thinning hair does hear "Time's winged Chariot hurrying near", but he does not "have the strength to force the moment to its crisis". The clear-cut contrast in Marvell's poem between the time of life and love and the "Deserts of vast Eternity" throws Prufrock's endless deliberations into almost caustic relief, but it was from the French Symbolists that Eliot had learnt the technique of applying such irony. For the model of Prufrock's personality and the style of the poem, most critics, no doubt rightly, point to Laforgue,[31] but Prufrock's experience of time is more closely related to Baudelaire than to any other Symbolist. Baudelaire's "morbid" experience of time has been analysed by Richard Glasser:

> Der Symbolist stellt sich dar als einer, der seine Haltung und seinen festen Willen gegenüber dem Strom der Zeit eingebüsst hat

[31] See *e.g.* Matthiessen, *The Achievement of T. S. Eliot*, p. 17.

und weder die Kraft noch die Lust besitzt, sie zu gestalten und zu ballen.[32]

This characterization applies to Prufrock as well as to Baudelaire and the other Symbolists. Time is an oppressive burden, crushing the shoulders of man, and, according to Baudelaire, the only means of liberation from the "horrible" burden lies in ecstatic intoxication:

> Il faut être toujours ivre. Tout est là: c'est l'unique question. Pour ne pas sentir l'horrible fardeau du Temps qui brise vos épaules et vous penche vers la terre, il faut vous enivrer sans trêve [...] Pour n'être pas les esclaves martyrisés du Temps, enivrez-vous sans cesse! [33]

This passage from *Le spleen de Paris* implies both aspects of Prufrock's experience of time – time as a wearisome burden, and the desire for a moment of ecstatic self-surrender that would redeem a life-time of temporal slavery.

In an essay written twenty years after "Prufrock", Eliot describes Baudelaire as a more or less unconscious explorer of Christianity. The glory and grandeur of the Christian life were unknown to Baudelaire, but he possessed a profound knowledge of Evil and of Sin – the first step, in Eliot's view, towards salvation. The world of evil was, to Baudelaire, the world of time, and the only way of escape was to be found in ecstasy – not the mystic ecstasy of divine love, but something much vaguer. "Baudelaire's notion of beatitude certainly tended to the wishy-washy", Eliot says, and "there is for him a gap between human love and divine love" [34] – a gap which Baudelaire never succeeded in bridging. His only positive creed lies in the *enivrez-vous.* With Eliot it is different. His poetry reveals an increasing tendency to identify the symbols of human and divine love. Just as Prufrock's hope of delivery from the burden of time is dependent upon his daring to make love to a woman, so, on a quite different level, the moments of bliss in Eliot's later poetry are repre-

[32] Glasser, R., *Studien zur Geschichte des französischen Zeitbegriffs,* München, 1936, p. 224.

[33] Baudelaire, C., *Le spleen de Paris,* ed. by A. v. Bever, 3rd ed., Paris, 1915, pp. 161 f.

[34] *Selected Essays,* p. 429.

sented as timeless moments. In his early poetry the idea and experience of the timeless are conveyed through the scenes and symbols of a more profane ecstasy – the "instant de puissance et de délire" in "Dans le Restaurant", and the Hyacinth garden episode in *The Waste Land* for instance – and one of the tasks Eliot set himself as a Christian poet seems to have been to relate those moments of supposedly profane love to his new vision of divine love. How to accomplish such a poetical achievement he could learn, not from Baudelaire, but from Dante.

The collection of poems of 1917, called *Prufrock and Other Observations*, is a very slender volume, as is its successor, the *Poems*, of 1920. Eliot is not known to have written any poems between 1911 and 1915, and after a spell of creative activity in 1915–1916, when he seems to have written most of the poems included in the first collection, he was afflicted by a feeling of barrenness. He has admitted that he thought he had "dried up completely".[35] As a way out of this affliction he started to write poems in French: "I think it was that when I was writing in French I didn't take the poems so seriously, and that, not taking them seriously, I wasn't so worried about not being able to write. I did these things as a sort of *tour de force* to see what I could do."[36] This was in 1917 and among these poems in French are "Dans le Restaurant", just mentioned, and "Lune de Miel".[37] As Eliot himself suggests, these pieces should not be taken too seriously, but anticipating as it does some of the subsequent poems in English, "Lune de Miel" is of special interest.

The sense of tradition and of history, which receives its fullest expression in *The Waste Land*, is noticeable as early as in "Lune de Miel". Describing a honeymoon tour on the Continent, this little poem is largely built on contrasts between the sordid present and the glorious past and between the sacred and the profane. Not far from the cheap hotel at Ravenna, where the couple has put up, is one of the most beautiful churches of Christendom:

[35] Hall, (Interview with Eliot), p. 56.

[36] Ibid.

[37] See Gallup, p. 81.

Ils restent sur le dos écartant les genoux
De quatre jambes molles tout gonflées de morsures.
On relève le drap pour mieux égratigner.
Moins d'une lieue d'ici est Saint Apollinaire
En Classe, basilique connue des amateurs
De chapitaux d'acanthe que tournoie le vent.[38]

About their visit to Milan, two things are mentioned – Leonardo da Vinci's masterpiece and a cheap restaurant:

Où se trouve la Cène, et un restaurant pas cher.

The religious overtones of the historical contrasts seem to anticipate *The Waste Land*, and "Lune de Miel" is also the first of Eliot's poems, in which carnal love is openly treated with that feeling of disgust so noticeable in many of his subsequent poems.

The creative power released by the experiments in French verse, resulted in a number of poems concerned with the historical sense of time. As a poet Eliot seems to have attempted to live up to his own principles, as laid down in "Tradition and the Individual Talent", to "write not merely with his own generation in his bones, but with a feeling that the whole of the literature of Europe from Homer and within it the whole of the literature of his own country has a simultaneous existence and composes a simultaneous order".[39] It may be doubted whether Eliot has ever written with the whole of European literature in his bones, but he has certainly written a number of poems with a great deal of it in his brain. Sometimes the impact of the mass of literary allusions obscures the immediate comprehension of a poem, but in other cases the allusions help to articulate and reinforce the historical sense.

Contemporary with the essay on tradition is the poem, "Burbank with a Baedeker: Bleistein with a Cigar", first published in 1919,[40] which is an example of Eliot's more excessive use of literary allusions. The epigraph to the poem, in this case an integral part of the whole piece, is composed out of quotations from not less than six different sources, from Gautier, Mantegna, Henry James, Shake-

[38] *Collected Poems 1909–1935*, p. 48.
[39] *Selected Essays*, p. 14.
[40] In *Art and Letters*, Vol. 2, 1919; cf. Gallup, p. 84.

speare, Robert Browning and John Marston,[41] and the eight stanzas of the poem include, in Grover Smith's interpretation, references to three more passages in Shakespeare, as well as to Tennyson, Byron, Seneca, Chapman and Kipling.[42] Even if some of Smith's identifications may be doubtful, the poem remains an impressive exhibition of scholarly erudition. But it is not merely the literary allusions that make "Burbank" an illustration of the historical sense. Several of the quotations are in various ways related to Venice, and the former glory of that city is contrasted with its later decline. The futility of modern civilization, in other poems a matter of subjective experience, is seen in "Burbank" as a historical phenomenon: "The smoky candle end of time / Declines." And in the concluding lines we find

> Burbank, meditating on
> Time's ruins, and the seven laws.

The seven laws involve, according to George Williamson, "Ruskin's laws of growth and decay, which depend upon the morals of the age".[43] The metaphor of "time's ruins" also seems particularly appropriate in a poem published shortly after the end of the first world war, when many feared that the European civilization and cultural tradition were ruined for ever. As a picture of the sterility and moral decay of modern metropolitan life, "Burbank" anticipates *The Waste Land*, in which the historical perspective is further developed.

The concluding piece in *Poems 1920* is "Sweeney Among the Nightingales", containing the startling juxtaposition of Sweeney and Agamemnon. Whether this juxtaposition is interpreted as an identity or as a contrast, it is clearly an instance of the historical sense at work. Here, however, it is not only a matter of equating or comparing different periods of history, but of a timeless, mythical pattern. The violent death of Agamemnon, alluded to in the epigraph and in the last stanza, has a certain affinity with the vegetation rites referred to in *The Waste Land*, the knowledge of which was derived from Frazer's *The Golden Bough*.[44] Again, in "Sweeney

[41] Williamson, G., *A Reader's Guide to T. S. Eliot*, New York, 1953, p. 101.

[42] Smith, G., *T. S. Eliot's Poetry and Plays*, Chicago, 1956, pp. 52 f.

[43] Williamson, p. 103.

[44] Frazer lists Agamemnon among the king priests; see *The Golden Bough*, 3rd ed., (1911) 1932, I: 1, p. 365; I: 2, p. 279.

Among the Nightingales" and even more in *The Waste Land*, this pattern of primitive myth and ritual serves the same purpose as do the historical parallels elsewhere – to suggest an interpenetration of past and present and to demonstrate the existence of identical psychological and spiritual patterns at different periods of history. Thus it seems that the mythological dimension of Eliot's early poetry is only an extension of the historical sense.

In *The Waste Land* (1922) Eliot combines the various aspects of the experience of time illustrated in his earlier poems, the central problem being that of the meaning of time and history. In *The Waste Land*, the historical sense is developed into a sense of simultaneity, or coexistence, of the identity, almost, of events and places of widely separate origins in time and space. The actual scene, the London of the early nineteen-twenties, is also the London of Elizabeth I; merging with the Paris of Baudelaire and the Carthage of St. Augustine, it becomes the prototype of a metropolis, whether ancient or modern, of

> Jerusalem Athens Alexandria
> Vienna London

The juxtaposition of different historical events sometimes amounts to identification – the battle of Mylae in the year 260 B.C. symbolizes a naval engagement of the first world war. Again, Cleopatra and Elizabeth, together with the nameless modern typist, symbolize certain eternal qualities of woman. The numerous commentaries on *The Waste Land* provide an abundance of further examplification, but the above instances may suffice to demonstrate Eliot's use of historical parallels and perspectives.

As regards the poetic technique of *The Waste Land*, Eliot was undoubtedly influenced by contemporary French literature. The school of Futurism indulged in a device intended to create a sense of what they called simultaneity, consisting in the throwing together in the same poem, or even in the same line, of place-names and names of persons widely separate in time and space.[45] The Futurists,

[45] See A. Lebois, "T. S. Eliot, les Imagistes et Jean de Boschère", *Revue de Littérature Comparée*, Vol. 26, 1952, pp. 365–379; these aspects of Futurist poetry

using juxtaposition in this way, were no doubt prompted by, and tried to impart the effect of, a triumphant, almost delirious admiration of the progress of the modern world, of the technical development and of the increasing speed of communication. Marinetti, the leader of the Futurists, used the word *modernolatria*, "the cult of the modern", to describe the spirit animating him and those who with him worshipped progress and speed.

How utterly different appears the spirit in which Eliot wrote *The Waste Land*! Far from extolling the value of modern life, he seems rather to have been possessed by a feeling of its futility and barrenness, and, turning to the glorious past of England and Europe, he beheld the same futility. This is not the only possible interpretation, however. According to Cleanth Brooks, "The popular view of the method used in *The Waste Land* may be described as follows: Eliot makes use of ironic contrasts between the glorious past and the sordid present".[46] This view Brooks rightly refutes. Although contrasts between past and present undoubtedly form a striking feature of *The Waste Land*, these contrasts in the end appear as superficialities obscuring the deeper identity of all the historical periods alluded to in the poem. This identity lies in the fundamental barrenness of temporal civilization at any period of history.

To the inhabitants of the "waste land" history has no meaning or purpose, and time is the wearisome burden that it was to Prufrock. This entire lack of purpose and meaning is reflected in exclamations and questions such as, "What shall I do now? What shall I do?", "What shall we do tomorrow?", "What shall we ever do?" And yet, the time is late and life is short, but no one heeds the one thing that is needful, to save one's soul, to pursue the quest for the Holy Grail. The only reminder of night drawing near is the barman's, "HURRY UP PLEASE ITS TIME".

In *The Waste Land*, as in "Prufrock", the only thing to be set against the tyranny of empty time is self-surrender, death and rebirth. Prufrock pictures himself as "Lazarus, come back from the

have also been fully treated by P. Bergman in an unpublished thesis (Univ. of Uppsala) on Simultaneity and Futurism.

[46] Brooks, C., "The Waste Land: An Analysis", *T. S. Eliot. A Study of his Writings by Several Hands*, ed. by B. Rajan, London, 1947, p. 32.

dead", corresponding to the drowning of Phlebas in *The Waste Land,* or "The awful daring of a moment's surrender". The episode in the Hyacinth garden at the beginning of the poem can be read as a kind of prefiguration of the life-giving death of Phlebas – "I was neither / Living nor dead" – set against the tedium of temporal existence implied in the earlier lines in the poem:

> And I will show you something different from either
> Your shadow at morning striding behind you
> Or your shadow at evening rising to meet you;
> I will show you fear in a handful of dust.

The two shadows may perhaps be interpreted as the successive alternation of day and night, as youth and old age, as the future and the past, interrupted by the fearful moment of light and silence.

The mythical and ritual patterns in *The Waste Land* serve, partly, the same purpose as the historical perspectives, to underline the fundamental uniformity of man's situation at all times. But the myth of the Holy Grail and the maimed king also conveys a hope unknown to secular history, the hope of spiritual rebirth of man and society. At the time of writing *The Waste Land* Eliot had rejected Christian beliefs, but in so far as the poem gives grounds for hope of salvation, it is a religious poem. The rain never falls, and Christ remains the unknown, the Hooded Man, and consequently the problem of the meaning of history and temporal existence, though indicated, remains unsolved. Eliot was later to find the solution in the doctrine of the Incarnation.

Holding that the meaning of temporal life belongs to a supernatural order, seen only in brief moments of timeless vision, Eliot regards any attempt to foretell the future as futile. Tiresias, who "Perceived the scene, and foretold the rest", is, in the author's own notes to *The Waste Land,* said to be "the most important personage in the poem, uniting all the rest. [. . .] What Tiresias *sees,* in fact, is the substance of the poem". But what he sees is not a meaning or a purpose, only the recurrence of identical events; all that his prophecy amounts to is that the future will be like the past. The same is true of Madame Sosostris, "famous clairvoyante", who, "with a wicked pack of cards", foretells what will happen to the characters in the poem. She well knows the card of the Wheel of Fortune – the endless cycle of temporal events, and the card of the "lady of situations" – the fate of all the women in the poem. She also knows that Phlebas, the Phoenician Sailor, will be drowned. But there is one she cannot find, and another she is forbidden to see – the ones which disclose the hope of salvation. Thus all attempts to read the future are futile, since the only thing worth knowing cannot be revealed that way. It lies, not in the future, not in time, but out of time.

III

Although in his poems written between 1922 and 1934 Eliot hardly touches on the problem of time, his return to it in *The Rock* and the *Four Quartets* shows that he had continued to concern himself with it. Eliot's later treatment of the experience of time is not only more mature, and showing a greater depth and range of ideas, but is expressed with clarity and vigour.

Eliot's development seems to have been caused only to a certain extent by sustained reflection on issues raised in his early work, for much of the new material is obviously related to the contemporary discussion of the problem of time, as raised in various philosophical works and periodicals.

It is important to note that Eliot was only one of many writers of poetry and fiction, influenced by this contemporary discussion, and, in order to be fully understood, Eliot's later poetical work has to be viewed in the light of that discussion and its immediate literary repercussions. Samuel Alexander, for example, said in 1921:

> If I were asked to name the most characteristic feature of the thought of the last twenty-five years, I should answer, the discovery of Time. I do not mean that we have waited until to-day to become familiar with Time; I mean that we have only just begun, in our speculation, to take Time seriously, and to realize that in some way or other Time is an essential ingredient in the constitution of things.[47]

This was true not only of England but also of Europe at large. Such

[47] Alexander, S., *Spinoza and Time*, London, 1921, p. 15.

an opinion may well appear exaggerated, but Alexander's statement, no doubt the result of his study of the history of time philosophy, is borne out by a mass of evidence in the form of books, pamphlets, and articles dealing with the problem of time.

Up to 1919 altogether about ten books, chiefly devoted to the subject of time, were published in England; among these are some early works on the fourth dimension and the principle of relativity. From 1919 to 1921 another ten books on time appeared. That is to say, the output of these three years equalled the collected output of the preceding one hundred years. The average number during the subsequent decade amounts to three books a year. The frequency of essays and articles in journals and periodicals shows a similar tendency, and to conclude this brief bibliographical note, it may be well to add that the continental development is almost identical, exhibiting, in France and Germany, an enormous increase of literature on time about 1921.[48]

This unparalleled interest in the problem of time then evinced by scientists, scholars and laymen alike, appeared to some to be an integrated intellectual movement, a school. Wyndham Lewis, for instance, a friend of Eliot's, in *Time and Western Man* (1927) set out to analyse and criticize what he called the "Time-school", but to group together Bergson, Joyce, Einstein, Charlie Chaplin and Bertrand Russell as a "school" is, of course, absurd, though typical of a common reaction in those literary and artistic circles whose interest in things new is apt to obscure their perception of the fundamental issues involved. The same sort of misunderstanding is to be found in Gertrude Stein's pamphlet, *Composition as Explanation* (1926), in which she suggests that the new notions of time were related in some way to "modernism" in art and social life. In the same way, and this time in relation to Eliot, Lawrence Durrell, himself a poet and novelist, in the chapter, "Space Time and Poetry" in his *Key to Modern Poetry* published in 1952, again sees in Eliot's poetry the traces of various aspects of the time problem of the nineteen-twenties, but does not attempt to relate these aspects to the

[48] The above statements are based on a thorough study of English bibliographies and book catalogues from the beginning of the nineteenth century up to the present date.

various sources that have influenced Eliot. No doubt the general interest in the problem of time increased Eliot's awareness of time as an intellectual problem, but the critical turn of his mind and his philosophical training certainly prevented him from an indiscriminate acceptance of the new ideas *in toto*. It may be well, therefore, to attempt to distinguish between the chief elements of the so-called "Time-school".

The problem of time is above all a philosophical problem, and as such it has occupied a number of eminent thinkers throughout history. It is nothing new, but in the present century a continuation rather, and in certain respects the conclusion, of a long philosophical tradition. This tradition was familiar to Eliot in its earlier Platonic form as well as in its later phases, the Idealist philosophy of Royce, MacTaggart and others. Apart from this tradition Bergson seems one of the chief sources of the modern philosophy of time. His work did much to arouse the interest of the intellectuals of the period, but broadly speaking Bergson's theory of time stimulated rather than shaped the subsequent speculation about the nature of time. A summary of the situation and a step forward in the Realist direction was taken in 1920 by Alexander in his comprehensive work, *Space, Time, and Deity*. The analytical empiricism in the subsequent decade rejected metaphysical speculation about time, in favour of a more purely scientific and mathematical approach to the problem. An attempt was made to estimate the progress of the philosophy of time by G. F. Goldsbrough in his pamphlet, *Recent Discussions on "Time"* (1927), while in 1929 appeared the most exhaustive historical and critical study of the subject in English, Alexander Gunn's *The Problem of Time*.

With the possible exception of Bergson, no one has influenced the modern philosophy of time more than Albert Einstein. Though not the first to conceive of time as a fourth dimension, it was really he who gave the idea its present form by integrating it with his Theory of Relativity. In fact Einstein made the fourth dimension an indispensable element in the description of physical reality. Einstein's theory was authoritatively introduced to the English public in 1920 by A. S. Eddington's *Space, Time and Gravitation: An Outline of the General Relativity Theory*. The purely scientific aspects of Relativity can hardly have been studied in detail by Eliot, but an indication of his general interest in the problems raised by Einstein is to be found in the fact that he translated a French essay, "On Reading Einstein", for the *Criterion*.[49] But no particular evidence is needed: as an editor and critic Eliot must have come across the name of Einstein again and again. The philosophical stir created by the Theory of Relativity was considerable. It worked as a challenge to the aging Bergson who, in his *Durée et simultanéité* (1922), tried to defeat Einstein with his own weapon – mathematical analysis. In England many of the leading philosophers of the day engaged in the debate on Einstein's concept of time, men like C. D. Broad, Bertrand Russell and A. N. Whitehead, whose views Eliot is likely to have studied closely.[50]

The effect of Einstein's theory of time on Eliot's poetry, if in fact it did affect his poetry, was probably similar to that produced by Bergson's philosophy – *i.e.* an increased awareness of time as an essential component in the order of things. But while Bergson's philosophy exercised a direct influence on poetry and fiction generally, Einstein's theory of time was unrelated to the immediate, psychological experience of time, and thus it entered into works of fiction as a speculative system, invariably vulgarized, and often transformed into some kind of pseudo-scientific occultism. In an anonymous commentary to the *Four Quartets* an attempt has been made to relate the theme of time in the *Quartets* to the "findings of modern mathematics as taught at universities today",[51] but it is quite unconvincing and fails to establish such a parallel.

Only a minority of the reading public could have grasped the full scientific meaning of Relativity, but a phrase such as the "fourth dimension" seems to some extent to have captured the popular imagination, and to have provoked several kinds of books – ranging from sincere scientific speculation to fantastic excursions into the domain of the occult, and even to stories written for sheer enter-

[49] Mauron, C., "On Reading Einstein", *Criterion*, Vol. 10, 1930.

[50] See *e.g.* Broad, C. D., *Scientific Thought*, London, 1923; Whitehead, A. N., *The Concept of Nature*, Cambridge, 1920; Russell, B., *The A.B.C. of Relativity*, London, 1925.

[51] [Anon.], *On the Four Quartets of T. S. Eliot*, London, 1953, p. 12. It is not the main object, however, of this pamphlet to establish such a parallel.

tainment. To the first category belongs J. W. Dunne's *An Experiment with Time*, first published in 1927, which ran through a number of editions during subsequent years. Dunne's experiment, based on the interpretations of dreams, aimed at proving a possibility of predicting future events. In order to support the supposed evidence of his experiments he elaborated a system of time series, further developed in *The Serial Universe* (1934), which, he believed, provided a scientific explanation of the gift of foresight. Dunne's theory has met with adverse criticism from scientists and philosophers alike,[52] which, naturally enough, did not diminish its popular appeal. To a certain extent Dunne's ideas suggest a continuation of the speculations of the French astronomer Camille Flammarion, whose *Death and its Mystery*, containing "evidence" of experiments in the prediction of future events, appeared in English translation in 1921–1923. Further instances of fantastic, pseudo-scientific explorations of the idea of a fourth dimension and the possibility of predicting the future, are John Hodgson's *The Time-Journey of Dr. Barton* (1929), and P. D. Ouspensky's ideas of time in *Tertium Organum* (1920) and *A New Model of the Universe* (1931). This idea of foreknowledge of events appears in novels as well. E. L. White's *The Eternal Journey* (1930) and J. Buchan's *The Gap in the Curtain* (1932) both derive their chief excitement from the introduction of the consequences of this popular concept of time as a fourth dimension into the events of everyday life.

The influence of these phantasies on Eliot's poetry, since it is hardly likely that he would take them seriously, is, if it exists at all, negative. The ironic repudiation of popular fortune-telling in *The Waste Land* has been discussed above. The theme recurs in the last Section of "The Dry Salvages", which opens with a list of occult practices. Astrology, telepathy, sortilege and the like, all "usual / Pastimes and drugs, and features of the press", are repudiated in the following words:

> Men's curiosity searches past and future
> And clings to that dimension. But to apprehend

[52] See C. D. Broad, "Mr. Dunne's Theory of Time in An Experiment with Time" (1935), reprinted in *Religion, Philosophy and Psychical Research*, London, 1953.

The point of intersection of the timeless
With time, is an occupation for the saint –

Against the dimension of past and future Eliot sets the timeless, and the only element of the discussion of time during the nineteen-twenties that could enrich his conception of the timeless, was the metaphysical element. In siding with the metaphysicians, Eliot took his stand against many of the contemporary philosophers, who refused to consider the metaphysical problem of time as a philosophical problem. But the supporters of traditional views were not altogether silenced. In science the problem of time is largely a problem of measurement, but as Alexander Gunn has observed, the "discussion of the *measurement* of time offers little or no clue to its *nature*. This remains a metaphysical problem".[53] The nature of time is clearly what interests Eliot, and in so far as his conception of time and the timeless in the *Four Quartets* is derived from philosophy, it is derived from the Platonic, Idealist tradition in metaphysics, and the modern theories have worked as a strong but negative stimulus, directing his attention to the treatment of time in classical philosophy.

Eliot's conception of the timeless is as much religious as philosophical, however. By being confirmed into the Church of England in 1927, Eliot affirmed his allegiance to the fundamental spiritual and theological tradition of Christianity. It is apparently largely in the light of this tradition that he chooses to regard the problems of time and history.

Although the theological implications of the problem of time have been discussed in a number of books, which have accompanied the widespread interest in the problem, most of them appeared after the publication of the *Four Quartets*, but some of the earlier ones, such as von Hügel's *Eternal Life* (1912),[54] and S. F. Davenport's *Immanence and Incarnation* (1925), may have influenced the *Quartets*. On the whole, however, Eliot seems to have based his Christian philosophy of time directly on the essentials of Christian doctrine, rather than the more formal expressions of Christian theology. Of some relevance – though it is doubtful whether Eliot ever read it – is J. H.

[53] Gunn, p. 239.

[54] Evidence of Eliot's admiration of von Hügel is found in his *Sermon Preached in Magdalene College Chapel*, p. 4.

Brown's *Eternity: is it a Biblical Idea?* (1926), which raises the question whether the concept of eternity in the sense of timelessness formed part of the original Christian doctrine. How far the concept of the timeless in the *Quartets* involves eternity in the traditional Christian sense, is a problem to be dealt with later, in the analysis of the *Quartets*. It might be added that the attempt of, for instance, Ilse Strömsdörfer to relate the *Four Quartets* to Existentialist philosophy and Heidegger's *Sein und Zeit* (1927), reveals a failure to understand Eliot's essentially Christian approach to the problems raised in these poems.[55]

Eliot thus rejects, especially in their more general and popular sense, the current philosophical and theological approaches to the problem of time. There remains, however, the psychological approach. Here he seems to have preferred its literary to its purely scientific expression and Marcel Proust to William James. Eliot is certain to have read Proust's novels – they were readily available both in English and in the original. The first part of *A la recherche du temps perdu*, *Swann's Way*, appeared in 1922, and the last, *Time Regained*, in 1931.[56] Furthermore, a number of critical studies of Proust's work appeared in England at the same time as the translations of the novels.

As the chief literary exponent of Bergson's philosophy of time, Proust subscribed to a view of life completely different from Eliot's, but their literary methods have certain affinities. In trying to recapture the past by means of the creative memory, Proust hoped to overcome the destructive power of time, which threatened to divide the identity of the self into discontinuous pieces of consciousness, and thus in the recollection of things past he saw the only guarantee of the unity and continuity of his own self.[57] A similar tendency to go back into the past for the purpose of connecting the mature per-

[55] Strömsdörfer, I., *Der Begriff der Zeit bei T. S. Eliot*, unpublished thesis, München, 1957.

[56] The first part of the original, *Du côté de chez Swann*, appeared in 1913, and the last part, *Le temps retrouvé*, posthumously in 1928.

[57] Cf. H. Meyerhoff, *Time in Literature*, Berkeley/Los Angeles, 1955, Ch. II: 4, pp. 42–51; Donner, H. W., "Marcel Proust och den litterära traditionen i Frankrike", *Finsk Tidskrift*, Vol. 105, 1928, pp. 153–159.

sonality with its roots and origins in childhood and youth, characterizes much of Eliot's poetry. In the *Quartets* the ideas, emotions and beliefs of the middle-aged poet are constantly related to his early experiences and his childhood background. To Proust the exercise of the creative memory was not only a means, but an end; his sole religion lay in the cultivation of the faculty of memory. To Eliot, on the other hand, it is merely a means of arriving at a better understanding of himself *sub specie aeternitatis*. Speaking of Dante's *Vita Nuova*, Eliot holds that it "can only be understood by accustoming ourselves to find meaning in *final causes* rather than in origins".[58] Proust looked for meaning in origins, psychological and biological, Eliot in final causes. The difference between Proust and Eliot as explorers of the past of the self has been cogently put by Georges Poulet:

> The search for lost time in Eliot is therefore totally different from what one finds in Proust, but no less important. It depends on a voluntary memory, on a continuous abnegation, on a patient effort to recover, to reassemble, to readapt under new conditions, what was lost. Far from being restored at one stroke by the affective memory, the past is regained only by the exercise of all the mental and physical powers. It is less a memory than a reacquired habit, the effect of a vow of fealty.[59]

The idea of returning to childhood as a means of integrating the self is also a common feature of romantic literature. Psychologically, the romanticist cult of childhood recollections may be related to Proust's search for lost time, but the underlying philosophy of life is very different. In a lecture on "Poetry and Time", Henry Newbolt has analysed the experience of time in a number of English poets from Crashaw to Yeats, and in common with what might be called a romantic tradition in English poetry he found the themes of exile and nostalgia, more or less directly dependent upon the Platonic doctrine of pre-existence.[60] Childhood is nearer than manhood to the pre-natal, heavenly existence. In consequence the child and me-

[58] *Selected Essays*, p. 274.

[59] Poulet, G., *Studies in Human Time*, (transl.) Baltimore, 1956, p. 356.

[60] Newbolt, H., "Poetry and Time", *Proceedings of the British Academy*, 1917–1918, pp. 487–503.

mories of childhood assumed a character of holiness in the eyes of the "Metaphysical" and romantic poets, and by returning to childhood in memory, they hoped to get a glimpse of eternal bliss. Well-read in poetry of this kind, Eliot is certainly aware of the meaning and implications of such romantic nostalgia, but reverting to childhood, he does so, not with nostalgia, but in a real and practical way, with an end in view, a search not for origins, but for ultimate causes.

Eliot's attitude of mind at the time of composing the *Quartets* has earlier in this chapter been defined in terms of contrasts and rejections, as in the case of Bergson and certain pseudo-scientific writers. Suffice it to add but one more instance of his rejection of contemporary ideas, in this case also related to the theme of childhood. Among the occult practices denounced in the last Section of "The Dry Salvages", one appears startling in such a context:

> dissect
> The recurrent image into pre-conscious terrors –
> To explore the womb, or tomb, or dreams;

This obvious reference to psychoanalysis expresses Eliot's rejection of the curiosity that "searches past and future / And clings to that dimension". The psychoanalyst's exploration of the subconscious is in many ways the counterpart of the exercise of the Bergsonian and Proustian creative memory. In striving to lay bare the hidden, psychological relations between past and present, both Proust and Bergson attempt in some way to integrate the self with time, but without raising the question of the relation of the soul to eternity. Eliot's poetical work has sometimes been interpreted in psychoanalytical terms, and far from denying the empiric reliability of Freud's discoveries – as is apparent from, for example, his essay on Dante [61] – Eliot is no doubt aware of the possibility of a Freudian interpretation of much of his imagery, but in fact he gives an altogether different meaning to the phenomena described by Freud. The Freudians explore the "low dreams" arising from the unconscious; against such dreams Eliot sets the "high dreams" of St. John and Dante.[62] Scientists and psychologists alike cling to what Eliot calls the dimension

[61] *Selected Essays*, p. 273.
[62] Ibid., p. 262; cf. p. 243.

of past and future, interpreting reality in temporal terms of origin and result, of cause and effect, whereas Eliot, as a Christian, strives to transcend that dimension, to apprehend the timeless pattern in time, to find an eternal purpose in temporal life.

Eliot's reaction to the theories of time outlined above can thus be said to be mainly negative, but they seem to have had a stimulating effect, opening his eyes to new aspects of old problems, and forcing him to define his own position. In 1935, the year of "Burnt Norton", as in 1919, the year of "Tradition and the Individual Talent", he turned to tradition for guidance and support in the midst of the flux and change of contemporary civilization.

CHAPTER II

The General Background of the Four Quartets

The cultural and spiritual tradition underlying the symbolism of the *Four Quartets* is to a large extent objective and historical, but not all of the ideas, writers and thinkers linked together in Eliot's thought constitute an actual unified tradition, at least not if orthodoxy is made a criterion. Often Eliot's notions of the development of Western civilization have their counterparts in secular scholarship, but not always, and simple references to histories of philosophy, literature and the like would be misleading. It is therefore necessary to indicate, not the complete structure of Eliot's thought and learning, which would be an immense undertaking, but the fundamental principles by which he appears to have sorted and classified, accepted and rejected ideas and authors. The following survey is greatly indebted to Kristian Smidt's conscientious research, presented in his *Poetry and Belief in the Work of T. S. Eliot.*

The present chapter aims at providing a general background for the *Quartets,* designed to serve as a guide to the origins of isolated ideas and symbols. It is in effect a survey leading to the interpretation of the *Quartets,* and as such concentrates on the period preceding the writing of the first of the *Quartets,* that is the early nineteen-thirties, and is largely based on Eliot's critical writings from that time. But before investigating the ideas and beliefs of the *Quartets,* their chronology must first be considered.

I

Much of the criticism of the *Four Quartets* attempts to show the fundamental unity of the sequence, relating themes and whole Sections of one poem to corresponding passages in others.[1] The outcome of such comparisons appears, at first sight, to give ample support for the notion of the unity of the *Quartets*. Thus all four poems are of identical formal construction, each containing five Sections, of which the fourth, being lyric in form and style, stands out from the rest, and the fifth Section in each is concerned with the problems and difficulties of literary composition. Each poem, it is maintained, represents one of the four elements; "Burnt Norton" air; "East Coker" earth; "The Dry Salvages" water; and "Little Gidding" fire. The names of the *Quartets* are all place-names with some special association with Eliot's own life. East Coker, for instance, was the homestead of the Eliot family before their emigration to America in the seventeenth century, and Little Gidding, the resort of an Anglican community founded by Nicolas Ferrar in 1625, stands for Eliot's spiritual return to his native soil by means of his conversion to Anglicanism. On a deeper level of interpretation the unity of the *Quartets* appears even more striking. Not only are many of the main themes and metaphors common to all the poems, but they are also developed so as to become increasingly suggestive and comprehensive, and reach, at the end of the last *Quartet*, a climax for which the author seems to have prepared from the very beginning of the sequence. This inner unity of the *Four Quartets*, revealed by critical interpretation, seems to have been emphasized by Eliot himself in putting the poems into one volume, the title of which suggests a unity, at least of form.

Certain objections, however, may be made to this generally held conception of the unity of the *Quartets*, and particularly on one point. In trying to relate the last three poems to each other, we are not confronted with any grave difficulties, but the attempt to fit "Burnt Norton" into the general pattern invariably leads to a forced

[1] See Rajan, B., "The Unity of the Quartets", *T. S. Eliot. A Study of his Writings by Several Hands*, ed. by B. Rajan, London, 1947; Gardner, H., "Four Quartets: A Commentary", in the same work.

interpretation. Would one, for instance, have thought of "Burnt Norton" as a poem representing the element of air, if the explicit references to specific elements in the other three *Quartets* had not evoked the idea of such symbolism? Furthermore, "Burnt Norton" gives the impression of being a unity in itself. The concluding lines form a real conclusion, and hardly leave the reader in expectation of more to come, as do the second and third poems of the sequence. It would seem, therefore, almost as if the author had considered "Burnt Norton" as a unity in itself, not the introductory piece in a set of four.

The solution of the problem, however, is clearly apparent from evidence which has been overlooked in most critical studies of the *Quartets*. It is simply that Eliot did in fact conceive "Burnt Norton" as a separate work with no view to appending further poems to it later. This appears beyond doubt from a statement made by Eliot in an interview as reported by John Lehmann. Speaking of *Murder in the Cathedral*, Eliot said:

> That was dramatic poetry, of course, and I thought pure, unapplied poetry was in the past for me, until a curious thing happened. There were lines and fragments that were discarded in the course of the production of "Murder in the Cathedral". "Can't get them over on the stage", said the producer, and I humbly bowed to his judgment. However, these fragments stayed in my mind, and gradually I saw a poem shaping itself round them: in the end it came out as "Burnt Norton". Even "Burnt Norton" might have remained by itself if it hadn't been for the war, because I had become very much absorbed in the problems of writing for the stage and might have gone straight on from "The Family Reunion" to another play. The war destroyed that interest for a time: you remember how the conditions of our lives changed, how much we were thrown in on ourselves in the early days? "East Coker" was the result – and it was only in writing "East Coker" that I began to see the Quartets as a set of four.[2]

[2] Lehmann, J., "T. S. Eliot Talks About Himself and the Drive to Create", *The New York Times Book Review*, Nov. 29, 1953, p. 5. This interview has been noticed by Grover Smith, *T. S. Eliot's Poetry and Plays*, Chicago, 1956, p. 321, note 11; Eliot has confirmed his earlier statement in an interview published by D. Hall under the title, "The Art of Poetry", in *The Paris Review*, No. 21, 1959, p. 57.

These circumstances need not necessarily affect the general reader's attitude towards the poems; as they stand they do form a unity, in a general sense. In a deeper sense, however, the *Quartets* should be approached rather differently; "Burnt Norton" should be considered primarily by itself and only secondarily as the first in a sequence of four poems. Furthermore, being composed at least to some extent round fragments of the original version of *Murder in the Cathedral*, the poem should be interpreted in the light of that play. In the passage quoted above Eliot gives no indication of his reasons for choosing the title, "Burnt Norton", and, moreover, the reference to the lines discarded from *Murder in the Cathedral* certainly suggests only part of the truth about the origin of the poem. True to his "impersonal" theory of what poetry should be, Eliot avoids stressing the purely personal elements in "Burnt Norton", wishing perhaps that his critics would do likewise. Nevertheless there are certain circumstances relating to the selection of the title which have to be considered, since they relate to the interpretation of the poem.

Burnt Norton is the name of a country house in Gloucestershire not far from Chipping Campden, which Eliot visited some time before writing the poem. This information, supplied by most critics, is undoubtedly perfectly correct, but it hardly explains why Eliot chose to apply the name of that house to this poem. The significance of the titles of the following three *Quartets* appears immediately from the relation of the places East Coker, the Dry Salvages and Little Gidding to the history of Eliot and his family, but since there exists no obvious connection between Eliot and Burnt Norton, either biographical or symbolical, the explanation of the title probably lies in the fact that, while visiting the house, he had some sort of experience to which he attached great importance, an experience so intense or unique as to be permanently associated, in the mind of the author, with the place where it occurred. Since the titles of the last three *Quartets* each represent a significant development in Eliot's spiritual life, it would not be unnatural to suppose that the title of the first *Quartet* was chosen because it represents some experience, which prompted the sustained meditation on the spiritual meaning of life that constitutes the *Four Quartets*.

Nothing is known of the nature of Eliot's experience at Burnt

Norton except for what may be inferred from the poem itself, and the First Section in particular, but concerning the time and the circumstances under which the experience took place some facts are available. According to Eliot's close friend John Hayward, who has supplied the notes to the French edition of the *Four Quartets*, Eliot visited Burnt Norton some time during the summer ("autumn heat" suggests late summer) of 1934. The house was uninhabited at the time and Eliot – one imagines – stole into the garden of the solitary house situated some distance from the main road.[3] The First Section of "Burnt Norton" contains a fairly accurate description of that garden, its flower-beds and shrubberies, the box circle and the concrete pool. It is easy to picture the setting of Eliot's experience that summer's day, the panoramic view over the slope of the Cotswold Hills, the neglected garden and the air "vibrant" with heat. But the experience itself can be imagined only from the strange and elusive atmosphere of the poem. No doubt it cost the author considerable spiritual and intellectual effort to transform the fleeting vision in the garden into the firm foundation of a bold poetic construction, and a similar effort is required of the reader who wants to penetrate to the deepest levels of its meaning. The author's approach was synthetic, the reader's has to be analytic.

That "Burnt Norton" was written one year after the visit, during the autumn of 1935, as Hayward says,[4] is confirmed by Eliot's statement, quoted above. The first acting edition of *Murder in the Cathedral* was published on May 10, 1935,[5] and by then all eliminations must have been made, leaving Eliot with the "lines and fragments" round which "Burnt Norton" was to be built. It would be interesting to know exactly which parts of the poem are based on these fragments, though any attempt to discover them can be but guesswork. It appears nevertheless that the phrase, "human kind / Cannot bear very much reality", at the end of the First Section of "Burnt Norton", is taken *verbatim* from the play.[6] Moreover, it seems reason-

[3] *Quatre Quatuors*, traduit par P. Leyris, notes de J. Hayward, Paris, 1950, p. 131. Hayward's statement has been orally confirmed by the present owner of Burnt Norton.

[4] Ibid., p. 156.

[5] Cf. Gallup, D., *T. S. Eliot. A Bibliography*, London, 1952, pp. 23 f.

[6] *Murder in the Cathedral*, 4th ed., p. 69.

able to suppose that the philosophical ideas embodied in the poem are related to the play, whereas the more purely poetic passages, such as the rose garden episode, derives from the experience in the garden of Burnt Norton.

The necessity of considering *Murder in the Cathedral* in any attempt to interpret "Burnt Norton" is thus obvious. Equally important is Eliot's "pageant play", *The Rock*, published on May 31, 1934.[7] Many central themes and images are common to both *The Rock*, *Murder in the Cathedral* and "Burnt Norton", which is quite natural since all three were written within the space of two years. The chronological connection between these three works is as follows: Some time after his return from a visit to America in 1932–1933, Eliot accepted a commission to write a play projected by the Forty-five Churches' Fund, and this work, *The Rock*, was completed and produced in May, 1934. During the following summer Eliot visited the garden of Burnt Norton. The winter of 1934–1935 was devoted to the writing of another commissioned play, *Murder in the Cathedral*, first printed in May, 1935. During the autumn of the same year he completed "Burnt Norton", which was published as the last item in the *Collected Poems 1909–1935*. Being more explicit in both their symbolism and doctrine, these plays form a convenient starting-point for an interpretation of "Burnt Norton".

II

The theme of time in the *Four Quartets* has two different aspects: the perceptual and the conceptual aspect, *i.e.* time as immediate experience and time as the subject of abstract speculation. As works of poetry the *Quartets* are primarily concerned with human experience, and such abstract categories as appear are the result of the poet's reflection upon experience, or an external order imposed upon experience. Accordingly the poems seem to be based on the one hand on introspection and intuitive vision and, on the other, on reading and thinking. This dualism in the *Quartets* is deliberate, as appears from Eliot's declaration that in the *Quartets* he was "seek-

[7] Cf. Gallup, p. 22.

ing the verbal equivalents for small experiences he had had, and for knowledge derived from reading".[8] The word "small" is used no doubt to minimize the personal element; the experiences were in any case sufficiently important to occupy the mind of the poet for several years. Our knowledge of what the experiences actually were can be derived only from the text of the poems, however, except for certain passages in Eliot's writings dealing with mysticism, in so far as these experiences are themselves mystic.

The "knowledge derived from reading", which is embodied in the *Quartets*, can be studied apart from the poems. Eliot's views and opinions in matters of theology and philosophy are expressed or implied in almost all of his writings. The relevant material in this connection can conveniently be grouped under four headings: Eliot's religious faith, his conception of a cultural tradition, his views on mysticism and his theory of the relation between poetry and belief.

Eliot's first public declaration of his new faith after his conversion to Anglo-Catholicism in 1927, is found in the Preface to *For Lancelot Andrewes* (1928), where he describes his general point of view as "classicist in literature, royalist in politics, and anglo-catholic in religion".[9] The vagueness of this famous declaration invited misunderstanding, and in 1933 Eliot pointed out that the three terms need not necessarily be related to each other; they only happened to be so in his mind.[10]

A more explicit statement is given by Eliot in a letter to a Sister Mary James Power dated December, 1932, and is worth quoting in full:

> Dear Sister,
>
> In reply to your letter of December 1st, perhaps the simplest account that I can give is to say that I was brought up as a Unitarian of the New England variety; that for many years I was without any definite religious faith, or without any at all; that in 1927 I was baptized and confirmed into the Church of England; and that I am associated with what is called the Catholic movement in that Church, as represented by Viscount Halifax and the

[8] Smidt, K., *Poetry and Belief in the Work of T. S. Eliot*, Oslo, 1949, pp. 155 f. The pronouncement was made in reply to a question put to Eliot by Smidt.

[9] *For Lancelot Andrewes*, p. ix.

[10] *After Strange Gods*, p. 28.

> English Church Union. I accordingly believe in the Creeds, the invocation of the Blessed Virgin and the Saints, the Sacrament of Penance, etc.
>
> Yours faithfully,
> T. S. Eliot.[11]

Eliot's attitude to the Christian faith in this letter is characteristic of his attitude in general. Always suspicious of subjectivity in thought and feeling, he emphasizes the dogmatic side of Christianity. His adherence to the classicist doctrine in literature is partly due to his wish to "escape from personality", as he put it in "Tradition and the Individual Talent",[12] and the same motive can be discerned behind his adherence to Christian orthodoxy. The theology of the Catholic Church provides a spiritual order more impersonal than any literary doctrine, but as even the strictest and seemingly most objective classicist poetry springs from the private, subjective experience of the poet, so Eliot's orthodox faith is an order emotionally derived from his private experience, from the same experience that is the source of his poetry. (It should be noted that, in the present study as well as in much of Eliot's critical writings, "orthodox" is taken to mean: conforming to a given theological system, not of subjective invention.) In the *Four Quartets* the two orders, the literary and the religious, come very close to each other and sometimes overlap. The formal structure of the poems corresponds in fact to the intellectual structure of Eliot's religion.

In his eagerness to be and to appear orthodox, Eliot sometimes over-simplifies his own case. In the letter quoted above he ignores, not only the emotional and personal side of his faith but shows no predilection for any particular aspect of the Christian doctrine – except for Anglicanism as a whole. But his almost impersonal references to the Church and creeds cannot obscure the fact, evident from all his later writings, that his theological thought is coloured by his personal background.

In his essay on Baudelaire (1930), Eliot subscribes to the notion of Baudelaire as an essentially Christian poet. The criterion adduced, however, is not submission to the Church or the creeds, but Baude-

[11] Quoted by Scott, N. A., *Rehearsals of Discomposure*, London, 1952, p. 201.
[12] *Selected Essays*, p. 21.

laire's recognition of "moral Good and Evil", of the reality of Original Sin.[13] Eliot emphasizes *moral* in contradistinction to "natural Good and Bad or Puritan Right and Wrong". He would probably not have felt called upon to make this differentiation, had he not been brought up to regard the Puritan conceptions of Right and Wrong as the fundamental principles of Christian morality. Seen from Eliot's own point of view this differentiation may well be essential, but seen in a larger perspective it appears perhaps less significant. The emphasis he lays on the moral side of religion is no doubt dependent on the influence of his early Puritan environment and also on the deep impression made on him by his university teacher Irving Babbitt, who, although an agnostic humanist, based his philosophy of life on a strict moral dualism. Babbitt's equating of romanticism with monism and of classicism with dualism is often reflected in Eliot's critical writings.

In Baudelaire Eliot perceived a moral dualism akin to his own and perhaps also a kindred poetic temperament, but for the full Christian interpretation of that dualism he seems to have turned to Pascal. Originally written as the Introduction to an English translation of Pascal,[14] Eliot's essay, "The 'Pensées' of Pascal" (1931), is mainly informative and impersonal in tone, but occasional passages disclose a deeply personal appreciation of Pascal, which is well worth investigating. In a sense the influence of Pascal can be said to pervade the *Four Quartets*, but is so fully assimilated as to make it difficult to indicate specific allusions or references. The extremes of despair and joy as stages of the spiritual progress of the soul, the burning desire for a higher meaning in life, the search for knowledge of the hidden God, these are some of the features common both to the *Pensées* and the *Quartets*.

In following Pascal Eliot deviates from strict Catholic orthodoxy. The question of Pascal's Jansenism is raised in the essay, and in spite of his declaration that "I do not wish to enter any further than necessary upon the question of the heterodoxy of Jansenism",[15] Eliot goes on to discuss the matter for some pages. Obviously he is worried to

[13] Ibid., p. 429.

[14] Cf. Gallup, p. 51.

[15] *Selected Essays*, p. 412.

find himself sympathizing with a doctrine that may be heterodox – the Jansenistic view of man as fundamentally corrupt is often reflected in Eliot's writings, and sometimes he even touches on the doctrine of predestination. The problem of Pascal's influence on the *Quartets* has a bearing on several of the topics of the present study, and will later be considered in some detail.

In one particular aspect Eliot is a typical exponent of Anglicanism. A well-known characteristic of Anglican theology is the emphasis laid on the doctrine of the Incarnation of Christ, and Incarnation is one of the central themes in the *Four Quartets*. The importance Eliot attaches to this doctrine cannot be over-estimated, and the following statement, published in 1937, reflects the view of revelation underlying his dramatic and poetic works from the previous years:

> I take for granted that Christian revelation is the only full revelation; and that the fullness of Christian revelation resides in the essential fact of the Incarnation, in relation to which all Christian revelation is to be understood.[16]

Already in the essay on Lancelot Andrewes we find the same insistence upon the Incarnation as the central dogma of the Christian faith,[17] and the same is true of Eliot's two ecclesiastical plays and of the *Quartets*.

What particular interpretation Eliot gives to the doctrine of the Incarnation, is difficult to tell, but if he sometimes seems to be vague on this point in his poetry, it is certainly not because he was unaware of the controversy that has raged for two thousand years. In *Christ the Word*, Eliot's friend Paul Elmer More gives an instructive account of the various forms the doctrine has assumed.[18] However, Eliot's unwillingness to commit himself to any particular interpretation of the doctrine of the Incarnation is probably a deliberate intention. He does not wish to narrow the range of associations too much, but rather to extend the symbolic meaning of the Incarnation so as

[16] *Revelation*, ed. by J. Baillie and H. Martin, New York, 1937, pp. 1 f.

[17] *Selected Essays*, p. 347.

[18] Eliot seems, for instance, to share More's appreciation of Athanasius; see More, P. E., *Christ the Word*, Princeton, 1927, pp. 180 ff.; and *After Strange Gods*, p. 30.

to include a wider field of experience which, though apparently wholly secular, reveals a deeply religious significance in the light of the Christian doctrine.

Thus although it may be difficult to define Eliot's views on particular points of theology, as a rule the general trend of his thought can be apprehended, and thus certain notions can be eliminated as foreign to his mind. Eliot's orthodoxy, closely related to his upholding a cultural tradition, is better understood in the light of this tradition as it appeared to him after his conversion.

III

The investigation of the literary sources of the images and symbols employed in the *Four Quartets* is not only of interest to the scholar, it is also necessary to the interpretation of the poems. So many different meanings can be, and have been, read into one and the same symbol that some standard of interpretation appears indispensable – some standard other than the individual critic's or reader's personal associations. The only practical method seems to be to relate the various meanings to what is known about Eliot's views and beliefs and thus rule out certain interpretations as impossible, *i.e.* not in accord with Eliot's intellectual intention. As will appear later, some of the wildest conjectures concerning the meaning of, say, the rose garden in "Burnt Norton" should be disregarded on this ground. But we need more than a negative or a restrictive method.

In most cases it is, of course, impossible to identify actual sources of metaphors or symbols with such final and convincing certainty that there can be no doubt that Eliot had this or that particular passage in mind when writing a certain line. Although this is occasionally possible, the student must generally content himself with a more or less limited range of likely texts with similar imagery expressing similar thoughts and experiences. Similar fundamental thoughts and experiences expressed in similar symbolic form – that might pass as a definition of a literary tradition, and a survey of Eliot's tradition in this sense is the first step towards solving the problem of the symbolic meaning of the *Quartets*. There are obviously Eliot's personal experiences and contacts – if they be called "sources" – but this is, of course, country closed to the explorer.

Eliot's definition of the concept of tradition is of minor importance in this context, but since a definition predicates attributes to a class, it may be well to draw attention to the development of Eliot's concept of tradition after he had written "Tradition and the Individual Talent" (1919). Reconsidering his doctrine of tradition in *After Strange Gods* (1934), Eliot observes that the problem no longer appears so simple to him, nor could he "treat it now as a purely literary one".[19] He emphasizes the religious side of tradition which, however, "is not solely, or even primarily, the maintenance of certain dogmatic beliefs".[20] Tradition is a way of feeling and behaving as much as a way of thinking and writing. Yet there is right and wrong thinking, leading to right and wrong action; by association with orthodoxy, tradition eventually becomes a philosophy of life.[21] The main development in Eliot's concept of tradition between 1919 and 1934 is thus his extension of the meaning of the literary tradition so as to include also philosophy and theology.

"Royalist in politics" was Eliot's second declaration in his creed of 1928, and hence it appears that his view of tradition has its political aspect as well. Eliot's association with Charles Maurras and *L'action française* and his conservative attitude towards ecclesiastical and educational matters, seem closely related to his activities as a man of letters, but in so far as the *Four Quartets* are political at all, they are only vaguely patriotic and the topic can therefore be set aside in this study.[22]

Eliot's conversion to Anglo-Catholicism had no doubt been prepared by his study of one of the great Anglo-Saxon humanists of this century, Irving Babbitt. Of all Eliot's teachers and spiritual mentors he seems to have done most to foster Eliot's sense of tradition, to open his eyes to the continuity of cultural development, and to encourage his search for ethical and literary standards. For many years

[19] Ibid., p. 15.

[20] Ibid., p. 18.

[21] Ibid., pp. 18 ff.

[22] For a full discussion of Eliot's political thought, see Beer, E., *Thomas Stearns Eliot und der Antiliberalismus des XX. Jahrhunderts*, Wien, 1953.

Eliot associated himself whole-heartedly with Babbitt's struggle against "romanticism" in literature and philosophy, and "Tradition and the Individual Talent" strongly suggests the influence of Babbitt's thought. It was characteristic, however, of Eliot's growing tendency to see everything in the light of the Christian religion and theology that, in *After Strange Gods*, he substituted the term "heresy" for "romanticism".[23] By the time of his conversion he had come to consider Babbitt's humanism insufficient both as *Weltanschauung* and as a standard of criticism.[24] In 1937 in his essay, "Revelation", Eliot criticizes his former teacher for having failed to discern the inherent truths of Christianity, truths which, Eliot suggests, place it above all other religions and philosophies.[25] Such a criticism does not, however, minimize the debt Eliot owes to the stimulus of Babbitt's teaching in earlier years.

While Eliot's conversion alienated him from Babbitt, it drew him closer to Paul Elmer More, once a friend of Babbitt's. More was also a friend of Eliot's, and from time to time until More's death in 1937, Eliot reviewed his books in English periodicals, and in a review of his posthumous *Pages from an Oxford Diary*, Eliot sums up the work and belief of his friend.[26]

"An Anglican Platonist", is Eliot's epithet for More, indicating the two main components in More's spiritual orientation – Greek idealism and Anglo-Catholicism combined with what Eliot calls "a passion for England, and especially for Oxford". More did not consider the amalgamation of these two elements of Anglicanism and Platonism in his own thought a matter of circumstance or personal inclination. They were rather successive stages in a continuous spiritual and philosophical development, and the tracing of this tradition is the object of his work, *The Greek Tradition* (1917–1931). This work in effect traces critically a line of development of thought from the death of Socrates to the council of Chalcedon in 451, with an

[23] *After Strange Gods*, p. 21.

[24] See "The Humanism of Irving Babbitt" (1928) in *Selected Essays*.

[25] *Revelation*, pp. 16 ff.

[26] *Times Literary Supplement*, Oct. 30, 1937, p. 792. For the attribution of this review to Eliot, see Gallup, p. 104. For other articles by Eliot on More, see Gallup, pp. 80, 96, 103 f.

additional volume, *The Catholic Faith.* But it is also an account of the dramatic struggle between two opposing trends in the classical world, the dualism of Plato and what More considers orthodox Christianity on the one hand, and the heretical schools of monism on the other. Philosophy and theology are inseparable elements in More's exposition. While, in More's view, Christianity would never have had the effect it has had without the influence of Platonism, neither would Platonism have had it without the aid of Christianity. Especially significant is the influence of Platonism on those Christian apologists who defended the orthodox doctrine of the Incarnation against the heresies of Gnostic and other sects. The philosophy and theology of the Incarnation is the subject of the fourth part of *The Greek Tradition, Christ the Word.*

Beginning as a humanist in the sense that Babbitt was a humanist, thence gradually approaching a definite Christian belief, More's spiritual progress suggests a striking parallel to Eliot's, but Eliot's tone when writing of More certainly suggests that he regarded him more as an honoured friend than as a teacher. But to go any further into this question of their personal relationship would be to stray too far from the point in question.

More's *The Greek Tradition* is in fact an exposition of a concept of tradition very much akin to Eliot's own, and even if More is by no means Eliot's sole or even main authority on ancient philosophy and theology, he almost certainly supplied Eliot with a special approach. A further instance of the coinciding interests of the two friends is to be found in their literary criticism, in both cases limited to shorter essays, usually rather personal in tone. More's *Shelburne Essays* (1904–1921) often deal with subjects and authors that also occur in Eliot's criticism, *e.g.* classicism as against romanticism, seventeenth century devotional poets, Pascal – to mention only a few instances. But there are also some important discrepancies between More's views and interests and Eliot's, shortly to be specified.

Eliot's acquaintance with Greek philosophy had been firmly established before his arrival in England, but when at Merton College, Oxford, in the winter of 1914–1915, he had an opportunity of renewing and deepening this acquaintance. However, it seems that after the year in Oxford he has never again had the time or inclination to devote himself whole-heartedly to systematic philosophical studies. Yet, as Kristian Smidt observes,

> The philosopher in him lingered on, as we can tell by the essays in *The Monist* and a number of reviews in the *International Journal of Ethics* of 1916 and 1917. But he was soon swallowed up by the poet and the literary critic. We may, however, discern many of the features of the philosopher in the physiognomy of the poet ...[27]

One of the aims of the present study is to relate the philosophical features of the *Four Quartets* to Eliot's philosophical reading, but if we expect to find the same orientation in the poet of 1935 as in the student and scholar of 1915, we shall be disappointed. The change brought about by his study of Dante and by his Anglican conversion did not necessarily imply a new philosophical outlook, since philosophy was no longer his chief concern. But it brought him into contact with philosophical systems which seem not to have interested him so much before. In these cases, it would seem, it is not the systematic categories of philosophy that are essential, but rather the imaginative force.

That Eliot is a Platonist, as the comparison with P. E. More suggests, is a view which perhaps needs some justification. It has become usual for Eliot's critics to place him on the side of Aristotelianism as against Platonism. Perhaps the most striking instance of such classification is provided by E. R. Curtius in his discussion of Eliot's criticism of Keats' "Ode on a Grecian Urn". Commenting on the line

Beauty is truth, truth beauty ...

Eliot says that "this statement of equivalence means nothing to me". Either he fails to understand it, he says, or it is untrue – he sees no other alternative.[28] On this Curtius comments:

> Armer Keats! Die „sinnlose" Gleichsetzung von Wahrheit und Schönheit war shon bei Shaftesbury zu finden, der gesagt hat: *Beauty is truth*. Die Quelle des Gedankens ist natürlich Platon.

[27] Smidt, p. 34.
[28] *Selected Essays*, p. 270.

> Eliot ist wahrscheinlich zu sehr Aristoteliker, um für platonisches Denken empfänglich zu sein.[29]

Divested of Curtius' irony the same idea recurs in many places, and that Eliot owes much to Aristotle can hardly be doubted. But nevertheless many of the major figures and symbols of the *Four Quartets* are best explained and understood in terms of Platonic and Neo-Platonic philosophy.

How far Aristotelianism and Platonism are to be considered as opposing philosophical systems, is a question not to be discussed here. With regard to Eliot, the difference between Plato and Aristotle on the one hand, and Neo-Platonism on the other, seems more relevant. In this respect Eliot is likely to have been influenced by Babbitt and More who were eager to emphasize and implant in their disciples the fundamental distinction between "true" Platonism, implying a strict moral and metaphysical dualism, and the monistic Neo-Platonism, the root of all "romantic" aberrations.[30] Being associated with romanticism in literature and with heresy in theology, Neo-Platonism is certainly opposed to what Eliot stands for.

Although Eliot is thus likely to disagree with the fundamental position of, for example, Plotinus, much of the imagery of the *Four Quartets* bears the imprint of Plotinian, or generally Neo-Platonic, influence. Eliot also seems to have been ready enough to accept many of the Neo-Platonic elements in the *Divine Comedy*, perhaps without realizing, or bothering about, the origin of these elements, for there is much to suggest that he believed Dante to be a good Thomist – a very interesting point which will presently be the subject of further discussion. It would seem as if, unconsciously, Eliot had made use of Neo-Platonic imagery in the *Quartets*. But he may also have been well aware of the fundamental difference between the Neo-Platonic point of view and his own, for it does seem clear that in order to derive poetically effective metaphors from another

[29] Curtius, E. R., *Kritische Essays zur europäischen Literatur*, 2nd ed., Bern, 1954, p. 354.

[30] Cf. More, P. E., *Hellenistic Philosophies*, p. 172; Babbitt, I., *The Dhammapada*, Oxf. Univ. Press, 1936, p. 105. The relation between Platonism and Neo-Platonism is of course a controversial topic.

writer, a poet need not necessarily accept his philosophy (or religion).

As regards Eliot's relation to Plato himself, there is hardly any real difficulty. "True" Platonism, in Babbitt's and More's sense of the term, seems fully compatible with Eliot's Christian belief. And Eliot has certainly read most of the dialogues of Plato – inevitably, as a university teacher of philosophy – and is likely to have studied possible readings in the original text. His ability to do so is confirmed by his statement: "I still think it [Greek] a much greater language [than Latin]: a language which has never been surpassed as a vehicle for the fullest range and the finest shades of thought and feeling."[31] But the question whether the philosophical reminiscences in the imagery of the *Four Quartets* were directly suggested by Eliot's academic studies or his general reading during subsequent years, is not only very difficult to decide, but anyway largely irrelevant to the actual interpretation of the *Quartets*.

Eliot's tradition is not only Greek; it is also Roman. He speaks of More's "lifelong Platonism, which gave him a bias towards the Greek fathers rather than the Latin".[32] In Eliot there seems to be more balance between the two, and there is no trace in his writings of the occasionally hostile tone of More in speaking of the Roman Catholic Church. In deliberate contrast to More's Greek tradition Eliot applied the title, "The Latin Tradition" to a book review in 1929, but in the end the contrast appears to be a complement; the right balance demands an equal stress on the Greek and the Latin elements.[33] Eliot's deep respect for the Latin elements of the spiritual tradition of the West is centred on two names, those of Virgil and Dante – to which perhaps a third, St. Augustine, might be added.

Virgil's direct influence on Eliot's poetry seems of minor significance, but in his critical work Eliot returns to Virgil time and again. Already at school he felt himself "at ease" with Virgil,[34] and the enormous importance he has come to attribute to him later in life

[31] *On Poetry and Poets*, p. 124.

[32] Vide supra, note 26.

[33] *Times Literary Supplement*, March 14, 1929, p. 200. For the attribution of this review to Eliot, see Gallup, p. 96.

[34] *On Poetry and Poets*, p. 124.

is manifest in the two essays, "What is a Classic?" (1944) and "Virgil and the Christian World" (1951). In the latter Eliot maintains that, in spite of the mistakes of the traditional medieval reading of the fourth *Eclogue*, the notion of Virgil as a forerunner of Christianity is well-grounded: "There is in Aeneas a virtue – an essential ingredient in his piety – which is an analogue and foreshadow of Christian humility" and "He is, in fact, the prototype of a Christian hero".[35] This view of Virgil not only echoes Dante's, but also illustrates Eliot's affirmation of the relationship between pagan thought and Christian theology. Without this interpretation of the works of the classical authors as analogous to and foreshadowing Christianity, it would be impossible to understand the place of, for example, Heracleitus' Logos and Aristotle's Unmoved Mover in the *Quartets*.

According to Eliot Virgil's chief anticipation of Christianity lies in his idea of a Roman empire, which later became the Holy Roman Empire, and it is perhaps as a philosopher of history and tradition in this sense that Virgil has influenced Eliot most. In an essay on "T. S. Eliot as a Classical Scholar", W. F. Jackson Knight quotes the following highly suggestive passage from Father E. J. Stormon:

> A sense of history does in fact play an important part in the poetry of men like Eliot and Yeats. [. . .] But for the perfect use of the time-dimension (not to speak of the past in its timeless aspect) we must go to Virgil. In the *Aeneid* it is everywhere [. . .], especially in single forward- or backward-looking words or phrases and in a certain consciousness of "things gone by" conveyed by tone and texture as much as by explicit statement. The sense of time as a factor partly constitutive of the reality apprehended by the poet is something to which the modern should be particularly responsive.[36]

The references to St. Augustine in Eliot's writings, though not many, are important. The *Confessions* are echoed in *The Waste Land* and also in the *Four Quartets*. St. Augustine to some extent exemplifies the deliberate tendency of many of the Fathers of the Church to translate pagan philosophy into Christian terms. This is true in particular of his cosmology and his metaphysics of time,

[35] Ibid., pp. 127, 128.

[36] Knight, W. F. J., "T. S. Eliot as a Classical Scholar", *T. S. Eliot. A Symposium for his Seventieth Birthday*, ed. by N. Braybrooke, London, 1958, p. 127.

which are variations on Plato's *Timaeus*. This aspect of St. Augustine's philosophy appears almost beyond doubt to have exercised a direct influence on Eliot, but in the case of St. Augustine as well as Virgil the indirect influence through the writings of Dante is often equally important.

Of all the influences that can be traced in Eliot's work there is probably no single author more important than Dante. Literary, philosophical and religious, his influence is manifest from "Prufrock" to the last of the *Quartets*, and the technical devices Eliot has learnt from Dante are as fundamental as the themes derived from the *Divine Comedy*. The problem of Dante's technical influence will be considered in a separate chapter.[37] The object of the present discussion is to estimate Dante's place in Eliot's literary tradition and his relation to certain themes in the *Four Quartets*.

The most important period in Eliot's lifelong study of Dante was the nineteen-twenties. During that period he published two essays on Dante, the first in 1920 in *The Sacred Wood* and the second as a separate pamphlet in 1929. The first is very thin and superficial compared with the second. The second also shows a marked change in attitude; so marked, in fact, as to justify the assumption that Eliot only came to realize Dante's full significance for him after he had written the earlier essay. This realization was not only Eliot's recognition of Dante as one of the greatest poets of the West, but his realization that Dante had more to teach him as a poet than any other writer before or since. Eliot's attitude to Dante might even be compared with Dante's attitude to Virgil:

O degli altri poeti onore e lume,
  Vagliami il lungo studio e il grande amore,
  Che m'ha fatto cercar lo tuo volume.
Tu se' lo mio maestro e il mio autore:
  Tu se' solo colui, da cui io tolsi
  Lo bello stile che m'ha fatto onore.[38]

[37] For a full account of the quotations and other verbal allusions to Dante in Eliot's poetry, see Praz, M., "T. S. Eliot and Dante", *T. S. Eliot. A Selected Critique*, ed. by L. Unger, New York, 1948.

[38] Dante, *Inferno*, I, 82–87.

The development of this deepening appreciation and understanding of Dante between 1920 and 1929 is reflected in Eliot's poetry during that period. His three major poetic works from that time, *The Waste Land* (1922), "The Hollow Men" (1925) and "Ash-Wednesday" (1928–30), all show the influence of Dante, but from appearing mainly in isolated metaphors and themes in the first two, in "Ash-Wednesday" the influence extends to the very structure of the poem, which is analogous to Dante's *via purgativa.*

It is deeply significant that Eliot's growing understanding of Dante was contemporary with his conversion, though it is difficult to decide which is the cause, and which the effect. On the one hand Eliot's study of the *Divine Comedy* no doubt prepared him for his final acceptance of Christianity, but on the other, his conviction of the truth of the Christian doctrine must have made him all the readier to accept Dante's view of life.

Dante's Christian faith cannot be doubted, but his orthodoxy seems more questionable. It is perhaps not quite appropriate to speak of an orthodox Christian doctrine in the West at the time of Dante, since, for example, St. Thomas Aquinas was not yet made an official authority of the Church. It has been maintained, however, by a number of Dante scholars that the *Divine Comedy* owes its main structure to the *Summa Theologiae,* and since Eliot seems to share this view at least to some extent, and since he has built his theory of the relation between poetry and belief partly on Dante, this question of Dante's "orthodoxy" is well worth considering.

There is ample evidence of Eliot's believing Dante to be an orthodox Christian poet in the sense that the intellectual framework of the *Divine Comedy* derives from such elements in the then contemporary theological and philosophical thought as were later to be accepted as the orthodox doctrine of the Roman Church. As regards Dante's relation to Thomas Aquinas, Eliot is not quite so positive as many other critics of Dante: "Dante's debt to St. Thomas Aquinas [. . .] can be easily exaggerated; for it must not be forgotten that Dante read and made use of other great mediaeval philosophers as well." [39] He also points out another aspect of Dante's poetic philosophy: the peculiar Dantesque pattern of the *Divine Comedy,* which

[39] *Selected Essays,* p. 257.

is not derived from any external system.[40] Recognizing these two elements in the *Comedy*, medieval and ancient philosophy in general and Dante's own original thought, Eliot yet regards Aquinas as one of Dante's main sources. And he never hints at any downright heterodox elements in the *Divine Comedy*.

Until quite recently Eliot's view of Dante's philosophical background seems to have been shared by the majority of Dante scholars, although some recent works on Dante have made this view appear doubtful – for instance, E. Gilson's *Dante et la philosophie* (1939), of which work E. R. Curtius firmly declares, "Sie hat uns endgültig von der Irrlehre befreit, Dante sei Thomist gewesen".[41] Instead of Thomist philosophy Curtius emphasizes two other components in Dante's thought. The first is one acknowledged also by Eliot, namely Dante's own original thought, what Eliot calls his private "pattern" and Curtius "myth and prophecy".[42] The second component is Neo-Platonism, sometimes with a Gnostic colouring.[43] The Platonic elements in the *Divine Comedy* have been further analysed by J. A. Mazzeo who, in confirming Dante's debt to Plato, Plotinus and Pseudo-Dionysius, convincingly demonstrates the heterodox character of Dante's view on such varied topics as, for instance, the function of metaphors and the nature of the beatific vision.[44] It is difficult to tell what Eliot would think of the criticism of these three scholars; in 1956 he expressed his great admiration of "that masterly work" of Curtius', *Europäische Literatur und lateinisches Mittelalter*,[45] but that was about twenty years after he wrote the first of the *Quartets*.

What does it matter, it might be argued, whether Eliot was aware of the origins of the thought and symbolism of the *Divine Comedy*

[40] Eliot's Introduction to G. Wilson Knight, *The Wheel of Fire*, Oxford, 1930, pp. xi f.

[41] Curtius, E. R., *Europäische Literatur und lateinisches Mittelalter*, Bern, 1948, p. 376.

[42] Ibid., pp. 376 ff.

[43] Ibid., p. 381 and passim.

[44] Mazzeo, J. A., *Structure and Thought in the Paradiso*, Ithaca, New York, 1958, pp. 11, 40 f., 97 ff.

[45] *Freundesausgabe für Ernst Robert Curtius zum 14. April 1956*, Bern, 1956, p. 27.

or not? Eliot believed that Dante was indebted to contemporary philosophers such as Aquinas rather than to Platonic and Neo-Platonic thought, and if subsequent scholarship has modified this view, that need not worry the student of Eliot's poetry. But it is not so simple. Dante's influence on Eliot seems to be deeper than is suggested by Eliot's own critical writings. Much of the Neo-Platonic material in the *Divine Comedy*, to which Mazzeo has drawn attention, has entered into the *Four Quartets*, probably without Eliot's full recognition of its origin, and Dante's use of allegory, heterodox in actual fact though not recognized as such by Eliot, is one of the keys to the understanding of the structure of the *Quartets*. In these ways Eliot has thus unconsciously imparted to the *Quartets* a force and imaginative power that redeems and counter-balances any deliberate, almost didactic tendencies.

Dante, as the preceding paragraphs show, may be regarded as combining something of the Greek as well as of the Latin tradition, the tradition on which Eliot builds. After Dante the different strands of the great tradition are no longer distinguishable in the work of a single author. It is superfluous to trace the various elements of this tradition in post-Renaissance literature, though a few schools and individual authors may be mentioned, whom Eliot, at some time or other, has recognized as upholders of the classical tradition in Christian literature: seventeenth century English poets and preachers of the Metaphysical school, Pascal, Racine and, in a way, Baudelaire. And it may surely be said that it is the ambition of the author of the *Four Quartets* to have his name added to this tradition, and that, equally surely, it will be the duty of the scholars of the future to consider his claim.

Something more should be said of Eliot's debt to the Metaphysical poets. Their contribution to the development of the Christian tradition in poetry is surely in itself remarkable enough, but their special relevance in the present context lies in the fact that they have consistently influenced Eliot both as a critic and as a poet. A number of his essays are devoted to these poets, and several of his earlier poems clearly show the influence of, for example, Donne and Marvell. In his later poetry the more devout ones of the Metaphysical poets seem to play an important part, which of course is natural enough.

Thus the title of the last of the *Quartets*, "Little Gidding", is associated with both Georg Herbert and Richard Crashaw. Herbert was a close friend of Nicolas Ferrar, the master of Little Gidding, with whom Herbert carried on a correspondence on spiritual matters for many years, and Crashaw was one of the visitors to the pious community at Little Gidding.[46] In view of these circumstances it seems appropriate to relate certain ideas and images in the *Four Quartets* to the works of the Metaphysical poets.

While the European Christian tradition forms the core of Eliot's vast reading and learning, there is among the more peripheral material one sphere of thought and literature that deserves special attention in this context: Indian philosophy. Eliot's study of Indian philosophy and religion and the use he has made of it, have been examined chiefly by two critics. Kristian Smidt discusses at some length Eliot's Hindu sources, and H. E. MacCarthy analyses his relation to Buddhism.[47] There is no need to rehearse the evidence they have adduced; Eliot's debt to Indian thought is a recognized fact. It is an interesting question, however, what place Eliot attributes to Indian thought and religion in relation to the Christian tradition.

Eliot's academic study of Indian philosophy is confined to his second, post-graduate period at Harvard from 1911 to 1914.[48] Behind this choice of study one divines the influence of Babbitt, who was an outstanding oriental scholar, and Eliot's own characterization of the insight gathered from this study has an air of urbane scepticism worthy of his famous teacher: "Two years spent in the study of Sanskrit under Charles Lanman", he wrote in 1934, "and a year in the mazes of Patanjali's metaphysics under the guidance of James Woods, left me in a state of enlightened mystification."[49] And he goes on to declare that Eastern and Western thought appeared to him in marked contrast as regards "philosophical categories and kinds

[46] See Hyde, A. G., *George Herbert and His Times*, London, 1906, pp. 197–222; and Walton, Izaak, *The Life of Mr. George Herbert*, London, 1670, pp. 100 ff.

[47] Smidt, pp. 166–172; MacCarthy, H. E., "T. S. Eliot and Buddhism", *Philosophy East and West*, Vol. 2, no. 1, pp. 31–55.

[48] Matthiessen, F. O., *The Achievement of T. S. Eliot*, 2nd ed., Oxford, 1947, p. xvi.

[49] *After Strange Gods*, p. 40.

of distinction". But however mystified, he evidently acquired an extensive knowledge of the various systems and the symbolic language in which they are expressed. From that point of view we are wholly justified in relating the imagery of the *Four Quartets* to Indian sources, whenever we are invited to do so by metaphors strikingly similar to those of Indian philosophy and religion.

It is relevant, however, to ask to what extent the metaphors thus derived retain the philosophical and religious implications they bear in their original contexts; or, in other words, whether Eliot has attempted to bring the Indian elements into harmony with the general Christian trend of the *Quartets*. Applied to most other authors such a question might appear pedantic, since most writers of poetry and fiction are not concerned with inconsistency of this kind in symbolic allusions, but Eliot the poet seems inseparable from the shadow of Eliot the scholar, and it is therefore very improbable that he was unaware of this problem in writing the *Quartets*.

An answer to the question is to be found in the seventh Chorus from *The Rock*, in which Eliot paraphrases the opening of Genesis. The second part of the Chorus runs as follows:

And the Spirit moved upon the face of the water.
And men who turned towards the light and were known of the light
Invented the Higher Religions; and the Higher Religions were good
And led men from light to light, to knowledge of Good and Evil.
But their light was ever surrounded and shot with darkness
As the air of temperate seas is pierced by the still dead breath of the Arctic Current;
And they came to an end, a dead end stirred with a flicker of life,
And they came to the withered ancient look of a child that has died of starvation.
Prayer wheels, worship of the dead, denial of this world, affirmation of rites with forgotten meanings
In the restless wind-whipped sand, or the hills where the wind will not let the snow rest.
Waste and void. Waste and void. And darkness on the face of the deep.
Then came, at a predetermined moment, a moment in time and of time . . .[50]

In this passage the "Higher Religions" seems to include both Hinduism and Buddhism as well as the mystery religions of classical

[50] *Collected Poems 1909–1935*, pp. 172 f.

antiquity. All these religions are seen as stages in a spiritual development leading up to the Incarnation of Christ, but here "development" is not equal to "evolution" or "progress" in the modern sense; it is the development of a divine intention. The Higher Religions are said to have been "invented" by men, that is true, but by "men who turned towards the light and were known of the light". That is to say man invented the outer forms of worship of a revealed deity. But the revelation granted to the Indians and the ancients was only a partial revelation, because the only full revelation, according to Eliot, is the Incarnation.

Paul Elmer More significantly put this same idea into rather laboured prose. In an essay on "Buddhism and Christianity" of 1931, he wrote:

> So, as I read the Buddhist books and am filled with admiring reverence for the Founder of the Dharma, it seems to me at times as if that great soul were searching on all the ways of the spirit for the dogma of the Incarnation, and that the fact of the historic Jesus, could it have been known to him, might have saved his religion in later ages from floundering helplessly, yet not ignobly, among the vanishing shadowy myths that so curiously resemble and multiply, while ever just missing, the story of the Word made flesh. Buddhism, I think, at the last may be accepted as a preface to the Gospel, "lovely in its origin, lovely in its progress, lovely in its end", and as the most convincing argument withal that truth to be clearly known waits upon revelation.[51]

Allowing for the fact that Buddhism undoubtedly meant more to P. E. More than it has ever done to Eliot, the statement seems in a general way to express Eliot's standpoint. The connection between the Indian religions and Christianity thus appears parallel to the connection between certain classical Greek and Latin authors and the Christian revelation, of which they were, in Eliot's view, "analogues and foreshadows". And consequently the allusions to Indian religion in the *Quartets* should be interpreted as foreshadowings or figures of the unequivocally Christian vision at the end of "Little Gidding". The dramatic structure of the *Quartets*, the gradual movement towards a full Christian interpretation of life, is thus founded

[51] More, P. E., *The Catholic Faith*, Princeton, 1931, p. 75.

on the conception of a divine pattern in history, a pattern which to Eliot was recognizable not only in the history of religions and civilizations, but also in his own life.[52]

IV

The insistence upon classicism and orthodoxy as ultimate standards of criticism, points to a fundamental trait of intellectualism, almost of rationalism, in Eliot's personality. But this trait is counter-balanced, not only by his obvious poetic sensibility, but also by an inclination towards religious mysticism. His poetry and prose writings contain numerous references to mystic literature, and one cannot go very far into the *Four Quartets* without encountering the influence of, for instance, St. John of the Cross. References to mystic literature are one thing, but it is quite a different matter to decide whether Eliot himself is to be regarded as mystic, *i.e.* whether he has had genuine mystic experiences, or only has a second-hand, literary knowledge of such experiences. This, of course, is not for his critics to decide, but an account of Eliot's own views on the matter may throw some light on the problem, and thus contribute towards a fuller understanding of the mystic elements in the *Four Quartets.*

The imagery used in Eliot's poetry shows a striking continuity, unbroken by his conversion. Since much of the mysticism of the *Quartets* is expressed in images recurring from earlier poems, it may be well to consider some of these images. In the rose garden scene of "Burnt Norton", for instance, such images recur several times, images which in Eliot's earlier poetry appear sometimes singly and

[52] In outlining Eliot's tradition above, it has been tacitly assumed that, in writing the *Four Quartets,* he was conscious of employing traditional figures and symbols, even if he did not bother about the exact source of particular symbols. But some critics have tried to interpret Eliot's imagery in terms of Jungian "archetypes" or "primordial images", emphasizing the unconscious or "mythical" patterns in his imagery. See Foster, G. W., "The Archetypal Imagery of T. S. Eliot", *PMLA,* Vol. 60, 1945, pp. 567–585; with a comment by Coomaraswamy, A, K., in *PMLA,* Vol. 61, pp. 601–602; cf. also Martin, P. W., *Experiment in Depth. A Study of the Work of Jung, Eliot and Toynbee,* London, 1955.

sometimes as a complex of symbols. An early instance of this complex use is the following passage from *The Waste Land*:

> "You gave me hyacinths first a year ago;
> "They called me the hyacinth girl."
> – Yet when we came back, late, from the Hyacinth garden,
> Your arms full, and your hair wet, I could not
> Speak, and my eyes failed, I was neither
> Living nor dead, and I knew nothing,
> Looking into the heart of light, the silence.
> *Oed' und leer das Meer.*

This is evidently a reminiscence of a significant emotional experience of some kind. In a transport of ecstasy the speaker is subject to a vision of light and silence, followed by a feeling of disappointment and emptiness. The difference of imagery between this scene and the corresponding one in "Burnt Norton" lies in the greater complexity of the imagery of the latter and in the substitution of roses for hyacinths. As roses frequently occur in many other poems, the whole complex will, for the sake of brevity, be called the rose garden symbol.

The content and meaning of this symbol before and after *The Waste Land* is the subject of a study by Leonard Unger. He suggests that the core of the complex symbol is an experience of a sexual character belonging to Eliot's early years. To this experience, he says, Eliot repeatedly alludes, each time ascribing new and deeper meaning to it.[53] Unger largely ignores the religious implications, which are not stated by Eliot in any final way, but gradually emerge and take form after his conversion. It is evident, however, that the vision of light in *The Waste Land* represents a mystic experience, though mystic only in the limited sense of being little more than supernatural.

It should be noticed that Eliot draws an important distinction between mysticism in a psychological sense and mysticism in a religious sense. To him a supernatural experience is not necessarily mystic in the religious sense. Against true, religious mysticism he sets the

[53] Unger, L., "T. S. Eliot's Rose Garden", *T. S. Eliot. A Selected Critique*. The theme is further developed by Wagner, R. D., "The Meaning of Eliot's Rose-Garden", *PMLA*, Vol. 69, 1954, pp. 22–33.

"*psychological mysticism* that is a phenomenon of decadence rather than of growth. This is the mysticism which seeks contact with the sources of supernatural power, divorced from religion and theology".[54] If we are justified in speaking of a mystic element in Eliot's pre-conversional poetry, this mysticism is by his own definition psychological, since, at that time, he had no definite religion or theology to relate it to. And yet the supernatural experience in *The Waste Land* *is* related to some sort of doctrine, if not religious at least philosophical. In the last part of the poem the author speaks of

> The awful daring of a moment's surrender
> Which an age of prudence can never retract
> By this, and this only, we have existed

The nature of this surrender is only vaguely suggested. A surrender of what to what? Thus much can be said that it means a breaking through of the dimension of ordinary life, leading to a contact with Absolute Reality (implied in the concept of existence as it is used here in contradistinction to everyday existence). Interpreted in this way, the supernatural experience of *The Waste Land* may be related to Bradley's system of metaphysics,[55] and in that case we may speak of philosophical mysticism rather than psychological. And in the *Four Quartets*, where religion has taken the place of philosophical metaphysics, and union with God that of absolute existence, it would seem reasonable to speak of Christian mysticism.

At this stage of the argument another distinction has to be drawn. Isolated mystic experiences may occur to a man who is not a mystic. Eliot makes this point quite clear in speaking of Pascal's famous illumination, and he seems to draw a parallel to his own experience in a passage that deserves quotation in full:

> We know quite well that he was at the time when he received his illumination from God in extremely poor health; but it is a commonplace that some forms of illness are extremely favourable, not only to religious illumination, but to artistic and literary composition. A piece of writing meditated, apparently without progress, for months or years, may suddenly take shape and word; and in this state long passages may be produced which require

[54] *Revelation*, p. 23.
[55] Cf. Smidt, pp. 129 f.

little or no retouch. I have no good word to say for the cultivation of automatic writing as the model of literary composition; I doubt whether these moments *can* be cultivated by the writer; but he to whom this happens assuredly has the sensation of being a vehicle rather than a maker. No masterpiece can be produced whole by such means: but neither does even the higher form of religious inspiration suffice for the religious life; even the most exalted mystic must return to the world, and use his reason to employ the results of his experience in daily life. You may call it communion with the Divine, or you may call it a temporary crystallization of the mind. Until science can teach us to reproduce such phenomena at will, science cannot claim to have explained them; and they can be judged only by their fruits.[56]

This passage is, by implication, most revealing. It seems to suggest that Eliot has received illumination similar to that of Pascal, but neither Pascal nor Eliot claim to be mystics. (By a mystic he probably here means one to whom illuminations are frequent rather than occasional.) Artistic inspiration is analogous to religious illumination, but neither can be cultivated by the non-mystic, though they may come to him. Furthermore, the experiences are sometimes concomitant with physical illness. Not sufficient in themselves for the religious life or artistic creation, they form the starting-point of an intellectual process that aims at finding the meaning of the experiences. Finally, whether this meaning is to be formulated in terms of psychology or religion, is a question to be decided, not by science, but by the individual man. In effect Eliot suggests that, while not a mystic, he, like Pascal, has had experiences of a special kind which border on the mystical and thus make mysticism comprehensible to him.

Although the essay on Pascal was written before Eliot had the idea of writing the first of the *Quartets*, there is no reason to believe that any fundamental change took place in his mind between 1931 and 1934. The essay thus has its relevance to a study of the *Quartets*, especially its reference to "crystallization".

If the reconstruction of the composition of "Burnt Norton" attempted at the beginning of this chapter is correct, "Burnt Norton" itself affords an example of "crystallization" in this sense. The in-

[56] *Selected Essays*, p. 405.

spiration of the poem lay in an illumination Eliot received in the garden of Burnt Norton, although it is essential to distinguish here between the experience underlying the symbol of the rose garden and the actual illumination or "crystallization" in the mind. The rose garden episode reverts beyond the early poems, probably to the author's childhood, and in "Burnt Norton" it clearly appears as a reminiscence. And it is upon this reminiscence that the mind of the poet is intent when the "crystallization" occurs: the same experience that has occupied his mind for years is suddenly seen in a new light, as part of a new pattern. But the fleeting illumination is not sufficient; the new meaning is barely touched, not firmly grasped. Thus this moment of "crystallization" impells the poet to seek its intimated and inner meaning, and the poem is the account of that search, and *is*, in fact, the search itself.

This attempt to reconstruct the essence of the experience in the garden of Burnt Norton may not be accepted by the reader, especially in the absence of any positive external evidence to support it. Nevertheless, it does seem consistent with the whole feeling of the poem, and at least to suggest lines along which the reader may, as Eliot means him to do, interpret the poem for himself. Even if the critic chooses not to identify the speaker of "Burnt Norton" with Eliot himself, there must be someone to whom the experience occurs and in whose mind the subsequent meditation is carried on; otherwise the poem is meaningless.

The question of the figurative and symbolic language derived from mystical literature has concerned many critics, and it seems appropriate at this point to attempt to estimate the extent to which Eliot's reading of mystical literature has projected itself into his poetry.

In the essay on Pascal, Eliot maintains that spontaneous illumination should be followed by spiritual and intellectual discipline. Even the mystic "must return to the world, and use his reason to employ the results of his experience in daily life". It is precisely to this end that Eliot seems to put his reading of mystical literature: to guide him, or supply him with the appropriate words with which to convey the essence of what he has divined.

Perhaps the most conspicuous mystic feature of the *Quartets* is the concept of the dark night, most clearly illustrated in the Third

Section of "East Coker" beginning, "O dark dark dark. They all go into the dark." (It is convenient to call this pattern the dark night of the soul, as suggested by a reference to one of the works of St. John of the Cross describing the negative way to union with God.) Eliot's debt specifically to St. John should, however, not be exaggerated, for there is a whole body of mystical literature with much the same theme. St. John was nevertheless not only a devout mystic, he was also a remarkable poet. Intellectual analysis and poetic synthesis blend in his work, and hence his appeal for Eliot is not difficult to understand. His actual influence on the *Quartets* may, however, better be gauged from the examples discussed in the following chapter.

The psychological phenomenon of the "dark night" was probably familiar to Eliot before he took any apparent interest in Christian mysticism. This is no doubt what is reflected in the essay on Pascal, when he says that illness may be favourable to literary composition: "A piece of writing meditated, apparently without progress, for months or years, may suddenly take shape and word." [57] Whether Eliot had any particular work of his own in mind in writing this, is impossible to say, but it applies very well to all that is known about the composition of *The Waste Land*. A French version of the fourth part of that poem appeared as early as 1918 (the conclusion of "Dans le Restaurant").[58] The work was not completed until the beginning of 1922, however, and these circumstances might be taken to correspond to Eliot's words, "meditated, apparently without progress, for months or years". Though nothing is known about an illumination previous to the final composition of *The Waste Land*, it does seem that it was preceded and followed by physical exhaustion and mental depression. This much at least is suggested by one of the published letters of Ezra Pound, dated March 18, 1922, which contains the following dramatic account of Eliot's situation: "Too tired to write, broke down; during convalescence in Switzerland did *Waste Land*, a masterpiece; one of most important 19 pages in English. Returned to bank, and is again gone to pieces, physically." [59] The

[57] *Selected Essays*, p. 405. [58] Cf. Gallup, p. 83.

[59] *The Letters of Ezra Pound 1907–1941*, ed. by D. D. Paige, London, 1951, p. 239.

letter begins, "The point is that Eliot is at the last gasp. Has had one breakdown. We have got to do something at once." And Pound and his friends did help Eliot, financially in the first place. The success of *The Waste Land* probably did something as well, and from 1922 Eliot's social and financial position seems to have been constantly improving. But judging from his poetic output the depression deepened: "The Hollow Men", published in 1924–25, marks the absolute zero of pessimism in Eliot's poetry, if not in his life. All this may well have been experienced by Eliot as something of a "dark night", for after it his development takes on a new direction, and his next work, "Ash-Wednesday", speaks of the pains and joys of spiritual rebirth and the tone of faith and confidence is never wholly lost in any of his subsequent poems.

Thus the psychological pattern of Eliot's creative activity during the nineteen-twenties forms a parallel to the dark night of the mystics: frustration, exhaustion, deprivation, followed by inspiration, illumination and perhaps grace. The analogy between his own experience and that of the traditional mystic experience he describes in the essay on Pascal. The psychological phenomena of which the mystics speak, were known to him before his conversion. But after his conversion he gave a new meaning to the same phenomena; instead of a psychological mechanism, he saw the hand of God. And consequently he did not again descend to such depths of despair. In the darkness lies the hope of grace.

The practice of such ascetic discipline as that prescribed by St. John of the Cross, so remote from the realities of his life, would no doubt have been without meaning to Eliot. Some of the discipline, circumstances had already imposed. The rest of the discipline, circumstances – his duties as publisher, editor, essayist, lecturer and poet – made impossible. It is therefore appropriate to regard Eliot's debt to St. John chiefly as a literary debt, manifest in verbal allusions and paraphrases.

Less easy to discover on the surface of Eliot's poetry, but more closely related to the core of his development into a Christian author, is the influence of Pascal. In Pascal, Eliot seems to see the counterpart and forerunner of the modern Christian mystic, the difference consisting in Pascal's being more intellectual than the traditional mystic, holding, as it were, a juster balance between human and Divine – one who thought as well as felt; saw a discipline and a purpose in it all:

> His [Pascal's] despair, his disillusion, are, however, no illustration of personal weakness; they are perfectly objective, because they are essential moments in the progress of the intellectual soul; and for the type of Pascal they are the analogue of the drought, the dark night, which is an essential stage in the progress of the Christian mystic.[60]

Thus Eliot regards Pascal in the deepest sense as an "intelligent believer"[61] rather than merely as an apologist or as a purely medieval mystic. An intelligent believer writing of the progress of the intellectual soul – that seems a perfect characterization of the later Eliot, and it is for these reasons that, as somebody has put it, Pascal's *Pensées* may be read as a preface to the *Four Quartets*.

Eliot's reading of mystical literature is very wide, however, and it would therefore be misleading to mention only St. John of the Cross and Pascal. His references to Yoga,[62] to Julian of Norwich, to the *Cloud of Unknowing*, and many others, amplify rather than deepen the understanding of his mysticism. The pattern is more or less the same, except for one aspect not hitherto discussed – the mystic doctrine of Divine love.

For his thought on Divine love Eliot is indebted to Dante more than to anyone else. It is Dante's doctrine of *amor* together with his symbolism of light that makes him into something of a mystic in Eliot's view.[63] Eliot's conception of Divine love is implicit in the last Section of "Burnt Norton" and in the conclusion of "Little Gidding", and becomes the counterpart, or rather the fulfilment, of the dark night. Yet Eliot does not seem to think that he has had any direct, mystic experience of Divine love. The experience involved seems to be the one underlying the rose garden symbol. When this symbol first occurs in his poetry, Eliot does not ascribe any religious significance to the experience behind it, but he came to do so "on mature

[60] *Selected Essays*, p. 412.
[61] Ibid., p. 408.
[62] Cf. Smidt, pp. 169 ff.
[63] *On Poetry and Poets*, p. 131.

reflection upon it", to borrow a phrase from his characterization of Dante's relation to Beatrice. Unger also has something to say of this relation between the rose garden symbol and Eliot's interpretation of Dante's love of Beatrice;[64] the relevant passage in Eliot's second essay on Dante does, in fact, contribute a great deal to the interpretation of the theme of love in the *Quartets*. Eliot assumes that the *Vita Nuova* is basically inspired by an experience of infantile sexuality. Whatever this experience was, it prompted that final expression of Dante's idea of love which culminated in the *Paradiso*. In order to understand this astounding development we have to accustom ourselves, Eliot holds, "to find meaning in *final causes* rather than in origins". Dante's attitude to the fundamental experience of the *Vita Nuova* is not "meant as a description of what he *consciously* felt on his meeting with Beatrice, but rather as a description of what that meant on mature reflection upon it. The final cause is the attraction towards God".[65]

Eliot's attempt to explore the meaning of the rose garden experience seems consciously and unconsciously to follow closely the lines of Dante's experience, and aims at establishing a connection between human love and something felt to be more Divine. The idea of the Final Cause being the attraction towards God recurs at the end of "Burnt Norton":

> Love is itself unmoving,
> Only the cause and end of movement

The analysis of that poem will show how closely the context of these lines is related to the rose garden episode.

The mystic doctrine of love in the *Quartets* therefore seems to be the outcome of long reflection and long contemplation rather than the immediate expression of direct experience, and thus lacks the force of Eliot's poetic rendering of the dark night. If he attempted to make "Little Gidding" a parallel of the *Paradiso*, he was not wholly successful, even if we allow for the difference of scope. Where, in Dante, we are dazzled by the profusion of light, in Eliot we still discern the intellectual scaffolding.

[64] Unger, pp. 374 f.

[65] *Selected Essays*, p. 274.

V

To attempt to isolate and analyse ideas and emotional attitudes in a poem is to attempt only half an interpretation; to complete it in any sense, some effort must be made to assemble these elements to conform with the general pattern that seems to underlie the poem as a whole. These two aspects, analysis and synthesis, cannot be wholly isolated from each other – the details of poetic technique naturally depend upon what the poet is trying to do – but for the sake of convenience, the technical problems will be considered later. At this juncture there remains the difficult problem of the relation of the poet's actual belief to the poetry in which he expresses it. As, however, Kristian Smidt has devoted his study to the problem of poetry and belief in Eliot, the details of the argument need not be rehearsed here. But Smidt is chiefly concerned with the question of the relation between the work and the reader, not of the relation between the author and his work. The second problem, Eliot's relation to his own poetical work with special reference to the *Four Quartets*, will therefore be briefly considered.

Eliot's views and beliefs have changed, but his ideas of the function of the writer seem never to have changed very much. As early as 1920 he passed the following judgment on Blake:

> What his genius required, and what it sadly lacked, was a framework of accepted and traditional ideas which would have prevented him from indulging in a philosophy of his own [...] The concentration resulting from a framework of mythology and theology and philosophy is one of the reasons why Dante is a classic, and Blake only a poet of genius.[66]

In 1930 the same notion reappears, but this time expressed in a less authoritative tone:

> Now it is only a personal prejudice of mine, that I prefer poetry with a clear philosophical pattern, if it has the other [private] pattern as well [...] I like a definite and dogmatic philosophy, preferably a Christian and Catholic one, but alternatively that of Epicurus or of the Forest Philosophers of India.[67]

[66] Ibid., p. 322.

[67] Introduction to *The Wheel of Fire*, p. xiv.

The last sentence is but another way of saying, what Eliot has clearly said elsewhere, that among philosophical poems on the epic scale, he likes the *Divine Comedy* best of all, but next to that come *De Rerum Natura* and that which includes the *Bhagavad-Gita*.

Thus purely as a *reader* of poetry Eliot can be assumed to enjoy Lucretius almost as much as Dante, but as a *writer* of poetry his choice is narrowed by philosophical and theological considerations. As far as the *Four Quartets* are consciously constructed on a "framework of accepted and traditional ideas", that framework is the Catholic Christian doctrine such as it appears to Eliot. Unconsciously he may have assimilated other ideas as well, but that is a different matter. There is, in other words, no deliberate or admitted discrepancy in the *Quartets* between poetic practice and the poet's belief. If some such discrepancy exists in actual fact, it is contrary to Eliot's intentions.

It would, however, be a great mistake to think that Eliot really believes that the poet should proselytize. Of *De Rerum Natura* and the *Divine Comedy* he says that they "were not designed to persuade the readers to an intellectual assent, but to convey an emotional equivalent for the ideas. What Lucretius and Dante teach you, in fact, is *what it feels like* to hold certain beliefs".[68] He has made a similar pronouncement of his intentions in writing the *Four Quartets*. He was "seeking the verbal equivalents for small experiences he had had, and for knowledge derived from reading".[69] According to this view, religious poetry is hardly concerned with the truth of a certain doctrine, still less with the propagation of that doctrine, but with the emotional experience of the poet in his capacity as a believer.

This theory is of course open to attack. It can be decided whether a doctrine is orthodox or not, but it is more difficult to estimate the degree of orthodoxy in an emotion. By shifting the stress from ideas to their emotional equivalents, Eliot concedes considerable liberty to the poet, although it is a liberty within certain limits. In fact, some of his pronouncements on the desirability of orthodoxy in poetry are more liberal than would be expected from the general

[68] Quoted from Smidt, p. 75.

[69] Ibid., pp. 155 f.

trend of his criticism. Thus the following passage from *After Strange Gods* (1934): "In my sense of the term, perfect orthodoxy in the individual artist is not always necessary, or even desirable. In many instances it is possible that an indulgence of eccentricities is the condition of the man's saying anything at all." [70]

It is quite obvious, however, that the situation of the Christian poet is essentially different to-day from what it was in the fourteenth century. Dante lived in, and wrote for, a society of Christians, and the *Divine Comedy* was certainly not designed to propagate the fundamental truths of Christianity, which were already known to and accepted by his readers. With Eliot it is different. Living in a world of scepticism and agnosticism he has more than any other contemporary writer of his standing striven to uphold Christian standards in English literature. In the essay, "Religion and Literature" (1935), he declares that what he believes "to be incumbent upon all Christians is the duty of maintaining consciously certain standards and criteria of criticism over and above those applied by the rest of the world".[71] If this duty is incumbent on the Christian reader and critic, it must also be incumbent on the Christian poet, and the author of *Murder in the Cathedral* and, still more, of *The Rock* is certainly something of a preacher.

The same basic view is set forth in another essay of the same year, "Literature and the Modern World", in which Eliot maintains that "the poet must assume his rôle of moralist" [72] and that "we must affirm the eternal against the transient".[73] It is significant that the second of these two pronouncements is levelled against the current notions of evolution, in particular against the "superficial philosophy" of H. G. Wells.[74] In the present study Eliot's intellectual and spiritual position has been defined mainly in terms of his positive views and beliefs, but it should be pointed out that there are important negative influences as well; that is to say, intellectual and

[70] *After Strange Gods*, p. 32.

[71] *Selected Essays*, p. 399.

[72] "Literature and the Modern World" (1935), reprinted in *The Literature of the United States*, an anthology ed. by W. Blair, T. Hornberger and R. Stewart, Chicago, 1949, p. 1299.

[73] Ibid., p. 1296.

[74] Ibid.

spiritual phenomena, such as the doctrines of evolution, against which Eliot has reacted strongly and which have forced him to revise and fortify his own positions. There are many such ideas and attitudes – religious, political, social and literary – which aroused Eliot's antagonism during the nineteen-thirties; most of them fall outside the scope of this study, but it may be relevant to mention another butt of Eliot's censure – the "philosophy" of D. H. Lawrence.[75] Eliot's idea of love, derived from Platonic and Christian mysticism, is in many ways the very opposite of that of Lawrence and the popular Freudian doctrine. To "affirm the eternal against the transient" thus involves, for Eliot, not only affirmation of positive values, but also denial of all that which threatens these values. And in *The Rock* as well as in *Murder in the Cathedral* there is a good deal of both.

Although contemporary with these two essays of 1935 and immediately following *Murder in the Cathedral,* "Burnt Norton" is yet different in kind. Containing hardly any explicit references to Christian conceptions it stands apart from the main tendency of Eliot's literary activity during the nineteen-thirties. In view of the suddenness and unexpectedness of the conception of that poem, this can well be understood. Eliot does not seem deliberately to have set aside his literary doctrines, he was simply overcome by an inspiration he had not dared to hope for any more. In fact, "Burnt Norton" stands, in almost every sense, apart from all other poems by Eliot. It is not manifestly religious as are "Ash-Wednesday" or "Little Gidding", and yet it is the most spiritual of them all. Elusive and paradoxical, enigmatic and fascinating, it represents the peak of Eliot's poetic achievement. The subsequent *Quartets* are gradually extended to include explicit Christian categories and "Little Gidding" wholly conforms to Eliot's theory of Christian literature.

[75] Ibid., p. 1297.

CHAPTER III

Time and Eternity in Mystic Philosophy

The purpose of the last chapter was, among other things, to give some indication of the philosophic tradition to which Eliot belongs, and some indication, in a general way, of the sources from which that tradition was derived. In the present chapter it is intended to develop this analysis in a more detailed way, with specific reference to the *Four Quartets*.

Eliot, as was shown in the previous chapter, is particularly careful to distinguish between versified philosophy and philosophical poetry, between the philosophy of the systematic philosopher and the philosophy of a poet; and he censures those poets who unwisely attempt to devise philosophic systems of their own. Accordingly, the *Four Quartets* set forth no original philosophic system, but a system, or rather a pattern, derived from various philosophical and other writings and the doctrines they express and imply. It is on the lines of this derived pattern that the *Four Quartets* are built up; and thus the *Quartets* constitute the only kind of philosophic poetry that Eliot fully approves.

This of course makes the task of developing the analysis of the *Quartets*, of identifying the constituent elements in the pattern, by no means easy. The critic of Lucretius, for example, has little difficulty in tracing the ideas in *De Rerum Natura* to their chief source – Epicurean philosophy. But with Eliot it is far otherwise, for he ranges over a complex of philosophical, theological and even mythological ideas that extend over thousands of years – a bewildering variety of ideas, images and notions, which is reflected in the bewildering variety of suggestions, hypotheses and explanations put forward by his critics as to what it all really means.

It was in order to avoid this confusion that some pains were taken in the last chapter to define Eliot's conception of tradition, and to give a survey of the main components of the particular tradition to which he belongs. In this way it should be possible, in analysing the *Four Quartets*, to distinguish the essential from the incidental – and not, as some critics have done, to attach almost equal weight to a vital passage from Dante and to a mere verbal reminiscence from Conan Doyle. For these reasons, in the following analysis only such ideas and symbols in the poems will be considered, as are clearly relevant to Eliot's broad philosophic tradition and its core of basic conceptions.

A further difficulty in analysing and understanding the *Four Quartets* arises from what might be called Eliot's symbolic use of significant metaphor; that is, he frequently adopts a metaphor which not only illustrates some particular experience described in the poem, but also retains something of the abstract, often almost metaphysical, significance that it has in the context from which Eliot has derived it. For example, there is Eliot's use of the metaphor of the wheel. In order to contrast the insatiable restlessness of the human spirit with the repose and serenity of Divine Grace, Eliot uses the image of the wheel, with its still point in the centre of the hub. There is however much more in the meaning of the metaphor than appears in the words themselves. To Eliot there is the whole background of the meaning of the symbol as he has found it used in philosophic and religious literature, and its special implications for the poet himself. Thus, however illuminating and apt the metaphor may be in the poem itself, if it is dissociated from its philosophic background in Eliot's reading, then much of its real significance is lost. A careful study of the significance of these metaphors is therefore essential in any analysis of the *Four Quartets*. In the present chapter a few only of these metaphors will be dealt with, fuller and more detailed discussion being reserved for later chapters.

It is perhaps relevant at this point to emphasize that it is not the purpose of the ensuing analysis to criticize or even fully to describe the various philosophic and other systems involved. What matters is the impact of the system, or ideas, on the mind of the poet; what precise meaning, for example, was given by Heracleitus to his Logos is of much less importance than the value and significance of the metaphor in the mind of Eliot.

It may be as well to note that the words "philosophy" and "philosophical" are to be taken in the following chapters in a wide connotation, including theology and mysticism. Eliot himself in his later writings does not always distinguish between them, and hence there is little to be gained in a critical study of this kind in preserving such distinctions, however relevant they might be to a purely philosophical or theological study.

I

One of the most remarkable and characteristic of the images that Eliot uses in the *Four Quartets* is that of "the still point of the turning world". The phrase had been used by Eliot before in "Triumphal March", but without the intellectual and symbolic background which gives it its special meaning in "Burnt Norton", a meaning which appears clearly in the light of what Eliot thought and wrote in the meantime. Between the composition of these two poems, "Triumphal March" and "Burnt Norton", Eliot wrote two plays, *The Rock* and *Murder in the Cathedral* which employ many of the themes that are fully developed in the *Quartets*. As was demonstrated in the foregoing chapter, "Burnt Norton" has a special connection with *Murder in the Cathedral*, the poem being built on lines originally intended for inclusion in that play. *Murder in the Cathedral* was written immediately after *The Rock* and very much in the same spirit as that play. The first production of *The Rock*, the writing of *Murder in the Cathedral* and the composition of "Burnt Norton", all took place within eighteen months – between the spring of 1934 and the autumn of 1935.[1] It sems therefore natural to turn to these plays for some elucidation of the *Quartets*.

The image underlying "the still point of the turning world" is of course that of the wheel. There are passages in *Murder in the Cathedral* where the symbol of the wheel serves to express ideas similar to those in the Second Section of "Burnt Norton":

[1] Vide supra, p. 43.

They know and do not know, that action is suffering
And suffering is action. Neither does the agent suffer
Nor the patient act. But both are fixed
In an eternal action, an eternal patience
To which all must consent that it may be willed
And which all must suffer that they may will it,
That the pattern may subsist, for the pattern is the action
And the suffering, that the wheel may turn and still
Be forever still.[2]

In other passages of the play the wheel seems to symbolize that inevitability of time and events, "the enchainment of past and future", which is the meaning of the recurrent burden of "Burnt Norton", "time past and time future":

Only
The fool, fixed in his folly, may think
He can turn the wheel on which he turns.[3]

That nothing lasts, but the wheel turns,[4]

The frequent use Eliot makes of the image of the wheel is not difficult to explain, for it combines the two main aspects of his philosophical and religious view of the world: matter and spirit, the temporal and the eternal. The perpetually moving circumference of the wheel is the material world, which is subject to change and temporal flux; the centre of the wheel, "the still point", is the world of the Absolute, of eternity, and yet the two are related to each other, as God to the world. The spokes possibly symbolize the way of the mystic leading up – or down – to the very hub. This interpretation may perhaps seem unwarranted in the light of the foregoing quotations, but the history of the wheel symbolism affords a good deal of evidence to support it. Eliot's use of the symbol lies within this tradition.

Other interpretations are of course possible. Philip Wheelwright, for example, has identified the wheel of "Burnt Norton" as the Wheel of Fortune,[5] (a very common significance of the image of the

[2] *Murder in the Cathedral*, 4th ed., p. 21.

[3] Ibid., p. 25.

[4] Ibid., p. 38.

[5] Wheelwright, P., "Eliot's Philosophical Themes", in *T. S. Eliot. A Study of his Writings by Several Hands*, ed. by B. Rajan, London, 1947, p. 100.

wheel in Shakespeare and other Renaissance authors), but this seems to pay too much attention to the popular, iconographic aspects of the symbol,[6] neglecting its primary philosophical meaning, a meaning closely related to ancient theories of time. A passage in T. E. Hulme's *Speculations* shows the connection between the Wheel of Fortune and the cyclic theory of history:

> It is the closing of all roads, this realisation of the *tragic* significance of life, which makes it legitimate to call all other attitudes shallow. Such a realisation has formed the basis of all the great religions, and is most conveniently remembered by the symbol of the *wheel*. This symbol of the futility of existence is absolutely lost to the modern world, nor can it be recovered without great difficulty.
>
> One modern method of disguising the issue should be noticed. In November 1829, a tragic date for those who see with regret the establishment of a lasting and devastating stupidity, Goethe – in answer to Eckermann's remark that human thought and action seemed to repeat itself, going round in a circle – said: "*No, it is not a circle, it is a spiral.*" You disguise the wheel by making it run up an inclined plane; it then becomes "Progress", which is the modern substitute for religion.[7]

The refutation of progress is the argument of the introduction to the first Chorus from *The Rock*, where captivity in time, in the cyclic movement of history, is contrasted with absolute stillness:

> The Eagle soars in the summit of Heaven,
> The Hunter with his dogs pursues his circuit.
> O perpetual revolution of configured stars,
> O perpetual recurrence of determined seasons,
> O world of spring and autumn, birth and dying!
> The endless cycle of idea and action,
> Endless invention, endless experiment,
> Brings knowledge of motion, but not of stillness . . .

The same theme is developed in the Second Section of "Burnt Norton" and in "East Coker".

What, then, are Eliot's sources for the wheel symbolism? As so

[6] Cf. Weinhold, K., *Glücksrad und Lebensrad*, Akademie der Wissenschaften, philos. u. hist. Abh., Berlin, 1892.

[7] Hulme, T. E., *Speculations. Essays on Humanism and the Philosophy of Art*, London, (1924) 1936, pp. 34 f.

often with Eliot, it is misleading to point out any single source. But if it can be shown that an idea or symbol is widespread within a school or tradition with which Eliot is, or has been familiar, then it may be correct to speak of sources. The symbol of the wheel happens to be common to two separate fields of thought, to both of which Eliot has devoted years of study – to Indian and to Greek philosophy.[8]

II

In Indian thought the Wheel of Existence, sometimes also called the Wheel of Rebirth, or Samsara, is a well-known image. The idea is that every living creature undergoes a number of deaths and rebirths until it attains perfection, *i.e.* when a man has liberated himself, not only from all earthly desires, but also from the delusion that the world of senses has any real existence. It is then that his true Self becomes one with the Absolute, with Brahman. This is the final object of contemplation, of Yoga. For those who do not attain this ultimate goal, there is no escape from the cycle of perpetual rebirths, nor is there any hope for them to be born into a world that has made some positive progress since they were last born. This sombre Indian view of history excludes the conception of a Redeemer or a future golden age. The events of history, it seems to affirm, return cyclically; salvation lies outside history, and is achieved only by the individual's attaining to Brahman. As we have seen above Eliot sometimes touches on the cyclic view of history, with the important modification that as a Christian he allows for the interpolation of the positive impulse of such events as the Incarnation of Christ in the negative Indian doctrine. Nevertheless the

[8] H. E. MacCarthy holds that Eliot is indebted to Buddhism for the image of the wheel: "T. S. Eliot and Buddhism", *Philosophy East and West* (Univ. of Hawaii), Vol. 2, pp. 31–55. The image is also to be found in the New Testament; the phrase in the Epistle of James (iii: 6), "setteth on fire the course of nature", is a free translation of "φλογίζουσα τὸν τροχὸν τῆς γενέσεως" -τροχός meaning wheel. The meaning of the image is fully discussed by M. Dibelius, *Der Brief des Jakobus*, 8th ed., Göttingen, 1956, (=W. Meyer, *Kommentar über das Neue Testament*, 15. Abt.), pp. 182–184.

conception of an incarnate god is well-known to Indian religious thinkers, though to them incarnation is not the unique event that it is in the Christian doctrine; for they believe that the same god can descend to earth on several historical occasions.[9] An essential difference between the Eastern and Western outlooks is indicated by Heinrich Zimmer:

> For the Western mind, which believes in single, epoch-making, historical events (such as, for instance, the coming of Christ, or the emergence of certain decisive sets of ideals, or the long development of invention during the course of man's mastery of nature) this casual comment of the ageless god [Vishnu] has a gently minimizing, annihilating effect. It vetoes conceptions of value that are intrinsic to our estimation of man, his life, his destiny and task.[10]

According to this view Indian philosophy of history seems irreconcilable with European, as indeed one would expect, and Eliot can hardly be said to have attempted a reconciliation. In his view, it seems, the Indian religions form a preparatory stage or an introduction to the full Christian revelation, and although not wholly compatible with the revealed truth, they contain many philosophical elements that can be embraced by a Christian.

In Indian thought, the symbol of the wheel is often used to illustrate the dualism of a philosophical system. The circumference of the wheel, Samsara, is the material, or sensuous world. Its opposite is Brahman. Though in classical Indian texts the Absolute is not often symbolized as the centre of a circle, in his book *Time and Eternity* Coomaraswamy has drawn a suggestive parallel between the numerous instances in Western literature of such symbolization and similar Indian conceptions. According to him, the following parallel may be drawn between conceptions that are common to Oriental as well as to Greek and Christian metaphysics:

> . . . temporal succession corresponding to motion along its [the circle's] circumference and the *ex tempore* motion of free-will to

[9] Cf. The *Bhagavad-Gita*, IV, 5–8. (In, for example, S. Radhakrishnan's and C. A. Moore's *A Source Book in Indian Philosophy*, Princeton, 1957, p. 116.)

[10] Zimmer, H., *Myths and Symbols in Indian Art and Civilization*, New York, 1946, pp. 18 f.

centrifugal motion (fall or descent into matter) and centripetal motion (ascension or resurrection).[11]

Here Coomaraswamy identifies the circumference of the wheel with time and its centre with the timeless. To escape the contradiction between free-will and predestination, free-will is here supposed to be exerted out of time. And in the same way, according to the Catholic doctrine, the perfect freedom of a Christian means his being ruled entirely by God, the Eternal. A suggestion of this concept is foreshadowed in one of Becket's speeches in *Murder in the Cathedral*:

It is not in time that my death shall be known;
It is out of time that my decision is taken
If you call that decision
To which my whole being gives entire consent.
I give my life
To the Law of God above the Law of Man.[12]

The distinction between the motion along the circumference of the wheel, Samsara, and the timeless centre, Brahman, is sometimes obscured by the monistic tendencies in Indian philosophy. "There are, indeed", writes Coomaraswamy, "two forms of Brahma; time, and the Timeless." [13] Both are aspects of Brahman, *are* Brahman, but the timeless is apprehended only by the mystic in his moments of ecstasy; to most men Brahman is obscured by the veil of temporal existence.

In one of its aspects, however, Indian philosophy may be regarded as having developed out of mythology and primitive cosmology. Kala, Time, sometimes appears more of a deity than an abstract concept.[14] And some hold that Kala is a substance which emanated from the Absolute at the creation of the Cosmos. This doctrine, by

[11] Coomaraswamy, A. K., *Time and Eternity*, (*Artibus Asiae*, Suppl. VIII), Ascona, 1947, p. 109.

[12] *Murder in the Cathedral*, p. 73. Considered apart from their religious context, these lines seem to owe something to the philosophy of Bergson.

[13] Coomaraswamy, *Time and Eternity*, p. 15.

[14] See J. Scheftelowitz, *Die Zeit als Schicksalsgottheit in der Indischen und Iranischen Religion*, Stuttgart, 1929.

Stanislaw Schayer called the "somatistic" conception of time,[15] is a striking parallel to Plato's in *Timaeus*, and supplies another illustration of the tendency to identify time with the created world, or to make time a prerequisite of material existence. Brahman itself remains, in most systems, timeless and eternal.

What has now been described is not only a static metaphysical pattern made up of logical antitheses resolved in the Absolute; it is also a religious creed involving a theory of man and his salvation. Man's true Self, his Atman, is eternal and will in the end become one with Brahman, but as long as man is chained to the Wheel of Rebirth, he is not aware of his Self, only of his ephemeral, temporal identity. Indian mysticism from the *Upanishads* to the Yoga of the present day seems to have but one object in life: the penetration into the Self of man, to the timeless, which means the end of reincarnation. This penetration can take place at any moment in time; salvation is a perpetual possibility independent of any historical event.

It is of course extremely difficult to translate Oriental concepts of these things into Occidental language. The Oriental background differs so much historically and sociologically that the possibilities of confusion are almost endless. All that can be attempted is to indicate what appear to be the elements that have influenced Eliot's poetic imagery. Much simplified, and expressed in the language of Western philosophy and theology, the fundamental conceptions Eliot seems to have derived from Indian sources are these: Time and the timeless are related to each other as the world to the Absolute, to God. Material existence means existence in time. The timeless is experienced only in the direct apprehension of the Divine. Though enacted in time, human life aspires to the timeless. To overcome the limitations of temporal existence and become one with God is the object and end of life. Thus expressed, the Indian conceptions of time and the timeless come very close to those of Western, in particular Platonic philosophy.

[15] Schayer, S., *Contributions to the Problem of Time in Indian Philosophy*, Krakow, 1938, Chapter I.

III

The question of Eliot's debt to Greek philosophy is difficult to decide. Eastern and Western philosophical systems as sources of the imagery of the *Four Quartets* often overlap, and as long as we are interested only in generalities, the differences may not be of much account.[16] As a Christian, however, and a writer of Christian poetry, Eliot repudiates certain Indian notions as he does many conceptions in Greek thought, though undoubtedly both types of philosophy have left deep impressions on the *Quartets*. By juxtaposing pagan and Christian ideas in the *Quartets*, Eliot seems to suggest a reinterpretation of the pagan doctrines in the spirit of Catholic theology. To the modern mind this lack of historical perspectives may seem almost outdated, as no doubt Eliot is fully aware, but in spite of his realizing, perhaps, how surprised Aristotle would have been to see the use Thomas Aquinas made of his philosophy, Eliot seems to hold, in agreement with Paul Elmer More, that the Christian interpretation of Greek metaphysics is justified, and like the medieval theologians, he regards the philosophical and religious thinkers of ancient times as forerunners of Christianity, but forerunners unconscious of their mission.[17]

The chief source of the imagery of the *Four Quartets* in Greek philosophy is the Platonic, or Neo-Platonic tradition, as has been pointed out in a previous chapter, rather than, as might perhaps have been expected of a writer in the orthodox Christian tradition, the purely Aristotelian scholastic tradition. The canon of all treatises on the problem of time up to the Renaissance was Plato's *Timaeus*. That dialogue contains Plato's cosmology, describes the creation of Cosmos out of Chaos. Together with the heavenly spheres, time was created and the motion of the spheres made to constitute the division of time into years, days, and hours. It was the equation of time with motion that formed the starting-point of Aristotle's analysis of time. Being part of, and one with, the Cosmos, Plato goes on to say in effect that time has its transcendent form, its παράδειγμα as have

[16] Cf. K. Smidt, *Poetry and Belief in the work of T. S. Eliot*, Oslo, 1949, pp. 166 f.

[17] Vide supra, pp. 55, 62.

all created things. The name of that form is eternity and thus time can be defined as "the moving image of eternity".[18]

The chapter on time in *Timaeus*, short but significant, contains the germ of many subsequent systems including those of the Schoolmen. The attribution of time to creation, and of eternity to God, is common to most post-Platonic philosophy. Many expounders of Plato's doctrine of time have found the wheel or the circle an appropriate symbol of this relation between time and eternity. The basis for this symbolism is in fact implicit in *Timaeus*, as a German writer on Neo-Platonism, Hans Leisegang, has shown:

> Gliedern wir nun in diesen Zusammenhang der dualistischen Ideenlehre die Begriffe der Zeit und Ewigkeit ein, wie Platon sie uns in Timäus darstellt, so erhalten wir folgendes Bild: Urbild, Ruhe, Sein, Ewigkeit stehen auf der einen, Abbild, Bewegung, Werden, Zeit auf der anderen Seite des Dualismus. Die erste Begriffsreihe ist intelligibel, sie braucht keine körperliche Ausdehnung und ist einem ruhenden Punkte zu vergleichen. Um diesen ewig ruhenden Punkt herum jedoch bewegt sich die körperliche Welt des Werdens in einem in sich geschlossenen Kreislauf. Zwischen beiden steht die Menschenseele, durch den Körper an die irdische Welt und damit auch an den Kreislauf der Zeit gebunden, durch ihre intelligible Natur jedoch stets nach der Ideenwelt, nach der Ruhe, dem Sein und der Ewigkeit strebend.[19]

This is a further possible interpretation of the meaning of "the still point of the turning world", which appears time and again in Neo-Platonic philosophy. Proclus has it in his commentary on *Timaeus*,[20] and Plotinus in his *Enneads*.[21] The philosophy of Plotinus deserves special attention as a possible source of Eliot's time specula-

[18] Plato's theory of time is found in *Timaeus*, 37–38. Cf. the chapter on Plato in J. F. Callahan's *Four Views of Time in Ancient Philosophy*, Harvard, 1948. A short exposition of *Timaeus*, 37–38, is given by J. Burnet in his *Greek Philosophy*, I, London, 1914, pp. 342 f., a book which Eliot has read and quoted in an article in *The Monist*, Vol. 26, 1916, p. 543.

[19] Leisegang, H., *Die Begriffe der Zeit und Ewigkeit im späteren Platonismus*, Münster i. W., 1913, p. 4.

[20] Proclus, *In Timaeum*, 243–247. Cf. Leisegang, p. 40, and W. Gent, *Die Philosophie des Raumes und der Zeit*, Bonn, 1926, p. 37.

[21] Plotinus, *Enneads*, III, 7, 11, and IV, 4, 16. Cf. Leisegang, pp. 20, 23.

tion, not least because of its deep influence on Dante.[22] That remarkable scholar on Plotinus, W. R. Inge has provided a detailed analysis of Plotinus' conception of time in his *Philosophy of Plotinus*, which appeared in 1918. He also contributed to the academic controversy concerning the nature of time that was carried on in English philosophical journals round 1920,[23] and Eliot cannot have failed to come into contact with his writings. In a book which ought to have interested Eliot, *The Platonic Tradition in English Religious Thought*, Inge gives the following characterization of what he considered a dominant tendency in the spiritual life of the early Christian era:

> The chief aim of mankind (it was now felt) is or should be to escape from the "weary wheel" of earthly existence, and to find rest in the bosom of the Eternal.[24]

What has been said earlier of Indian philosophy is true also of Plotinus; his concern was not only with abstract speculation as such but also with the salvation of the soul. Plotinus appears as the great mystic in Western philosophy. The demand for peace and rest, in the same spirit as that implied in the quotation from Inge, is one aspect of his mysticism; the other, and perhaps more representative one, is the positive demand for direct apprehension of divine Beauty and Goodness.

There is an obvious element of mysticism in the *Four Quartets* that gives poetic force to the intellectual argument of the poems; *i.e.* a mysticism devoid of emotionalism and based on the realization of the theoretical possibilities of mystic intuition. Eliot's interpretation of the meaning of the mystic insight appears to become more definitely Christian for each new *Quartet*, culminating in "Little Gidding". In "Burnt Norton" the Christian elements are not made so explicit; they exist, but only as hints and allusions, and the teaching of that poem is uniformly religious rather than Christian. This there-

[22] An English translation of the *Enneads* by S. MacKenna appeared in 1917–1930, 2nd revised ed., London, 1956.

[23] Cf. W. R. Inge, "Is the Time Series Reversible?", *Proceedings of the Aristotelian Society*, Vol. 21, London, 1920–1921.

[24] Inge, W. R., *The Platonic Tradition in English Religious Thought*, London, 1926, p. 8.

fore is another instance of how misleading it is to single out any particular source for Eliot's poetic symbolism.

Plotinian mysticism deserves special attention, not as a source more important than others, but as a source representative of a certain combination of different qualities also peculiar to the *Four Quartets*. The significance attached by Plotinus to mystic ecstasy cannot be understood independently of his philosophical system in general. The symbol of the wheel, or the circle, will once more serve as the best illustration of the philosopher's picture of the universe. The relation between the three parts of Plotinus' Trinity, the One, the Spirit, and the Soul, can be described as the relation between two concentric circles and their centre, the centre being the One, the inner circle the Spirit, and the outer the Soul.[25] The One is the still, the timeless point of the ever-turning outer circle, for the Soul is itself time, time presupposing motion. The created universe is contained in the Soul, and is, consequently, permeated by time.[26] Being part of the Cosmos, man exists in time but his soul has, like the Soul, emanated from the One, has been "sent down" to earth by God.[27] This descent of the soul implies that it has once dwelt at the timeless centre and it always retains a faint memory, a reminiscence, of that state. In its temporal degradation the soul aspires to its origin, to the One. After death, liberated from the encumbering body, the soul will return to the One along the path of its descent, but this centripetal journey can also be undertaken while the soul is still an inhabitant of the earth: that is what happens in the divine ecstasy.[28]

[25] *Enneads*, IV, 4, 16. Cf. Leisegang, loc. cit.

[26] *Enneads*, III, 7, 11.

[27] Cf. W. R. Inge, *The Philosophy of Plotinus*, I, pp. 254 ff.

[28] Cf. ibid., II, p. 145. In the Metaphysical poets Eliot has been confronted with similar metaphors deriving from similar sources; cf. the following lines from Donne's "The second Anniversarie":

> Then, Soule, to thy first pitch worke up againe;
> Know that all lines which circles doe containe,
> For once that they the Center touch, doe touch
> Twice the circumference; and be thou such;
> Double on heaven thy thoughts on earth emploid;
> All will not serve; Only who have enjoy'd
> The sight of God, in fulnesse, can thinke it;
> For it is both the object, and the wit.

The Poems of John Donne, ed. by H. Grierson, Oxf. Univ. Press, 1949, p. 239.

This Plotinian pattern is very similiar to the one used by Eliot in the *Four Quartets*. He, too, seems to imagine the divine ecstasy as an escape from the temporal sphere to the timeless. The "Descent of the Soul" is the phrase used by Inge to describe Plotinus' notion of the Soul's emanating from the One; in consequence of this, the Soul's "homeward" journey to the One should be styled the "Ascent of the Soul". This is perfectly clear if we adopt the image underlying Inge's argument, that of heaven and earth. If, on the other hand, we substitute the circumference of the circle for the earth, and the centre of the circle for heaven – which is fully justified by the passage from the *Enneads* cited above – the concepts of descent and ascent lose their absolute meanings and become interchangeable, both involving centripetal movement. It seems probable that, among many other things, Eliot had this geometrical relativism in mind when prefixing the second Heracleitian epigraph to "Burnt Norton": "The way up and the way down are one and the same."

However, the interpretation of Heracleitus' Fragments is always a precarious undertaking. Louis Martz, commenting on Eliot's wheel symbolism, arrives at a slightly different conclusion concerning the meaning of the above Fragment. He quotes the Fragment that comes next in the Loeb edition of Heracleitus, "The beginning and end are common", and an editorial note in which it is maintained that "Heracleitus is referring to a point on the circumference of a circle".[29] This might well be the case as far as the second Fragment is concerned, but Eliot's application of the first one to "Burnt Norton" is better understood in the light of the above interpretation of that Fragment. Besides, Eliot quotes from Diels' edition of Heracleitus.

The juxtaposition of ascent and descent occurs in the Second Section of "Burnt Norton", though in negation: "Neither movement from nor towards, / Neither ascent nor decline." This movement that is no movement takes place at the centre, at the still point, and if we compare the passage from which it is quoted with the following extract from the *Enneads* it becomes clear that what Eliot is talking about is the beatific vision.

[29] Martz, L. L., "The Wheel and the Point: Aspects of Imagery and Theme in Eliot's Later Poetry", *T. S. Eliot. A Selected Critique*, ed. by L. Unger, New York, 1948, p. 446.

We must remember that our "circles" and "centres" are only metaphors. The Soul is no "circle" like the geometrical figure; we call it a circle because the archetypal nature is in it and around it, and because it is derived from this first principle, [. . .] The One does not strive to encircle us, but we strive to encircle it. We always move round the One, but we do not always fix our gaze upon it: we are like a choir of singers who stand round the conductor, but do not always sing in time because their attention is diverted to some external object; when they look at the conductor they sing well and are really with him. So we always move round the One; if we did not, we should be dissolved and no longer exist; but we do not always look towards the One. When we do, we attain the end of our existence, and our repose, and we no longer sing out of tune, but form in very truth a divine chorus round the One. In this choral dance the Soul sees the fountain of life and the fountain of Spirit, the Source of Being, the cause of Good, the root of Soul.[30]

Where motion is, there is time, and consequently the timeless must be free from motion; yet Eliot stops short of drawing this conclusion with adding the important qualification that the timeless is unmoving in the temporal sense of the word but yet it is not fixity, for that would mean death. So he arrives at a paradoxical solution to the dilemma. The unmoving motion of the timeless he calls "the dance":

At the still point of the turning world. Neither flesh nor fleshless;
Neither from nor towards; at the still point, there the dance is,
But neither arrest nor movement. And do not call it fixity,
Where past and future are gathered. Neither movement from nor towards,
Neither ascent nor decline. Except for the point, the still point,
There would be no dance, and there is only the dance.

("Burnt Norton", II)

Thus Eliot may have been, consciously or unconsciously, influenced by Plotinus in his use of the symbol of the dance. He may or may not have read the passage. As Plotinus says, these figures are only metaphors, but similar experiences sometimes seem to have a tendency to manifest themselves, independently of each other, in similar symbolic forms – a fact well-known to many psychologists. It

[30] Inge, *The Philosophy of Plotinus*, II, pp. 137 f.

is worth noticing that Eliot's symbol of the wheel has been interpreted in Jungian categories as a "mandala".[31]

It should be added that the symbol of the dance seems to imply a new paradox. The rotation of the wheel stands for motion in time, but the dance, also figured as a circular movement round the centre, stands for the apprehension of the timeless. Plotinus dismisses the figures of the circle and the dance, as has been shown, as mere metaphors, and makes no attempt to reconcile the contradictory elements. If we turn to Indian philosophy, however, we shall find the reconciliation at least attempted. The Dance of Shiva is, in one sense, the dance of the supreme god himself, and, in another sense, the ritual dance of the worshippers of Shiva. The ritual dance leads its performers into ecstasy and hence to union with God. As a ritual the dance has been interpreted thus in the holy books of India:

> The Essential Significance of Śiva's Dance is threefold: First, it is the image of his Rhythmic Play as the Source of all Movement within the Cosmos, which is Represented by the Arch: Secondly, the Purpose of his Dance is to Release the Countless souls of men from the Snare of Illusion: Thirdly the Place of the Dance, Chidambaram, the Centre of the Universe, is within the Heart.[32]

Coomaraswamy's comment on this passage is interesting: "If we would reconcile Time with Eternity, we can scarcely do so otherwise than by the conception of alterations of phase extending over vast regions of space and great tracts of time." Zimmer has a similar interpretation of Shiva's dance. He sees in it a tension "of Eternity

[31] "He [Jung] says that mandala is a Sanskrit word meaning magic circle, and that the basic design includes always a circle, having a centre, and divided into four equal parts. 'This design has turned up in every cultural region, more or less, and we find it today not only in Christian churches, but in Tibetan monasteries as well. It is the so-called sun-wheel, and as it dates from a time when no one had thought of wheels as a mechanical device, it cannot have its source in any experience of the external world. It is rather a symbol that stands for a psychic happening; it covers an experience of the inner world.' Jung asserts that the mandala dream image always combines the elements of a circular rotation (frequently of rotating light), some element of 'fourness', and the all-important centre." – Drew, E., *T. S. Eliot. The Design of his Poetry*, London, 1950, p. 175. The quotation from Jung is from *Modern Man in Search of a Soul*, New York, 1933, p. 188.

[32] Coomaraswamy, A. K., *The Dance of Śiva. Fourteen Indian Essays*, London, 1924, p. 65.

and Time, the paradox – the silent, mutual confutation – of the Absolute and the Phenomenal . . ." [33]

Some aspects of Plotinus' mystic philosophy, concerning its emotional colouring, may be added. Many mystics, and among them many Christians, have described their experience of the Absolute in words reminiscent of hymns of earthly love. Much of the esoteric language of this kind derives from the *Song of Solomon*, but there is also an unmistakable element of Platonism in Christian mysticism. Diotima's famous speech in the *Symposium* is a further example of the erotic symbolism involved in the mystic experience, and one of the most pronounced representatives of this tendency is another Platonist, Dionysius the Areopagite. Plotinus himself is obscure in this respect. He does call the power that attracts the soul to God love, it is true, but it is not imagined so much as the love of a bride for her spouse but as that of a daughter for her father.[34] In the end every trace of personal relationship is extinguished, subject and object become one. Inge sums up the difference thus:

> There is therefore, in the Plotinian mysticism, none of that deep personal loyalty, none of that intimate dialogue between soul and soul, none of that passion of love – resembling often too closely in its expression the earthly love of the sexes – which are so prominent in later mystical literature. Compare, as a favourable example of this type, the exquisite *Revelations of Julian of Norwich*, full of tender reverent affection for the heavenly Christ.[35]

Eliot in so far as he is a mystic is, on the whole, rather as Plotinus seems to have been – detached, abstract, reflective, yet at times warm and deep, inclining towards the close personal relationship with the Absolute that Inge associates with Julian of Norwich; in "Little Gidding", for instance, Eliot quotes from her.[36] In his striving to reconcile the antithesis of time and eternity, Eliot approaches purely philosophical mysticism, but being a poet rather than a thinker, he has to resolve the antithesis in a way that is emotionally comprehensible. The natural attraction of the detached intellectual

[33] Zimmer, p. 156.

[34] Cf. Inge, *The Philosophy of Plotinus*, II, p. 139.

[35] Ibid., p. 161.

[36] Cf. H. Gardner, *The Art of T. S. Eliot*, London, 1949, p. 182.

towards a more intimate and affectionate way of life, should also be taken into account. In the *Four Quartets*, both aspects of mysticism are represented and the possibility of uniting them in one poetic work had earlier been demonstrated by Dante. There are other features of the mystic way, such as it is set forth in the *Four Quartets*, that might be illustrated with passages from the writings of Plotinus – the conception of the *via negativa* is one – but these features will be dealt with later, in connection with St. John of the Cross.

In his insistence on love as the highest manifestation of the divine, Eliot is perhaps more Christian than Platonist, at least if we translate the concept of love in "Little Gidding" with Agape rather than Eros. But Eliot's Christian God of Love is often identified with the Absolute of Greek philosophy. Take for instance these lines from the last Section of "Burnt Norton":

> Desire itself is movement
> Not in itself desirable;
> Love is itself unmoving,
> Only the cause and end of movement,
> Timeless, and undesiring

Derived from the Aristotelian conception of the Unmoved Mover, as several critics have pointed out,[37] this is but another way of expressing the Plotinian relation between temporal motion and timeless stillness.

IV

"Eternity" and the "Absolute" are essentially metaphysical concepts rather than experienced realities. As such they are both concepts which are in a sense intellectually comprehended in an inferential way; the concept of the "Eternal Now", however, which forms the next step in the present investigation of Eliot's philosophical sources, involves certain difficulties. The apparent inconsistency of predicating eternity to a moment in time makes intellectual analysis difficult, and the idea of the Eternal Now is thus hardly susceptible to definition. The full comprehension of it cannot be achieved, it seems,

[37] Cf. Kristian Smidt, p. 140.

except by mystic intuition. In the *Four Quartets*, at least, it appears to be in the nature of a mystic intuition. In this sense the idea of the Eternal Now is clearly stated in the following passages from "Burnt Norton":

> If all time is eternally present

And

> the co-existence,
> Or say that the end precedes the beginning,
> And the end and the beginning were always there
> Before the beginning and after the end.
> And all is always now.

It seems relevant at this stage to point out that in philosophical discourse the concept of the timeless can have various meanings more or less closely related to Eliot's idea of the timeless. Eliot does not draw any distinction between different kinds of timelessness, but for the better understanding of his use of the idea it may be well to mention the possibility of such distinctions.

In the first place comes the actual experience in which the immediate, psychological apprehension of the stream of time is superseded by a feeling of something which seems to lie outside the dimension of time. This may be a purely psychological phenomenon by no means restricted to mystics. The next step in the definition of the timeless is taken when someone attempts to analyse and explain what his timeless experience really was, and at this point various possibilities present themselves. There is, for example, the Kantian conception of a transcendent reality to which the category of time is inapplicable, but besides being expressed in a language very remote from that of poetry however speculative, this conception of the timeless appears as the result of pure logical analysis rather than as an attempt to express something experienced. Then there is the mystic idea of the interpenetration of all times, of past, present and future, which is another form of timelessness – one very close to Eliot's own idea, and by the mystics themselves often expressed in almost poetic language. Again, this idea is not wholly unrelated to the more purely philosophical conception of time as a series of events, past, present and future, all equally real, which series, apprehended as a whole, amounts to a kind of timelessness. Eliot's idea of the timeless seems to be a kind of amalgamation of all these ideas, and this amalgamation will here be called the idea of the Eternal Now. Throughout the analysis of the *Four Quartets* that follows later in this study, it should be borne in mind that this idea of the Eternal Now is something different from the immediate apprehension of a timeless dimension in a particular experience, something which, as it were, is read into such an experience.

In our everyday experience things and events are presented to us as belonging to the dimension of time; things happen after each other in temporal succession, and the present moment, the now, is often pictured as a point moving along the line of time, from the past into the future. Time, then, involves motion, and motion time. As pointed out earlier in this chapter, time and motion appeared to the ancient Greek philosophers to be closely interrelated, time being the measure of motion, and motion the measure of time. The first to make systematic scientific use of this aspect of time was Aristotle,[38] and in our day Einstein has emphasized, more strongly than anyone before him, that time is an indispensable aspect, not only of events but of things; a thing without extension or duration in time does not exist to the scientific mind. Against this notion of the temporality of things and events, implied in immediate experience as well as in physics, Eliot sets the idea of the co-existence of past and future, of beginning and end. This idea is not original, however, not one invented by Eliot, as he was no doubt aware in using it. It goes back to classical Greek and Latin philosophy, and, emerging at intervals throughout the history of Western philosophy, it was subject to renewed and intense discussion during the first decades of the present century. Regarding the idea of the Eternal Now, such as it appears in the *Four Quartets*, in the light of this tradition, ancient and modern, we may hope to approach its meaning.

The idea had appeared already in *The Rock*, and is perhaps even more explicitly stated there:

> There's some new notion about time, what says that the past – what's be'ind you – is what's goin' to 'appen in the future, bein' as the future 'as already 'appened.[39]

[38] Cf. Gent, pp. 6 ff.

[39] *The Rock*, pp. 15 f.

As Grover Smith has observed, this "new notion about time" does not imply recurrence,[40] *i.e.* cyclic recurrence of the same events as in certain Indian and Platonic theories of history, but simultaneity, by which word is here meant "the co-existence of past and future". To Eliot this notion was far from new. Spoken as they are by an ordinary workman, the words quoted may be intended to refer to the "scientific" theories of time current during the nineteen-twenties – Dunne's *An Experiment with Time*, for instance, seems to have exercised a certain popular influence, and that work together with other similar ones, discussed in Chapter I of this study, can be taken to form the background of the saying of the workman in *The Rock*.

A current expression of the idea of the simultaneity of past, present, and future is found in an article in *Mind* of 1917:

> All parts of time are parts of an eternal "now", and [. . .] we cannot fix any limits to the present or exclude from it any part of what we wrongly call "the past" and "the future".[41]

This view belongs to an old tradition, and perhaps owes something to Plotinus who, according to Inge, believed that

> The form of existence in the world of Time is succession (τὸ ἄλλο μετ'ἄλλο); the stages follow each other. But in Eternity the whole is in each part; all is present together in its realised meaning and achieved perfection.[42]

The most elaborate expression of this idea of absolute simultaneity in classical philosophy is found in the eleventh book of St. Augustine's *Confessions*, which is devoted to an analysis of the problem of time. His analysis, on the metaphysical level, follows the author of *Timaeus* in regarding time as one with Creation. Before the Cosmos was created, there was no time. But God, the Eternal, was before the world and shall be after its annihilation, if we can speak of "before" and "after" where no time exists. In God is gathered all that which to man appears as change and succession. Everything exists at the same time, or rather without time, in God's Eternal Now, His *nunc stans*; such is St. Augstine's glimpse of the Eternal:

[40] Smith, Grover, *T. S. Eliot's Poetry and Plays*, Chicago, 1956, p. 177.

[41] Wordsworth, J. C., "Time as Succession", *Mind*, Vol. 26, 1917, p. 328.

[42] Inge, *The Philosophy of Plotinus*, I, p. 170.

Dies tuus non cotidie, sed hodie, quia hodiernus tuus non cedit crastino; neque enim succedit hesterno. Hodiernus tuus aeternitas.[43]

To the ordinary man every immediate experience belongs to the dimension of temporal succession and the *nunc stans* may therefore seem an unreal abstraction, but St. Augustine's analysis of the concept of time suggests the opposite. He starts with the concept of the instant, of the now, which seems to be the only real dimension of time. For the past is past and is no more, and the future is yet to come. Thus the now is the only thing that is real. But if both past and future are non-existent, what is left of the now? It loses extension, is reduced to an abstraction void of counterpart in reality. St. Augustine's solution of the problem is therefore essentially a kind of compromise. Strictly speaking only the now exists, he argues, but in that now are gathered past and future in the form of memory on the one hand and hope or presentiment on the other.[44] The extension of the now is essentially mental. The metaphysical contradiction is thus resolved on the "psychological" level. The introduction of a "psychological" point of view is St. Augustine's great contribution to the philosophy of time.

It is this idea of St. Augustine's that seems to be the basis of Eliot's meditations in the first part of "Burnt Norton". Louis Martz has drawn attention to some lines in that part which he regards as a verbal reminiscence from the *Confessions*. "Footfalls echo in the memory" and "My words echo / Thus, in your mind" ring like an echo of St. Augustine's "Out of the memory are drawn not the things themselves [. . .] but such words as being conceived by the images of those things, they, in their passing through our senses, have, as their footsteps, left imprinted in our minds".[45]

Thus to Eliot time is the moving image of eternity, and the now of human experience is the moving image of God's Eternal Now. What to the mind is a presentiment of the future, is present to God because past and future are gathered in Him. "If all time is eternally present", Eliot argues in "Burnt Norton", then "All time is un-

[43] *St. Augustine's Confessions*, II, Loeb ed., London, 1946, p. 236.

[44] Cf. Callahan, pp. 151 ff.

[45] *St. Augustine's Confessions*, II, p. 249; Martz, p. 451.

redeemable". That is to say that if past, present, and future do not follow each other as cause and effect, but are fixed in a static Eternal Now, then nothing can be changed, nothing atoned for, nothing redeemed; pleasure and pain, good and evil co-exist for ever and the hope of salvation is dissolved into thin air – an idea most people would reject as the product of a morbid mind. But Eliot considers it very seriously. It is this tendency of Eliot to push a concept or doctrine to its bitter conclusion, regardless of philosophic consequences, that has repelled some of his critics.[46]

Had the interpretation of the *nunc stans* as a rigidly unredeemable simultaneity been the only possible one, the *Four Quartets* would not have been what they are, a triumphant affirmation of divine Grace. But more than that they form a mystic interpretation along the lines of Meister Eckhart's description of his vision of eternity:

> He [God] makes the world and all things in this present Now (*gegenwürtig nû*) ... what was a thousand years ago and what shall be a thousand years hence, all that is there in the present, – all that is overseas as much as what is here ... In eternity, there is no before and after ... To live in that eternity, so help us God![47]

Thus what seems almost terrible to "natural man" is the supreme bliss of the mystic. Through acceptance and humility the damnation of temporal existence is transformed, by the divine Grace, into a joy eternal. The *Four Quartets* form, in one of their aspects, an account of such a gradual transformation.

The Eternal Now is sometimes called the *totum simul*, and as such this concept appears in the philosophy of Boethius and of the Schoolmen.[48] The concept of the Eternal Now has often been brought to bear, by medieval philosophers, on the problem of divine foreknowledge and free-will. If God knows all that is going to happen in the future life of a man, how, then, can this man's actions be free? If God knows what he will do, there is no choice left for him. This problem has perplexed the theologians ever since it was raised: God's foreknowledge and man's free-will constitute a paradox which the

[46] Cf. R. H. Robbins, *The T. S. Eliot Myth*, New York, 1951, p. 25.

[47] Quoted from Coomaraswamy, *Time and Eternity*, p. 117.

[48] Cf. A. Gunn, *The Problem of Time*, London, 1929, pp. 38 ff.

orthodox Christian seems driven to accept without comprehending it. There are many ways, it is true, in which the apparent contradictions can at least be made to appear reconcilable – man's subjective experience of freedom of choice is enough to make him morally responsible for his actions, is an argument favoured by some theologians – though the paradox seems to many no doubt to remain a paradox still.[49]

On the whole, Eliot seems to evade this difficult issue, preferring to accept the solution offered by the Church, to accept, that is, both God's timeless omniscience and the free-will of man, but making no attempt to explain away the difficulties. When the concept of freedom appears in his poetry, it is less a question of freedom of choice to act in time than a mystic freedom implying complete harmony with the will of God; as, for instance, in these lines from the last Section of "The Dry Salvages":

And right action is freedom
From past and future also.

Eliot's sympathy for the "Jansenist" type of theology is well-known,[50] and with that sympathy goes a latent affirmation of the doctrine of predestination. But for Eliot, predestination applies only to temporal existence, to the "enchainment of past and future". The nearer man comes to God, to the timeless, the freer he is. The experience of freedom and release expressed in the following passage from "Burnt Norton" II, is said to take place out of time:

And I cannot say, how long, for that is to place it in time.
The inner freedom from the practical desire,
The release from action and suffering, release from the inner
And the outer compulsion, yet surrounded
By a grace of sense, a white light still and moving

The different degrees of freedom depending on the nearness to God has been illustrated by Boethius in his *Consolation of Philo-*

[49] Cf. F. H. Brabant, *Time and Eternity in Christian Thought*, London, 1937; Murray, R., *Time and the Timeless*, London, 1942; Stace, W. T., *Time and Eternity. An Essay in the Philosophy of Religion*, Princeton, 1952; Stocks, J. L., *Time, Cause and Eternity*, London, 1938.

[50] Vide supra, pp. 46 f.

sophy under the familiar symbol of the circle and its centre. Divine Providence, Boethius argues, can be apprehended from two different aspects; either directly or indirectly. The indirect manifestation of Providence he calls Fate, which, in Boethius, involves predestination. Providence is sometimes defined so as to include the Eternal Now. Fate is the unrolling in time of all that which is gathered in the Eternal Now:

> For Providence embraceth all things together, though diverse, though infinite; but Fate putteth every particular thing into motion being distributed by places, forms, and time; so that this unfolding of temporal order being united into the foresight of God's mind is Providence, and the same uniting, being digested and unfolded in time, is called Fate.[51]

Adopting the traditional symbol of the circle, Boethius pictures Fate as movement along the circumference, and Providence as the centre of the circle; the nearer to the central point, the greater freedom from the necessity of Fate. Among the antitheses symbolized by the circle and the point Boethius also lists that of time and eternity:

> Wherefore in what sort discourse of reason is compared to pure understanding, that which is produced to that which is, time to eternity, a circle to the centre, such is the course of movable Fate to the stable simplicity of Providence.[52]

In this passage eternity is, of course, the equivalent of the timeless, and Boethius thus continues the traditional Platonic dualism in the field of time philosophy. It should be added that Boethius introduced a third term, an intermediary between time and eternity, which he called *aevum* and which was further developed by Thomas Aquinas.[53] The conception of *aevum* bears to the modern mind the impression of rather detached and academic speculation. It altogether lacks the imaginative force of the Platonic ideas, has never been fruitful in poetry, and is of no relevance to the *Four Quartets*.

The conception of the Eternal Now forms part of the philosophy of the English school of post-Kantian idealists, with which Eliot was

[51] Boethius, *The Consolation of Philosophy*, Loeb ed., London, 1918, p. 341.

[52] Ibid., pp. 343 f.

[53] Cf. Gunn, pp. 38 ff.

closely connected in his youth. Francis Herbert Bradley, for instance, exercised a strong influence on Eliot, and it may therefore be well to give a brief summary of his view of time.

Influenced by Hegel, Bradley continues the German dialectic tradition. Indirectly he builds his time philosophy on Kant's doctrine of time and space as *Anschauungen*.[54] Kant's distinction between the phenomenal world and the "thing in itself" is developed in Bradley's distinction between Appearance and Reality. Appearance stands for the phenomenal world as distinct from the ultimate Reality that "is such that it does not contradict itself; here", Bradley says, "is an absolute criterion".[55] In consequence of this, everything that contradicts itself belongs to the world of Appearance. Among the concepts which, as a result of Bradley's analysis, are found to be contradictory is that of change. It is hardly relevant to follow his argument in detail but the real point he makes is that if something changes, it becomes something else; what, then, is it that has undergone the change? Thus it is impossible to speak of change and at the same time of permanence or identity. Change is contradictory, and consequently, by definition, unreal. Time involves change, and falls under the same judgment: "Time [. . .] has most evidently proved not to be real, but to be a contradictory appearance."[56] Whether Bradley's argument is logically sound, may be debatable, but the problem is irrelevant here. Alexander Gunn, for instance, holds that Bradley confuses time as a fact, as part of our experience, with philosophical propositions about time: only a proposition can be contradictory, not a fact.[57]

Yet Bradley does not altogether deny the reality of time. At this stage of his argument he introduces the Absolute, which in his system comes near to Reality, but goes beyond it and comprises both Appearance and Reality. Thus the contradiction is resolved: "The Absolute is timeless, but it possesses time as an isolated aspect, an aspect which, in ceasing to be isolated, loses its special character."[58]

[54] Gent, W., *Die Raum-Zeit-Philosophie des 19. Jahrhunderts*, Bonn, 1930, pp. 46 ff.

[55] Bradley, F. H., *Appearance and Reality*, London, 1893, p. 136.

[56] Ibid., p. 43.

[57] Gunn, pp. 343 f.

[58] Bradley, p. 210.

In consequence of this Bradley reached a conception of time within the Absolute which comes very near to the Eternal Now. Every individual arranges his experience in a temporal order having a definite direction from the past towards some point in the future, though this order is valid only for that particular individual. Why could not some other man go through the same experience but in a different order of succession? Bradley considers this quite possible: "There is a man who traverses the same history with ourselves, but in the opposite direction." [59]

Bradley's affirmation of the co-existence in the Absolute of several time-series running in opposite directions is but one step removed from the affirmation of an Eternal Now. How near he comes to that conception he reveals in conceding that the belief in foresight and prophecy can find support in his philosophy.[60] Already St. Augustine claimed to have proved the possibility of prophecy: As all that which shall happen, seen from the human point of view, already exists to God, it is in principle available to the one who can read the divine writ in the book of nature, to the prophet.[61]

Eliot does not indicate his view of the logic of Bradley's discourse on time; he may well concur in Gunn's censure of it. Long after he had finished his academic study of Bradley, Eliot wrote an essay on him which suggests his appreciation of the semi-religious metaphysician rather than the logician.[62] The religious element underlying Bradley's concept of the Absolute had been noticed before, and it is significant that his philosophy has been compared with Vedic philosophy – as the bewildering illusions of Maya are brought to harmony in Brahman, so are the contradictions of Appearance in the Absolute.[63]

[59] Ibid., p. 217.

[60] Ibid.

[61] *St. Augustine's Confessions*, II, p. 250.

[62] "Francis Herbert Bradley" (1927) in *Selected Essays*; cf. Eliot's essay, "Leibniz's Monads and Bradley's Finite Centres", *The Monist*, Vol. 26, 1916, p. 571.

[63] See W. James, "Bradley or Bergson?" in *Collected Essays and Reviews*, London, 1920, p. 496; Leone, H., "The Vedantic Absolute", *Mind*, Vol. 21, 1912; Mackenzie, J. S., "Time and the Absolute", *Mind*, Vol. 36, 1927.

V

Such then are some of the ideas and symbols that Eliot appears to have derived from non-Christian sources. The transition from pagan to Christian is in Eliot's thought and poetry, as it is in history, something more than crossing a finely drawn line. There is so much in early Christian thought, both apostolic and patristic, that suggests a community and intermixture of ideas that it is not altogether easy to separate pagan from Christian thought. Of this Eliot seems well aware. The pagan element is to be found perpetuating itself well into the Middle Ages, as is testified by the writings of St. Augustine and St. Thomas Aquinas, and many others.

Accordingly Eliot in the imagery and thought of his later poetry avoids using ideas associated with purely speculative philosophy. The various philosophical ideas of which he does make use are always related to, or interpreted in terms of Christian ideas. And as far as ancient philosophy is concerned, the amalgamation of pagan and Christian elements has long before been completed within the Catholic Church and Eliot can thus build on an existing tradition, only with a more than usually acute discernment of the historical origins of the various components of that tradition. Where the Church has no such accepted synthesis to offer, Eliot does not hesitate to work out one of his own, as for instance in the case of Bradley and others. The interrelating of non-Christian and Christian ideas in the *Four Quartets* is a process which seems to have been deliberately planned and carefully accomplished by Eliot. It is thus possible for the reader to bring about a synthesis of these two elements in his own mind. This is true even of "Burnt Norton", although the author had not yet wholly committed himself when he wrote it. What appears as a possibility in "Burnt Norton" is gradually realized in the subsequent poems. The reconciliation of pagan and Christian ideas is not, however, always possible, for Eliot sometimes introduces conceptions that are incompatible with classical philosophy, conceptions in some special sense derived from the Christian revelation.

An instance of such an exclusively Christian idea is what Eliot calls the intersection of time with the timeless, which is not consistent with the Platonic doctrine of time and eternity. In the Platonic and Neo-Platonic systems time and the timeless, the Phenomenal and the Absolute, are related to each other as image to archetype, as creation to the Creator. That the soul of man has the innate ability to rise above temporal existence, is true only in a psychic sense; it is a process during which the soul travels from one sphere to the other, while time remains time and is unaffected by eternity. The idea of the Incarnation in the Christian sense, which for Eliot involves the idea of intersection as well, is foreign to Platonism. It will, however, be remembered that Paul Elmer More, in *The Greek Tradition*, maintains that Plato had already approached that idea, more or less consciously, despite its apparent contradiction to the rest of his thought. The idea of intersection can thus be said to be the fulfilment of Platonism.

The intersection of time with the timeless is an idea common both to the *Four Quartets* and to the two preceding plays, *The Rock* and *Murder in the Cathedral*. It is sometimes more easily comprehended, intellectually, in the form in which it appears in the plays. The idea of the following lines from the last Section of "The Dry Salvages" had already been fully developed in *The Rock*.

> But to apprehend
> The point of intersection of the timeless
> With time, is an occupation for the saint –

The dogmatic content of this idea is clearly stated by the Rock in the following speech:

> Remember, all you who are numbered for God,
> In every moment of time you live where two worlds cross,
> In every moment you live at the point of intersection,
> Remember, living in time, you must live also now in Eternity.[64]

Again, there is another variation of the theme in the same play:

> But come, you must put your thoughts once more to this season of sowing,
> So with much pain shall you see Eternity crossing the current of time.[65]

These quotations emphasize both man's moral responsibility and the intersection of eternity with time which is said to take place at every moment of life. In this secondary sense, the intersection becomes a

[64] *The Rock*, p. 52.
[65] Ibid., p. 53.

constantly repeated phenomenon. But primarily it is the unique event in the history of mankind when God the Eternal descended to earth and endured mortality:

Then came, at a predetermined moment, a moment in time and of time,
A moment not out of time, but in time, in what we call
  history: transecting, bisecting the world of time, a
  moment in time but not like a moment of time,
A moment in time but time was made through that moment:
  for without the meaning there is no time, and that moment
  of time gave the meaning.[66]

The doctrine of Incarnation is a dominant theme in many of Eliot's later poetical works. It appears conspicuously in the fifth part of "Ash-Wednesday", is the central theme in the "Journey of the Magi", and in the *Four Quartets* it is sometimes directly referred to and always present in the form of hints, allusions and implications. This emphasis on the idea of the Incarnation is no special characteristic of Eliot's, but is found again and again in the teaching of Anglican divines, and indeed, of the Christian Church as a whole.

There appears to be no consistent doctrine of the Church concerning the relation of the Incarnation to the categories of time and the timeless. Though in a general way Eliot's speculations in that field are paralleled elsewhere, certain aspects add so significantly to the ideas hitherto expressed that they deserve special attention. It may be well to keep Plotinus' words in mind that "our 'circles' and 'centres' are only metaphors", for the idea of the intersection of time with the timeless can hardly be imagined when the two intersecting elements are pictured as the circumference and centre of a circle. Eliot permits himself to use different, geometrically incompatible metaphors in the same poem. The concept of intersection implies different lines or planes crossing each other; the place where the lines intersect is a point, but one cannot speak of a point intersecting a line. Eliot wavers between the two metaphors. In "Ash-Wednesday" V, for instance, Christ, the Word, is pictured as the still point at the centre of the world:

Against the World the unstilled world still whirled
About the centre of the silent Word.

[66] *Collected Poems 1909–1935*, (Chorus from *The Rock*), p. 173.

In "The Dry Salvages", however, Incarnation is the point of intersection:

> But to apprehend
> The point of intersection of the timeless
> With time, is an occupation for the saint –
> – – –
> For most of us, there is only the unattended
> Moment, the moment in and out of time,
> The distraction fit, lost in a shaft of sunlight,
> – – –
> These are only hints and guesses,
> Hints followed by guesses; and the rest
> Is prayer, observance, discipline, thought and action.
> The hint half guessed, the gift half understood, is Incarnation.

Eliot's idea of Incarnation hardly seems to have Scriptural sanction. On the whole, such metaphysical speculation is alien to the spirit of the Scriptures, nor is it possible to extract any coherent theory of time and eternity from them. There are the well-known words of the Ecclesiast (iii: 1–8) which are echoed in the First Section of "East Coker":

> there is a time for building
> And a time for living and for generation
> And a time for the wind to break the loosened pane

The corresponding passage in *Ecclesiastes* must be seen as the formulation of human experience, not as a set of metaphysical propositions. When we come to the New Testament the words "time" and "eternity" become more frequent, but what meaning exactly did the writers of the New Testament put into these words? That is a question which has not seriously been raised until quite recently. In the Catholic doctrine as it is expounded by, for example, St. Thomas Aquinas, the question of the actual connotation given to words in Biblical times never arises; the text that he used was the *Vulgate* and his interpretation appears to have been based on the conceptual system of Greek philosophy.

The very considerable interest in, and study devoted to, the problem of time during the present century includes several theological revisions of established conceptions of time and eternity. The chief work perhaps in this field, *Christus und die Zeit*, was written as late as 1946 by the Swiss theologian Oscar Cullmann, but some of the most startling ideas of this book had already been put forward in 1926 in J. H. Brown's little-known pamphlet, *Eternity: Is It a Biblical Idea?* Brown's answer to that question is that eternity as something different in kind from time is not a Biblical idea.

Although Cullmann's work appeared after the completion of the *Four Quartets*, a brief summary of his argument is not irrelevant, since it throws some light on Eliot's conception of the Incarnation. Cullmann's work is based on a close reading of the New Testament, but whether that reading is historically correct, may be debated. Being radically different from Catholic teaching, however, it throws Eliot's ideas into relief.

According to Cullmann the dichotomy between time and eternity in ancient philosophy is not to be found in Scripture. The word for eternity used in the Greek New Testament is ἀιών. Plato uses the same word, in his *Timaeus*, for instance, to denote eternity, but with quite a different connotation. In the New Testament the word means simply time without a foreseeable end – just as "eternity" sometimes does in ordinary usage. So when God is said to be eternal, it means that His existence has no foreseeable end, that He exists throughout infinitely successive periods, "*in aeternitate aeternitatis*", and will be world without end, and not that He is a being above time and space, Absolute and Other, in the Platonic sense. Accordingly the Biblical view of history differs from the Platonic, cyclic theory. Plato conceived of history as moving round in a circle, as it were: after a certain lapse of time the same events recur in identical order and form; history repeats itself while God remains above both time and history. The Jews and early Christians on the other hand, Cullmann maintains, conceived of time and history as an infinite progression of successive events following the Creation, and they conceived of God as inherent in time.[67] Cullmann perhaps pretends to know more of the way in which the early Christians imagined time than can, in fact, be known. Nevertheless he certainly draws attention to an essential concept about which the Jewish-Christian religion and the contemporary Hellenistic religions may have been at variance.

The idea of salvation is closely connected with the idea of time.

[67] Cullmann, O., *Christus und die Zeit*, Zürich, 1946, pp. 43 ff.

In Hellenistic religious philosophy, salvation seems to have been conceived as a liberation from time, and escape from temporal existence to complete union with a timeless deity. The Apostles and other early Christian teachers, lacking the idea of a timeless dimension, thought of salvation as taking place *in* time – the immortal life of the redeemed soul is eternal only in the sense that it has no end. Ultimately the idea of Redemption depends on a single event in time, the appearance of Christ as the Incarnation of God Himself. The Incarnation is one of the three decisive events in the history of mankind, the other two being its beginning, the Creation and the Fall, and its end, the Last Judgment. The Incarnation divides history into two parts, forms a line of division between the Old and the New Covenant. The Last Judgment does not mean the end of time, only the end of history. The well-known words from the *Revelation of St. John,* (x: 6), "there should be time no longer", can be taken to refer to the end of temporal existence as such, but Cullmann regards the word for time, χρόνος, in this context as a synonym for the other Greek word for time, καιρός, and hence interprets the phrase to mean that there should no longer be opportunity – for man to save his soul.

The interpretation of time and the Incarnation in this sense is suggested by the words previously quoted from *The Rock*:

> A moment not out of time, but in time, in what we call
> history: transecting, bisecting the world of time

To the notion of the Incarnation bisecting history – in harmony with Cullmann's interpretation – Eliot seems to add the notion of something *trans tempus,* a timeless or eternal dimension. If "transecting" and "bisecting" are not merely meant to reinforce each other, the juxtaposition of these two words forms an illustrative example of the amalgamation in Eliot's thought and poetry of Greek and Christian elements.

The Incarnation not only bisected history, but changed the conditions of temporal existence – made time into something different. This idea, implicit in Cullmann's interpretation of the New Testament, has received poetic expression by George Herbert. The opening stanzas of his poem, "Time", illustrate this aspect of the Incarnation:

Meeting with Time, Slack thing, said I,
Thy sithe is dull; whet it for shame.
No marvell Sir, he did replie,
If it at length deserve some blame:
  But where one man would have me grinde it,
  Twentie for one too sharp do finde it.

Perhaps some such of old did passe,
Who above all things lov'd this life;
To whom thy sithe a hatchet was,
Which now is but a pruning-knife.
  Christs coming hath made man thy debter,
  Since by thy cutting he grows better.

And in his blessing thou art blest:
For where thou onely wert before
An executioner at best;
Thou art a gard'ner now, and more,
  An usher to convey our souls
  Beyond the utmost starres and poles.[68]

Another term for the point of intersection in Eliot's poetry is the Word. Though Eliot rarely speaks of Christ as the Word, the notion of the Logos is often implied in the *Four Quartets*. The theological and other issues raised by the concept of the Logos are vast, and only certain of the more significant and relevant aspects can be mentioned here. It was a notion that especially attracted Greek thinkers of the late Roman period, but it is also found as early as in the philosophy of Heracleitus; the meaning of his Logos is much disputed, however. The first of the two Heracleitian epigraphs to "Burnt Norton" concerns the Logos; whatever its original context may have been, its meaning for the *Quartets* should be judged from the context in which it appears in Diels' edition of Heracleitus, from which Eliot has quoted. The first two Fragments, in Diels' translation, are:

> Für dies Wort aber, ob es gleich ewig ist, haben die Menschen kein Verständnis weder ehe sie es vernommen noch sobald sie es vernommen. Alles geschiet nach diesem Wort, und doch geberden sie sich wie die Unerfahrenen, so oft sie sich versuchen in solchen Worten und Werken, wie ich sie künde, ein jegliches nach seiner

[68] *The Works of George Herbert*, ed. by F. E. Hutchinson, Oxford, 1941, pp. 122 f.

> Natur auslegend und deutend, wie sich's damit verhält. Die anderen Menschen wissen freilich nicht, was sie im Wachen thun, wie sie ja auch vergessen, was sie im Schlafe thun.
>
> Drum ist's Pflicht dem Gemeinsamen zu folgen. Aber obschon das Wort allen gemein ist, leben die meisten so, als ob sie eine eigene Einsicht hätten.[69]

It is difficult to say whether Eliot subscribes to the unhistorical but traditional view of Heracleitus as a forerunner of the Christian Logos philosophy. He seems to use the second quotation from Heracleitus to illustrate the opposition between words and the Word, as in "Burnt Norton", V, or between knowledge and wisdom, as in the first Chorus from *The Rock*. It is only in "Burnt Norton" that Eliot refers directly to the Word; but discussing the art of poetry, the proper use of words, in the last Section of each *Quartet*, he alludes indirectly to the "common Word" of Heracleitus, and it is quite natural that Eliot the Christian should identify this "common Word" with Christ, the highest wisdom.

It is interesting to note that St. Augustine also seems to have been concerned with the relation between words and the Word. The somewhat obscure passage in the ninth book of *De Trinitate*[70] seems to argue an analogy between the Word spoken by God and words spoken by men. It is perhaps dangerous to attach too much importance to this reference – the analogy, almost identification, of divine and human creative activity suggests a "romanticism" inconsistent with Eliot's general view.

Heracleitus' notion of the Logos was systematized by the Stoic school, which more or less identified the Logos with the Absolute. Eliot, however, apparently uninfluenced by this school, interpreted the Logos in the sense generally accepted by Christian theologians – though they by no means speak with one voice. Eliot does not seem much concerned with such things as the distinction between Judaistic and Hellenistic elements in the Gospel of St. John. His general approach is along broadly Christian lines, and it is in this sense that the Logos philosophy is relevant to the *Four Quartets*, and such

[69] Diels, H., *Die Fragmente der Vorsokratiker*, Berlin, 1903, p. 66.

[70] St. Augustine, *De Trinitate*, Book IX, vii, 12–13.

questions as the gnostic or other heretical influences do not seem to have bothered him.

The function of the divine Word, according to the above doctrines, is to be the temporal manifestation of God's will. God created the world by His Word, and in making the Word flesh He announced the beginning of the second era in the history of mankind, the New Covenant. This Incarnation of the Word in time was generally conceived as an emanation from God, the timeless, in accordance with the Neo-Platonic picture of the universe. Thus Incarnation can properly be called the transection of time by the timeless. Christ, the Word, is the Mediator between man and God, between time and eternity. The relation between the unique transection, or intersection, of the Incarnation of Christ and the perpetual incarnation, or intersection of the timeless with the temporal life of man, will be discussed in the following chapter, in connection with Dante.

Eliot's twofold interpretation of the Incarnation has perturbed his critics. Some maintain that his allusions to Incarnation must refer to the Incarnation of God in Christ, others have maintained that they refer to the immanence of the Divine in time at any moment of history – as in Blake's well-known lines:

> To see a World in a Grain of Sand,
> And a Heaven in a Wild Flower,
> Hold Infinity in the palm of your hand,
> And Eternity in an hour.[71]

It is quite clear, however, that both aspects concern Eliot and that in the *Four Quartets* he has attempted to reconcile them.[72] Yet theologians may maintain that the doctrine of the Incarnation has to be interpreted either in one way or the other. But what appears incompatible in systematic theology may not be so in poetry.

Eliot's idea of the Incarnation has immediate bearings on his speculations on history. A cyclic theory of history cannot be reconciled with the unique mission of Christ. And yet Eliot seems to employ the idea of recurrence in, for example, the first part of "East Coker",

[71] "Auguries of Innocence", *The Poetical Works of William Blake*, ed. by J. Sampson, Oxford, 1905, p. 288.

[72] The controversy has been summarized by H. E. Butz in *The Relation of T. S. Eliot to the Christian Tradition*, unpubl. thesis, Univ. of Ann Arbor, 1953.

opening with the words, "In my beginning is my end" and, again, ending with these words, "In my end is my beginning". The circle is closed, the end means a homecoming to the point of departure. The imagery of the whole passage varies the theme of rise and fall, birth and death, of the perpetual recurrence of the different phases of human and social life. Strictly speaking, this is not meant to be taken as a philosophy of history; as Eliot himself suggests in the final Section of "East Coker" it is rather the formulation of personal experience accumulated during the span of one life. Nevertheless Eliot sometimes seems to allude to cyclic theories of history, but however near he comes to such theories in some places in the *Four Quartets*, in the end he always transcends the historical, temporal dimension. The opening words of "East Coker" are inverted at the end of the poem: "In my end is my beginning." And the new beginning is not only that of another cycle in time, it is also the transfigured life of the reborn soul. The way through death to new life is the fundamental pattern of Eliot's poetry from "Prufrock" to the *Four Quartets*.

VI

In Eliot's earlier poetry the theme of death and rebirth was illustrated chiefly with symbols derived from fertility myths and rites, and in "Ash-Wednesday" the imagery is basically liturgical. In the *Four Quartets*, however, Eliot makes direct use of the language of the mystic tradition which is most apparent in the second and third parts of "Burnt Norton" and in the third of "East Coker". In these passages his attitude is more consistent, while the quotations from mystic writers in "Little Gidding" are more varied, no doubt in order to emphasize the effect of religious synthesis that Eliot is trying to achieve at the end of this poem. The mystic doctrine of both "Burnt Norton" and "East Coker" is that of the *via negativa*, a doctrine by no means peculiar to Christian mysticism. It is found in an extreme form in Indian Yoga, and in Plotinus in the notion that the way to union with the One is through negation of everything sensuous and temporal. Although either or both of these forms of mysticism have been Eliot's source, most critics seem agreed that more important than any other source is the teaching of St. John of the Cross.[73] It is his teaching that inspires many of the passages in "Burnt Norton" and in "East Coker"; the metaphors and the symbolism of darkness derive from him, as is confirmed by the closing lines of the Third Section of "East Coker" – an almost word for word rendering of a passage from *The Ascent of Mount Carmel.*[74] An English translation of the complete works of St. John appeared in 1934, the year before "Burnt Norton".

The basic teachings of St. John of the Cross, to be found in *The Ascent of Mount Carmel* and *The Dark Night of the Soul,* are relevant in certain respects to the *Four Quartets. The Ascent* deals with the active striving of the soul, describes the road of self-discipline and self-negation. *The Dark Night* represents the passive state of the soul, the necessary spiritual vacuum preliminary to the reception of God's grace. In Eliot's early poetry the passive condition of the soul waiting for rebirth was symbolized by "Death By Water", the title of the fourth part of *The Waste Land.* In the later religious poetry this image of the violent killing of the natural self by drowning is replaced, no doubt through the influence of St. John, by the idea of the rigid discipline of gradual progress along the road of negation, and so instead of drowning, Eliot uses the same image as St. John, total darkness. And as the life-giving rain at the end of *The Waste Land* corresponds to the deep currents of the sea into which Phlebas was submerged, so the darkness of the dark night corresponds to the dazzling flames of divine grace.

The distinction between actively striving and passively waiting applies in particular to "Burnt Norton". The passage in the Third Section beginning "Descend lower . . .", is a paraphrase of the teaching of *The Ascent of Mount Carmel,* and of this Eliot says:

> This is the one way, and the other
> Is the same, not in movement
> But abstention from movement

Movement is the striving of the soul, but abstention from movement

[73] Cf. Gardner, pp. 167 f., and Smidt, pp. 169 ff. For Plotinus' negative way, see Inge, *The Philosophy of Plotinus,* II, pp. 145 f.

[74] Cf. Gardner, loc. cit.

is submission to grace. Once more we seem to hear an echo of Heracleitus' words, "The way up and the way down are one and the same". The ascent of the mount of purgation is also a descent into utter darkness.

At the end of *The Dark Night*, St. John introduces a new metaphor. The very last part of the road to blessedness is likened to a stair of ten steps. The steps symbolize the mounting degrees of the soul's reception of divine love, and the last step on this stair of love leads to complete union with God, and those who are chosen to reach the top in this life need not go through Purgatory after death, but go straight to Paradise.[75] There is a direct allusion to this metaphor in "Burnt Norton" V:

> The detail of the pattern is movement,
> As in the figure of the ten stairs.

And, following the lines of St. John, Eliot goes on to expound the Aristotelian doctrine of the Unmoved Mover:

> Love is itself unmoving,
> Only the cause and end of movement.

Or, in St. John's terms, man's active purgation of his soul is worked by the drawing love of God.

The form in which St. John presents his mystic doctrine is itself a remarkable literary achievement. *The Ascent of Mount Carmel* and *The Dark Night of the Soul* are balanced against each other with perfect symmetry, treating the same topics in the same order but from different standpoints. The disciplined style of St. John has no doubt contributed to making him Eliot's favourite mystic writer. But, as do so many other mystic writers, he often describes divine ecstasy in terms of earthly love. This is true in particular of his poems, among which are the "Song Between the Soul and the Spouse" in which the bride praises her beloved in metaphors almost reminiscent of the *Song of Solomon*. Such extravagant imagery is perhaps too unrestrained for Eliot, though not actually foreign to him. He by no means rejects the analogy, but like St. John of the Cross, employs

[75] *The Complete Works of St. John of the Cross*, transl. by E. Allison Peers, London, 1934, I, pp. 463 ff.

for divine love the metaphors of "flame" and "light". A striking example from the writings of St. John are the "Songs of the Soul in the Intimate Communion of the Union of the Love of God":

O living flame of love
That, burning, dost assail
My inmost soul with tenderness untold,
Since thou dost freely move
Deign to consume the veil
Which sunders this sweet converse that we hold.[76]

The image of the flame, or light, comes readily to St. John of the Cross, suggesting as it does the antithesis of the darkness of the soul – though the image is also frequently used by other mystic writers without any such antithetical suggestion.

Eliot's use of the images of flame and light to express various aspects of divine love is as varied as the sources from which he seems to have derived them. In "Burnt Norton" II, for example, the beatific vision is described as "a white light still and moving". Again, the "shaft of sunlight" in the First and Fifth Sections of the same poem, and in "The Dry Salvages" V, carries a related meaning. The Fourth Section of "Little Gidding" combines the themes of love and fire, and the last lines of the whole cycle of poems are built on the light and fire symbolism:

And all shall be well and
All manner of thing shall be well
When the tongues of flame are in-folded
Into the crowned knot of fire
And the fire and the rose are one.

These concluding lines have generally been interpreted as a conscious imitation of, or at least parallel to, the last part of Dante's *Paradiso*, in the last canto of which Dante describes his vision of the Person of God Himself, using, among other metaphors, that of the "circle of light". He uses a similar figure in the twenty-eighth canto where he sees a shining wheel of light and, moreover, significantly combines with the figure of the circle the symbol of fire and the still point:

[76] Ibid., II, p. 448.

E poi che le parole sue restaro,
   Non altrimenti ferro disfavilla
   Che bolle, come i cerchi sfavillaro.
Lo incendio lor seguiva ogni scintilla;
   Ed eran tante, che il numero loro
   Più che il doppiar degli scacchi s'immilla.
Io sentiva osannar di coro in coro
   Al punto fisso che li tiene all'ubi,
   E terrà sempre, nel qual sempre foro; [77]

The figure of the wheel recurs in the very last lines of the *Paradiso*; the whole universe circles round God, moved by the unmoved Love.

Though all this may seem far removed from the topic of time and eternity, the descriptions of the beatific vision given by Dante and St. John of the Cross represent attempts resembling Eliot's to find adequate metaphors to describe the vision of eternity. Again, in seventeenth century English poetry we find an example of a direct combination of the two themes, in Vaughan's well-known poem:

   I saw Eternity the other night
Like a great *Ring* of pure and endless light,
   All calm, as it was bright,
And round beneath it, Time in hours, days, years
   Driv'n by the spheres
Like a vast shadow mov'd, In which the world
   And all her train were hurl'd.[78]

Not all the possible sources of Eliot's fire symbolism are Christian. Heracleitus' idea of fire as the chief element or principle of life is, as Matthiessen points out, paraphrased at the beginning of the Second Section of "Little Gidding". He also quotes an annotation on Heracleitus from the note-book of Eliot when he was a student of philosophy at Oxford: "By God he meant fire." [79]

To round off this search for the origins of Eliot's symbolism, something should be said of the significance of the ring of flames which, in Indian art, sometimes surrounds the figure of Shiva. There are

[77] *Paradiso*, XXVIII, 88–96.

[78] *The Works of Henry Vaughan*, ed. by L. C. Martin, 2nd ed., Oxford, 1957, p. 466.

[79] Matthiessen, F. O., *The Achievement of T. S. Eliot*, p. 190.

many possible interpretations of the meaning of this ring, suggesting affinities with both Heracleitus and Dante. According to Zimmer, the ring

> is said to signify the vital processes of the universe and its creatures, nature's dance as moved by the dancing god within. Simultaneously it is said to signify the energy of Wisdom, the transcendental light of the knowledge of truth, dancing forth from the personification of the All.[80]

Shiva is also the God of the Dance. It will be recalled that Plotinus employed the image of the dance to describe the immediate vision of the One, a circular dance round the still centre. Thus the three images of the wheel and the still point, the dance, and the ring of flames are combined in one complex symbol. Some writers have used only one or two of these symbolic elements in their representation of the highest vision; others, and among those Dante, use all three. In the *Four Quartets* the symbol appears, in all its complexity, as one of the chief expressions of the spiritual meaning of the poems.

It should be noticed that this review of the possible sources of certain of Eliot's images has, with the exception of Bradley, dealt almost exclusively with pre-Renaissance philosophy and mysticism. As has been shown there seem to be some good reasons for doing so – the Catholic Christian tradition was firmly established and well-defined at the end of the Middle Ages, and most subsequent developments in philosophic thought fall within the field of secular philosophy. Furthermore, whether regarded as "orthodox" or not, Dante's work epitomizes the medieval tradition. No attempt has been made to show the continuity of the development of the philosophy of time and eternity. Only such ideas and symbols as seem relevant to Eliot's poetry, have been selected, and arranged in chronological order only in so far as convenient. For it is permanence rather than development that is of importance to Eliot. What he needed for his *Quartets* was not a sketch of the history of time philosophy, but a framework of permanent conceptions represented by a set of consistent metaphors.

For Eliot the Catholic tradition extends well outside the walls of Rome. He recognizes its succession in the Church of England. His

[80] Zimmer, p. 153.

chief literary source of inspiration, next to Dante, is, in his later years, seventeenth century English literature.

It may be worth noting at this point that one of the characteristics of the seventeenth century is its acute awareness of the transience of life and the tyranny of time. The medieval allegorical figures of Time and Death make their reappearance in art and literature at the end of the Renaissance, and Time has been called "the uncanny goddess of the Baroque".[81] Very many examples could be cited from English literature of that period. Time as the Man with the Scythe appears occasionally in Shakespeare's Sonnets; even Marvell ironically speaks of the approach of "Time's winged Chariot". Essential to the baroque mind is its love of contrasts and antitheses, and against the transience of the temporal world is set the stillness of eternity. Naturally enough the eternal dimension is emphasized in particular by the religious poets, as in the poem of Vaughan on the vision of eternity, and the triumph of eternity over time and death affirmed in Donne's *Holy Sonnets.* Again, among the works of the contemporary theologians are some devoted to the idea of eternity – V. Typing's *Discourse of Eternity* of 1633, W. Brent's *Discourse upon the Nature of Eternity* of 1655, and many other works which, although not exclusively devoted to the idea of time and eternity, touch upon the subject, showing the traditional attitude towards the problem. There is, for example, Sir Thomas Browne, from whose *Religio Medici* the following passage is taken:

> Who can speake of eternitie without a soloecisme, or thinke thereof without an extasie? Time we may comprehend; 'tis but five dayes elder than our selves, and hath the same Horoscope with the world; but to retire so farre backe as to apprehend a beginning [. . .] What to us is to come, to his [God's] Eternitie is present, his whole duration being but one permanent point, without succession, parts, flux, or division.[82]

This is a clear statement of the two familiar notions of time as one with Cosmos, and of the Eternal Now, the one descending from

[81] Strich, F., "Der europäische Barock", *Der Dichter und die Zeit*, Bern, 1947, p. 93.

[82] Browne, Th., *Religio Medici*, ed. by J.-J. Denonain, Cambridge, 1953, pp. 17 f.

Timaeus, the other from Neo-Platonic and Augustinian philosophy. Thus, although seventeenth century English literature added nothing to the classical conceptions of time and eternity, it may nevertheless have worked as a stimulant to Eliot's metaphysical speculation.

In conclusion, then, the *Four Quartets* are neither theological tracts nor philosophical essays. They are much more. The abstract doctrines, both implied and expressed in them, are only means to an end. The *Quartets* may be enjoyed at various levels. They are poetry first of all, and hence may be enjoyed purely for the euphony of the verse, but the deeper level of their psychological and philosophical structure and pattern asks of the reader a deeper comprehension of the language and imagery used, and of the implications of Eliot's own philosophical and theological reading and thought. The whole structure of the *Quartets* is, indeed, based on the fundamental antithesis of appearance and reality, of time and eternity. The actual words "timeless" and "eternal" each appear only once in "Burnt Norton", yet without this understanding of the special significance of these words and the ideas behind them in Eliot's mind and experience, the whole poem loses its deepest meaning.

More than that even, there is something almost dramatic underlying the dialectical structure of the *Four Quartets*. The eye is, as it were, constantly drawn towards the vision of eternity; each Section of "Burnt Norton" (except for the lyric Fourth) may be divided into two parts – one concerned with human experience *sub specie temporis*, the other, *sub specie aeternitatis*. The transition from the one to the other is gradual – it is at first foreshadowed, then suggested, and finally realized in language of ever-increasing poetic force.

CHAPTER IV

The Structural Problem in the Four Quartets

I

The *Four Quartets* represent the culmination of Eliot's craftsmanship as a poet. He may have achieved greater lyric intensity for example in the "Ariel Poems", and more trenchant analysis of contemporary life in *The Waste Land,* but never before did he set himself such a difficult task as the writing of the *Quartets.* The construction of "Burnt Norton" is in itself both bold and complex, but the rigorous application of its form to the three subsequent *Quartets* must have involved still greater technical problems. Of the same average length, developing the same themes, each consisting of five Sections each of almost identical form, the *Four Quartets* display a formal unity and a technical virtuosity which, quite apart from the complexity of the subject-matter, represent a remarkable achievement. As Eliot does not believe in art for art's sake, but prefers to present and explore life itself – intellectual and spiritual experience – mere experiments in poetic technique have no interest for him; they are but means to an end that lies beyond the normal categories of literary achievement. It would be a mistake, however, to think that Eliot could, or thought he could, achieve that end in a medium of representation other than that of poetry. The *Four Quartets* are religious poetry, but Eliot has firmly declined the suggestion that he was disclosing a revelation in writing them.[1] As a formulation of experience – religious though it be – the *Quartets* employ ideas in a different way and for a different purpose than the analytic discourse of Eliot's

[1] Smidt, K., *Poetry and Belief in the Work of T. S. Eliot,* Oslo, 1949, p. 155.

prose writings. They are concerned with ideas as part of human experience and with the integration of ideas with other forms of experience. Thus they are not merely versified philosophy and theology, but poetry. The *Quartets,* it seems, cannot properly be said to form a representation of experience, if this is taken to mean that the author knew from the outset exactly what he would represent in them. An exploration of experience would be a more appropriate term, implying that the meaning Eliot set out to discover emerged as he worked on the *Quartets,* partly as a result of the application of structural patterns to the experiential material. This, of course, applies to any kind of poetry, but in view of the complexity of the *Quartets,* the problem of the creative process itself calls for some consideration here. It may be impossible to distinguish clearly between form and content, between structure and subject-matter, but allowing for the close and constant interrelation of the two, an attempt will be made in the present chapter to analyse the fundamental structure and methods employed by Eliot in writing the *Quartets.*

Eliot's deep concern with the technical problems of the art of poetry is manifest in most of his critical writings, and ever since 1915, when he first began to publish his poems, he has been one of the chief experimenters in English verse forms. But not until the *Four Quartets* did the art of poetry itself form part of the subject-matter of his poetry. The Fifth Section of each *Quartet* (with the exception, perhaps, of "The Dry Salvages") contains a passage discussing the problems and difficulties of employing words to artistic ends. By his allusions to the art of writing poetry in the *Quartets,* Eliot shows his belief in the close connection between form and content. The actual connection is clear enough in "Burnt Norton", for in the Fifth Section of that poem, there is a return to the idea of the contrasts of time and eternity, of motion and stillness, which were, in the previous chapter, found to be the central theme of the *Quartets.* These contrasts, as was pointed out, imply two different metaphysical categories and modes of apprehension, two different aspects of reality. In returning to these contrasts in the Fifth Section of "Burnt Norton", Eliot explains their connection with the composition of the work of art generally, especially with poetry:

Words move, music moves
Only in time; but that which is only living
Can only die. Words, after speech, reach
Into the silence. Only by the form, the pattern,
Can words or music reach
The stillness, as a Chinese jar still
Moves perpetually in its stillness.
Not the stillness of the violin, while the note lasts,
Not that only, but the co-existence,
Or say that the end precedes the beginning,
And the end and the beginning were always there
Before the beginning and after the end.
And all is always now.

In this passage Eliot suggests that fundamental truth can be expressed "only by the form, the pattern": as the simultaneous co-existence of everything in the Eternal Now reconciles the opposition of motion in time and timeless stillness, so the pattern of a work of art reconciles its temporal limitations and instability and its striving towards perfection. Thus the analysis of the form, the pattern – the actual structure of the *Quartets* – is itself essential if the meaning of the poems is to be fully understood.

The *Four Quartets* are commonly regarded as "difficult" poetry, in the sense that their meaning does not lie on the surface, expressed in readily comprehensible images and familiar language, as in traditional poetry.

Although the first considerable contemporary English poet to do so, Eliot was in fact but one of a whole group of European writers attempting to write poetry of this new and "difficult" kind. The work which perhaps most closely resembles his, and which may have influenced him, was that of the contemporary French school. Paul Valéry, for instance, who broke his long silence at about the same time as Eliot wrote *The Waste Land,* strove to express himself in a style very like that of the *Quartets* – appealing to and at the same time defying the analytic intellect. Eliot is thoroughly familiar with Valéry's work, and often refers to him in his critical writings. "The self-consciousness of poets thinking about poetry"[2] was in Eliot's

[2] *The Use of Poetry and the Use of Criticism,* p. 121.

view one of the characteristics of the time, and especially characteristic in Valéry: "In the end, the question [in Valéry's critical writings] is simply: how did I write *La Jeune Parque* (or *Le Cimetière marin*)? The questions with which he is concerned are questions which no poet of an earlier generation would have raised; they are questions that belong to the present self-conscious century."[3] The self-consciousness of the poet leads him to explore, intellectually, new means of expression, and Eliot holds that "another important contribution by Valéry to the education of the poet is his emphasis upon *structure*."[4] Although published as late as 1958, these comments on Valéry are perhaps relevant to the analysis of the *Four Quartets*. There is no real external evidence of Eliot's debt to Valéry, but it seems likely that the self-consciousness and the emphasis on technique, so noticeable in the *Quartets*, owe something to the influence of Valéry.

Another exponent of modernism in this sense in French poetry is Guillaume Apollinaire, whom Eliot is reported to have met during his stay in Paris in 1910–1911.[5] In a study of Eliot's relation to Apollinaire, B. A. Morrissette draws attention to certain similarities between phrases and passages in Eliot's early work, particularly in *The Waste Land*, and passages in Apollinaire's poetry. Their descriptions of modern metropolitan life, for example, have much in common. Morrissette allows for the possibility of direct influence by Apollinaire on Eliot, but the correspondences can also be seen as "accidental parallels".[6] Since Apollinaire was in many ways associated with the Futurist movement, which Eliot indirectly denounced in "Tradition and the Individual Talent", the question of influence is more complex than appears from Morrissette's essay, but for the

[3] Introduction to Valéry, P., *The Art of Poetry*, New York, 1958, p. XI.

[4] Ibid., pp. XIII f.

[5] Taupin, R., *L'Influence du symbolisme français sur la poésie américaine (de 1910 à 1920)*, diss., Paris, 1929, p. 220; Taupin does not mention his source of information. M.-J.-J. Laboulle, however, says that "Mr. Eliot assures me that he has never read anything by Appollinaire". "T. S. Eliot and Some French Poets", *Revue de littérature comparée*, Vol. 16, 1936, p. 389.

[6] Morrissette, B. A., "T. S. Eliot and Guillaume Apollinaire", *Comparative Literature*, Vol. 5, 1953, p. 262.

present purpose it is sufficient to note the affinities between their respective works.

The new and "difficult" poetry was, then, an essentially European literary movement including writers not only from France and England, but from Italy, Russia, the Scandinavian countries and Germany as well. The most noteworthy German writer was, of course, Rainer Maria Rilke, whose *Duineser Elegien* and *Sonette an Orpheus* appeared in 1922, in the same year as *The Waste Land* and Valéry's *Charmes*. Although it is both enlightening and rewarding to compare, as some critics have done, the symbolism and the elements of mysticism in their work, it can hardly be maintained that Eliot was influenced by Rilke.[7]

Eliot, Valéry, Rilke and the rest of their company, have one thing in common – they all share in what Lawrence Durrell calls "the Semantic Disturbance" – or, as he explains it, "the disturbance of meaning within the structure of language".[8] Although these writers are not of one school and hold widely divergent beliefs and opinions, they are all united in their assault upon the traditional forms of poetry. Subordinating and even disregarding rigidly grammatical expression and conventional prosody, they employ an associative method which many of their contemporary readers found impossible to understand. Nowadays this poetry may not appear so difficult. Thirty years of critical analysis may have contributed something to the understanding of such poems as *The Waste Land,* although this criticism has sometimes stressed the superficial and hence obscured the fundamental. The *Four Quartets,* on the other hand, present difficulties of an altogether different kind. *The Waste Land* can be seen in some sort of historical perspective, and time has permitted the assimilation of most of the ideas and feelings there expressed. But the *Quartets* belong to a later generation, reflect other ideas and a different technique, and therefore require special analysis. Before attempting such an analysis, however, it is necessary to do more than

[7] Wood, F., "Rilke and Eliot: Tradition and Poetry", *Germanic Review*, Vol. 27, 1952, pp. 246–259; Weigand, E., "Rilke and Eliot: The Articulation of the Mystic Experience", *Germanic Review*, Vol. 30, 1955, pp. 198–210; Durrell, L., *Key to Modern Poetry*, London, 1952, pp. 37 ff.

[8] Durrell, p. 39.

merely consider Eliot in relation to his contemporaries, and treat his poetic technique as a manifestation of the general "Semantic Disturbance" of twentieth century literature. The origins and sources of this technique must also be traced.

The background Eliot shares with writers like Apollinaire and Valéry, is the Symbolist movement as it developed in France. Although Eliot's debt to Symbolism has been carefully studied by a number of critics, the importance of Stéphane Mallarmé seems generally to have been insufficiently emphasized. His influence on Eliot has probably been both direct and indirect – for many years the central figure in the literary life of Paris, Mallarmé influenced a whole generation of Symbolist writers, whom Eliot has read.

Mallarmé was among the first to write what may be called discontinuous or disconnected poetry – that is, poetry which rejects the usual means of ensuring that continuity of idea essential to the poem, if it is to have the unity of a great work of art. In dispensing with these means – the obvious emotional association, the facile metaphor, the patent sequence of events, of cause and effect – Mallarmé, together with certain other poets who wrote about this time, instead confronts the reader with a series of apparently disconnected phrases and even words, which at first sight appear wholly unintelligible.

The poem is in fact intended to achieve its unity in quite another way. The unity is not that of grammatical construction and the semantic equivalence of words. The words and phrases are superficially disconnected and dissociated. Nevertheless they represent images which suggest certain feelings and experiences. These feelings and experiences suggested to the reader correspond closely to those in the mind of the poet; for it is in the poet's mind, and not necessarily in his life, that the original experiences and feelings reside.[9]

Mallarmé was by no means the only poet to use this "symbolist"

[9] This aspect of Mallarmé's poetry has been discussed by several critics; for example by Svend Johansen in *Le Symbolisme. Etude sur le style des symbolistes français*, Copenhagen, 1945, particularly in the chapters on "le symbole" and "l'image". In a recent study Sven Lövgren has compared this aspect of Mallarmé with similar features in contemporary painting: *The Genesis of Modernism. Seurat, Gaugain, van Gogh and French Symbolism in the 1880's*, Stockholm, 1959. Mallarmé's influence on Eliot generally has been noted by Wallace Fowlie, *Mallarmé*, Chicago, 1953, pp. 278 ff.

technique, but as the most explicit and consistent of them, his influence on Eliot appears to have been deeper than that of the others. There is direct evidence of this influence in "Burnt Norton" II and in "Little Gidding" II. Here, the "dead master", "both one and many" meeting the speaker of "Little Gidding", seems to speak with the tongue of Mallarmé:

> Since our concern was speech, and speech impelled us
> To purify the dialect of the tribe.

The second line is a translation of Mallarmé's "donner un sens plus pur aux mots de la tribu",[10] and implies an acknowledgement of Mallarmé's significance as an originator of new forms of poetic expression. Again, Eliot's short poem, "Lines for an Old Man", in its manuscript form opens with the two lines that now begin "Burnt Norton" II, while the poem as a whole strongly suggests the allusive, terse, haunting obscurity of Mallarmé; it has even been suggested that the poem is addressed to Mallarmé.[11]

The actual form of the *Four Quartets* presents certain problems. The dramatic monologue as a poetic form in Eliot's work appears to have been derived from several sources; in his early work, from Elizabethan and Jacobean drama, Robert Browning and the French Symbolists, and in "Ash-Wednesday" and the *Four Quartets* also from Dante.[12] There is a wide difference between the Laforguian irony of "Prufrock", for example, and the Dantean pathos of the *Quartets,* which should warn us not to make any rash identification of the speakers of the monologues with the actual author. The speaker in the *Quartets* can readily enough be identified with Eliot himself, but the middle-aged J. Alfred Prufrock hardly suggests the young Eliot – nor does Gerontion. Nevertheless it is quite possible that even in such characters as Prufrock there is an element, a sardonic reflection, as it were, of the poet himself. Be that as it may, in the *Quartets*

[10] From Mallarmé's "Le Tombeau d'Edgar Poe". Cf. Gardner, H., "Four Quartets: A Commentary", *T. S. Eliot. A Study of his Writings by Several Hands,* ed. by B. Rajan, London, 1947, p. 74, note.

[11] Smith, G., *T. S. Eliot's Poetry and Plays,* Chicago, 1956, p. 257. The "Lines" were written in 1934.

[12] For a full discussion of "Gerontion" from this point of view, see Grover Smith, p. 57, and the references given in note 1 to his Chapter 4.

there is much to suggest a projection of the mind and experience of the poet, especially if due allowance is made for that element of objectivity that must necessarily insert itself between a poet and his work, and which necessarily precludes complete identification. It seems probable that the putative speaker of the *Quartets* is intended to be a projection of Eliot's own personality in much the same way as the Dante of the *Comedy* was intended to represent Dante as he actually was. In neither case is there any autobiographical intention, and hence it would be as futile to attempt to reconstruct Eliot's life from the *Quartets* as it would be to regard the *Comedy* as a series of episodes to be interpreted and included in a life of Dante. Although it is evident that the monologist in Eliot's poems is not to be wholly identified with the poet himself, it is equally evident that the monologist is not to be wholly dissociated from the mind and experience of the poet. Something of a poet's life and experience, emotions, feelings and beliefs must necessarily pass into any character he may create. The very titles of each of the *Quartets* suggest an association with the poet's own life – in fact a close association.[13]

The dramatic monologue as used by Eliot and the Symbolists who have influenced him technically resembles the "internal monologue" or "stream of consciousness" of James Joyce and other writers of his school, though there are important differences. In *Ulysses,* for example, Joyce intends the monologue to express the actual images, words and phrases passing through the mind of the monologist – as in Molly Bloom's famous monologue between sleeping and waking. It is, in fact, something between the conscious and the unconscious mind that Joyce is here concerned with, and the long monologue is supposed to be a direct reflection of the speaker's mind. In Eliot and Mallarmé, however, the words and phrases refer, not to conscious thoughts in the mind of the monologist, but to symbols, complex images and metaphors, which indirectly represent those conscious thoughts and feelings.

'Tis a figure, a symbol, say;
A thing's sign: now for the thing signified.[14]

[13] Cf. Kristian Smidt, "Point of View in T. S. Eliot's Poetry", *Orbis Litterarum,* Vol. 14, 1959, pp. 38–53.

[14] Browning, R., *The Ring and the Book,* London, 1912, p. 2.

The "thing signified" is indicated partly by the contextual imagery and associations in the monologue, and partly by what the poet has projected of his own ideas and feelings into the poem. In the *Four Quartets,* the ideas and feelings of the poet and the monologist are so closely associated as to be almost indistinguishable, but they are still not identical.

This essential difference, whether obvious or obscure, indicates the two different ways in which the reader and critic can approach such poetry as the *Four Quartets*. The one is to explore the meaning of the poem from within by means of regarding the whole from the putative speaker's point of view, attempting to follow his chain of thought and associations, in which case empathy is one of the chief critical virtues. The other approach consists in regarding a poem from without, attempting to discover patterns and forms which, independently of the putative speaker, provide logical connections between apparently disparate elements. This approach, which can be called the structural approach, relies in the first place on intellectual analysis and is, quite naturally, greatly facilitated by an understanding of the structural methods employed by the poet.

One of the most conspicuous structural methods employed by Eliot and some of his contemporaries, is the so-called mythical method. Mallarmé had already used myths to provide a symbolic framework for his poetry, and the later Symbolists developed this technique further – in England Yeats is a good example – but no one had hitherto gone to such lengths as Eliot in *The Waste Land.* The different parts of that poem cannot possibly be related to a single mind, and the structural methods employed to integrate the fragments into a whole, depend on myths familiar to the author and referred to in the notes, but not explicitly presented in the poem itself. In 1922, the same year as *The Waste Land,* appeared James Joyce's novel *Ulysses,* which also makes evident use of mythical elements. Reviewing *Ulysses* in 1923, Eliot emphasized the value and usefulness of the "mythical" method:

> In using the myth, in manipulating a continuous parallel between contemporaneity and antiquity, Mr. Joyce is pursuing a method which others must pursue after him. They will not be imitators, any more than the scientist who uses the discoveries of an Ein-

stein in pursuing his own, independent, further investigations. It is simply a way of controlling, of ordering, of giving a shape and a significance to the immense panorama of futility and anarchy which is contemporary history . . . It is a method for which the horoscope is auspicious. Psychology (such as it is, and whether our reaction to it be comic or serious), ethnology and *The Golden Bough* have concurred to make possible what was impossible even a few years ago. Instead of narrative method, we may now use the mythical method. It is, I seriously believe, a step towards making the modern world possible for art, towards . . . order and form.[15]

Eliot's enthusiasm, probably coloured by his own experiences in writing *The Waste Land,* can well be understood. Literary order and form were no doubt employed, in *The Waste Land,* to master "the immense panorama of futility and anarchy which is contemporary history", but it must not be forgotten that the demand for form and order in modern poetry was called forth by the literary development itself. The "Semantic Disturbance", distorting the immediately apprehensible surface meaning of modern poetry, necessitated some organizing principle that could save poetry from chaos. Disappearing from the surface, the logical and associative connections in poetry sank into the depths, from there directing the apparently incoherent verbal texture. Since modern poets, as Eliot has pointed out, tend to be self-conscious as artists, the submerged structures in their works tend to be one of their primary technical concerns. The whole idea of *structure,* so fashionable among modern critics, is perhaps the best term for these methods of organization that follow almost as a corollary of the "Semantic Disturbance". Eliot soon abandoned the mythical method, however, replacing it by even more complex structures, which find their consummation in the *Four Quartets.*

II

The formal structure of the *Four Quartets* can be analysed in three different ways. First, as a pattern of verbal, conceptual and sym-

[15] *The Dial,* Nov., 1923; quoted from Drew, E., *T. S. Eliot: The Design of his Poetry,* London, 1950, p. 19.

bolical relations, that is, as a strictly literary structure; secondly, as an analogue of musical composition; and thirdly, as an allegorical construction modelled upon Dante. While the analytical terminology depends on the approach selected, the structural relations subject to analysis remain the same in each case, and it would be meaningless to discuss which approach is most adequate – the deepest insight into the structure of the *Quartets* is gathered by the application of all three methods of analysis, each revealing a new aspect of the meaning of the poems. Several terms may be used to denote the objects of such analysis – "formal patterns" and "principles of organization", for example, are used by some critics – but in the present context "structure" is used throughout.

The appropriateness of the first method, employing a traditionally literary terminology, is immediately recognized, and it has been used by several critics.

A striking feature of the *Four Quartets* is the homogeneity and continuity of imagery and themes. Details from the rose garden scene in the First Section of the first *Quartet,* for example, recur time and again, interrelated or contrasted with other recurrent images. Abstract words such as time and the timeless are used to associate particular contexts, perpetually modified and modifying; in the same way references to one or more of the four elements, air, earth, water and fire, recur throughout the *Quartets.* These examples represent a kind of persistent imagery, called by John Bradbury the "structural symbolism" of the *Four Quartets.*[16] But the use of recurrent images is not sufficient in itself; the structure lies in the principles of interrelating the images.

Verbal antithesis is a frequent stylistic device in the *Quartets,* forming the most obvious surface reflection of the submerged structure. J. Levý holds that "outright *contrast* is the basic constructive principle of the quartet form."[17] This view he develops in an essay entitled "Synthesis of Antitheses in the Poetry of T. S. Eliot", in which he analyses verbal contrasts like "death-birth", "rising-falling",

[16] Bradbury, J. M., "*Four Quartets*: The Structural Symbolism", *Sewanee Review*, Vol. 59, 1951.

[17] Levý, J., "Synthesis of Antitheses in the Poetry of T. S. Eliot", *Essays in Criticism*, Vol. 2, 1952, p. 438.

"man-woman" and parallels such as "heavy-clumsy" and "earth-loam". Sometimes Eliot reinforces a contrast by using rhyming words: "womb-tomb", "decision-revision", "grief-relief". In Levý's interpretation Eliot never wholly reconciles the antitheses in the *Quartets*, but he approaches reconciliation by means of "transitory symbols", uniting the two terms of an antithesis. The extreme contrast between life and death, for instance, is bridged by referring to death as a point of departure – "In my end is my beginning" – and thus the contrast becomes threefold, life-death-rebirth, in which the third term synthesizes, as it were, the other two. The most significant contrasts in the *Quartets* are, however, not isolated single concepts expressed in single words but comprehensive themes expressed in whole passages. In "Burnt Norton", for example, each Section, apart from the lyric Fourth, can be divided into two parts, each dealing with the same basic experience or feeling, but seen from two opposed aspects. Applying the categories deduced in the last chapter, the first part of each Section can be said to represent the temporal aspect, and the second the eternal aspect. That is to say that the antitheses in the *Quartets* correspond to the fundamental antithesis of the metaphysical framework of the poems, the antithesis of appearance and reality, or of time and eternity.

Levý's approach has been further elaborated by B. H. Fussell and Reid MacCallum, and all these critics reveal, in their analyses of the *Quartets*, Eliot's preoccupation with the idea of time.[18] The phrases "time past and time future" and "time before and time after" recur throughout the *Quartets*, most noticeably in "Burnt Norton" and "The Dry Salvages", but echoed in the other two as well. The effect produced by these recurring phrases might be called musical, suggesting as they do a relation between the scenes and passages in which they occur and the temporal aspect of the subject-matter of these passages; a relation not specifically stated, only inferred or

[18] Fussell, B. H., "Structural Methods in *Four Quartets*", *A Journal of English Literary History*, Vol. 22, 1955. (Fussell's essay is one of the most noteworthy contributions to the understanding of the structure of the *Quartets*.) MacCallum, R., "Time Lost & Regained", in *Imitation & Design & Other Essays*, ed. by W. Blissett, Toronto, 1953. Cf. also Kenner, H., "Eliot's Moral Dialectic", *Hudson Review*, Vol. 2, 1949.

hinted at by the introduction of the burden-like phrase. In the opening lines of "Burnt Norton" III,

> Here is a place of disaffection
> Time before and time after
> In a dim light: neither daylight . . .

the second line indicates, by its mere presence, that the whole passage deals with existence in the dimension of past and future.

However, the analysis of antitheses and verbal contrasts in the *Four Quartets* is not enough. The very word "quartet" in the title of these poems suggests that Eliot wished to evoke the analogy of music, a fact which has naturally not escaped the attention of his critics. Various conjectures have been offered, ranging from strictly technical details of musical composition to vague notions of an intimate atmosphere often connected with chamber music. Compared with the "symphonic" scope and elaboration of *The Waste Land*, the *Four Quartets* are certainly more intimate, but probably Eliot wished to suggest a more definite musical analogy. Again, the impulse may have come from French Symbolism.

The analogy of poetry and music was an idea much cherished by the Symbolist poets. Théophile Gautier had already suggested such an analogy by calling one of his poems "Symphonie en Blanc Majeur", though this is an example of the synaesthetic experiments so popular among the Symbolists proper, rather than an example of the application to poetry of musical forms of composition. A more strictly technical device was taken over from music by literature apparently as a result of the influence of Richard Wagner on the Symbolist movement; but the musical character of the Wagnerian *Leitmotif* technique is much more noticeable in fiction than in poetry, and it is a technique adopted mainly by novelists. Thus it may well have been that Symbolist writing first impressed the analogy on Eliot.[19]

[19] Certain critics are inclined to doubt the influence of music on literature. Thus, *e.g.* R. Wellek & A. Warren in *Theory of Literature*, New York, 1949, p. 126: "Literary imitations of musical structures like leitmotiv, the sonata or symphonic form seem to be more concrete; but it is hard to see why repetitive motifs or a certain contrasting and balancing of moods, though by avowed intention

Writing on Valéry, Eliot made some observations concerning the relation of poetry to music that have immediate bearings on the *Four Quartets*. Comparing poetry to architecture and to the dance, Valéry maintained "that assimilation of Poetry to Music [. . .] was a Symbolist tenet." And "between these analogies there is no contradiction", Eliot remarks,

> For Music itself may be conceived as striving towards an unattainable timelessness; and if the other arts may be thought of as yearning for duration, so Music may be thought of as yearning for the stillness of painting or sculpture. I speak as one with no technical training in music, but I find that I enjoy, and "understand", a piece of music better for knowing it well, simply because I have at any moment during its performance a memory of the part that has preceded and a memory of the part that is still to come. Ideally, I should like to be able to hold the whole of a great symphony in my mind at once.[20]

This paradox of music "as yearning for stillness" suggests an important aspect of the "music" of the *Four Quartets*. The striving towards stillness and timelessness involves, in Eliot's view, not only literary technique, but spiritual discipline, as appears from, for instance, the Fifth Section of "Burnt Norton".

Eliot's views on the relationship between music and literature are developed in a lecture, "The Music of Poetry", delivered in 1942, shortly after the completion of the last of the *Quartets*. The date of the lecture is of special interest, since the author maintains that the critical writings of poets "owe a great deal of their interest to the fact that the poet [. . .] is always trying to defend the kind of poetry he is writing, or to formulate the kind that he wants to write".[21] In "The Music of Poetry" Eliot might then be expected to draw upon his experience in writing the *Four Quartets*, and certain of the ideas in that lecture seem particularly applicable to these poems.

imitative of musical composition, are not essentially the familiar literary devices of recurrence, contrast, and the like, which are common to all the arts."

The same basic opinion is set forth in C. S. Brown's critical survey, *Music and Literature*, Athens, Georgia, 1949. In spite of this it seems appropriate to speak of "musical" elements in the *Quartets*, since Eliot himself has applied musical terminology to poetry, *e.g.* in "The Music of Poetry".

20 Introd. to Valéry, *The Art of Poetry*, p. XIV.

21 *On Poetry and Poets*, p. 26.

Eliot emphasizes that "the music of verse is not a line by line matter, but a question of the whole poem."[22] In Eliot's view musical structure, in traditional literature, is achieved by the use of recurrent and dominant imagery, which is also a conspicuous feature of the *Quartets*. Other examples of musical structure are, Eliot maintains, forms like the sonnet or the formal ode. Such forms are not employed in the *Quartets,* however, which are written mainly in "free verse". But "free verse", Eliot holds, does not allow the poet greater freedom than the traditional metres which provided poetry with an outer unity. The revolt of the *vers-libristes* was "an insistence upon the inner unity which is unique to every poem, against the outer unity which is typical".[23] A poetic feature often found together with the use of "free verse" is what may be described as ellipsis, both in grammar and the logical association of ideas. It is a feature which was called, above, the "Semantic Disturbance", and the words "pattern" and "structure" as used in that context are but different words for Eliot's "inner unity" in the present context – unification made all the more necessary by the abandonment of outer form.

It is important to decide exactly what it is that gives unity to the *Four Quartets;* unity that is, in the sense that a sonata has unity.

"I think," Eliot says in "The Music of Poetry", "that a poet may gain much from the study of music: how much technical knowledge of musical form is desirable I do not know, for I have not that technical knowledge myself".[24] Thus the critic of the *Four Quartets* should be careful not to make too much of elaborate musical parallels in the analysis of these poems, but should rather attempt to discover some simple fundamental analogy. This at least is what Eliot seems to suggest towards the end of his lecture. It is true of course that in doing so, he contradicts his admitted lack of technical knowledge:

> There are possibilities for verse which bear some analogy to the development of a theme by different groups of instruments; there are possibilities of transitions in a poem comparable to the different movements of a symphony or a quartet; there are possibilities of contrapuntal arrangement of subject-matter.[25]

[22] Ibid., p. 36.
[23] Ibid., p. 37.
[24] Ibid., p. 38.
[25] Ibid., p. 38.

Eliot may well not know very much of the detailed laws of strict counterpoint and of the various modulations employed in the development section of, say, a Beethoven sonata, but he obviously has some notion of what concepts like counterpoint and development imply, which is quite sufficient as far as the *Four Quartets* are concerned. He certainly had some definite analogy in mind when applying the concept of quartet to his last sequence of poems.

The significance of the concept of quartet as used by Eliot has been variously interpreted. Some hold that the analogy is with the string quartet as a musical form in general, others that Eliot refers to one particular composer's treatment of that form, namely Beethoven's. The starting-point of the conjectures as to the relation of Beethoven to the *Four Quartets* is a pronouncement made by Eliot in 1933 in an unpublished lecture, mentioned by F. O. Matthiessen. Eliot said that to write "poetry so transparent that in reading it we are intent on what the poem *points at,* and not on the poetry, this seems to me the thing to try for. To get *beyond poetry,* as Beethoven, in his later works, strove to get *beyond music.*"[26] It may have some meaning to say that Eliot strove to get beyond poetry in the *Four Quartets* – an idea suggested above in slightly different terms[27] – and that would, critics maintain, imply that the title of the *Four Quartets* is an allusion to Beethoven's last string quartets. Many think of his five last quartets as *the* quartets, and in contemporary English fiction they have sometimes been used as a symbol of wholly spiritualized, or "transparent" art.[28] Furthermore, some of these compositions contain one movement more than the ordinary four, thus forming a parallel of the five Sections of each of Eliot's *Quartets.* The reference to Beethoven may be justified, but it certainly seems that the analogy should not be pressed any further.[29]

Several attempts have been made to analyse the *Quartets* in terms

[26] Matthiessen, F. O., *The Achievement of T. S. Eliot,* 2nd ed., Oxford, 1947, p. 90.

[27] Cf. supra, p. 120.

[28] See Huxley, A., *Point Counter Point,* London, (1928) 1947, p. 591; Wilder, T., *The Cabala,* London, 1928, pp. 164 f.

[29] Cf. the wild conjectures offered by H. Howarth, "Eliot, Beethoven, and J. W. N. Sullivan", *Comparative Literature,* Vol. 9, 1957.

of musical composition. I. A. Richards has characterized Eliot's earlier poetry as "a music of ideas", by which he means that the ideas and images in the poems are linked together in the same way as themes in a piece of music and not as concepts in a logical argument. He also emphasizes the unity of content and form and repudiates the search for an isolated conceptual meaning as an inappropriate approach.[30] This notion of "a music of ideas" applies to the *Quartets* as well, and Helen Gardner and Frank Wilson have developed it into a more definite analogy. Wilson, for instance, thinks that many Sections of the *Quartets* are modelled upon the sonata form and tries to show that these Sections contain two principal subjects which undergo a kind of development or modulation.[31] It is difficult to see why this kind of structure should resemble that of the sonata form more closely than any other musical form based on two main themes or subjects. It is not the musical terminology, however, that is of importance, but the realization that the meaning of the *Quartets* is not to be found by regarding the imagery, phrases and ideas in them as logically connected, with obvious emotional or intellectual continuity, but is rather to be found in the pattern of contrasted and interrelated themes and images, by looking for connections in form as well as in content. And, as Helen Gardner has observed, it is not only the ordinary, "poetic" symbols such as the rose and the yew-tree, or significant concepts such as time and the timeless, that are treated as "thematic material", but prepositions and adverbs such as "before", "after", "here", "there" and "now", are also integrated into a formal pattern and convey an accumulated meaning when occurring at the end of the poems.[32] Though contributing greatly to our understanding of the poems, this "thematic" approach does not account for Eliot's use of the word "quartet". The musical terminology used by Helen Gardner and Frank Wilson is applicable to analyses of symphonies, sonatas and trios as well, to mention only a few examples.

[30] Richards, I. A., *Principles of Literary Criticism*, 2nd ed., London, (1926) 1949, p. 293.

[31] Wilson, F., *Six Essays on the Development of T. S. Eliot*, London, 1948, pp. 54 ff. Gardner, H., *The Art of T. S. Eliot*, London, 1949, pp. 36–56.

[32] Gardner, *The Art of T. S. Eliot*, p. 53.

Why then "quartet"? What essentially is implied? Some critics have been misled by the fact that the *Four Quartets* consist of four separate poems,[33] but it is evident that the "fourness" implied in the word "quartet" is to be sought within each separate poem, and not in the number of poems. Since Eliot himself has not explained what exactly he means by the word quartet, any solution of the problem must be tentative. It is in fact possible to offer several solutions which by no means contradict or exclude each other.

The very beginning of the first of the *Quartets* suggests a kind of "fourness":

> Time present and time past
> Are both perhaps present in time future,
> And time future contained in time past.
> If all time is eternally present

Time past, time present, time future and eternity – these four terms, interrelated and interpenetrating, recur throughout the poems, indicating four different aspects of reality. In the *Quartets,* time present appears in two forms. One is the intense moment of deep insight – "the moment in the garden", "the moment in the draughty church at smokefall", "the moment of the rose and the moment of the yew-tree" – and in these moments the poet relives his past, foresees his future and also apprehends a timeless dimension – eternity. The other form is time present in the sense of the actual period in history in which the poet lives. Written during the first years of the war, the later *Quartets* contain several allusions to the contemporary political situation. The poet's meditation on that apparently desperate situation is closely connected with his meditation on history, on the past and future of his own country and civilization, and on the meaning of history, which is to be found in the dimension of eternity: "history is a pattern / Of timeless moments".

Regarded in this way the four "dimensions" of time are not merely four recurrent concepts or themes, but constitute four different

[33] See MacCallum, p. 161: "What are we to say: that it ["Burnt Norton"] was written as a solo, became a duet in 1940 with 'East Coker', a trio in 1941 with 'The Dry Salvages', and at last a quartet in 1942 with the writing of 'Little Gidding'?" This is only one example of this kind of misunderstanding.

aspects of the experience expressed in the *Quartets*. In the actual moments of insight, in time present, and in the symbols expressing these moments, the other dimensions of time are contained as levels of meaning. The moment in the garden in "Burnt Norton" I contains "echoes" of the poet's past, his vision of eternity and perhaps also his hopes for the future. All these levels of meaning are contained in the same symbol. Another complex symbol of this kind is that of the dove in "Little Gidding". In the Second Section it appears as a bomber attacking London – "the dark dove with the flickering tongue" – but in the Fourth Section the dove is not only a symbol of the destructive war, but of the Holy Spirit – a manifestation of the Eternal bringing "the only hope" for the future.

At this point it may be appropriate to connect the four "dimensions" of time with the musical structure of the *Quartets*. If by the word "quartet" Eliot intended to allude to a musical form of composition, then it seems natural to regard the different levels of meaning in the poems as a counterpart of the different voices or instruments in a string quartet, for example. Applied to poetry the division into voices or parts is, of course, unreal; what Eliot had in mind may perhaps be inferred from his remark quoted above: "there are possibilities of contrapuntal arrangement of subject-matter". Counterpoint, according to a neat definition, is "the combination of simultaneous voice-parts, each independent, but all conducing to a result of uniform coherent texture."[34] The only conceivable way in which poetry can be said to contain a combination of simultaneous voice-parts is as levels of meaning within the same image or passage.

In the *Quartets* there are many such images containing several levels of meaning. The dove in "Little Gidding" has already been mentioned; another exampel is the rose. It sometimes refers to the actual flower in a particular garden, sometimes to the rose of medieval allegory and sometimes to the royal emblem of the Stuarts – to mention only some of its meanings. When at the end of the *Quartets* the word "rose" appears, it conveys something of all its previous meanings, while at the same time it is also related to the immediate context in which it occurs. The use of these images, conveying as they do a wide range of meanings, may thus be

[34] *The Oxford Companion to Music*, 5th ed., p. 233.

regarded as the poetic equivalent of musical counterpoint. Each separate meaning, or rather implication or connotation, of the words or images is related to the same level of meaning in other words and images, and at the same time to all the different levels of meaning within the same word or image. One relation is horizontal, as it were, and the other vertical, exactly as in musical counterpoint.

This seems to be Eliot's own idea of literary counterpoint, applying in its simplest form, to the individual word:

> The music of a word is, so to speak, at a point of intersection: it arises from its relation first to the words immediately preceding and following it, and indefinitely to the rest of its context; and from another relation, that of its immediate meaning in that context to all the other meanings which it has had in other contexts, to its greater or less wealth of association.[35]

This double relation applies not only to individual words, however, but also to complex symbols and comprehensive abstract themes.

Thus the vertical meaning, so to speak, the cross-section of the different levels of meaning in an isolated passage, cannot be fully apprehended apart from its horizontal relations. A criterion of strict counterpoint is the independence of the different parts, but such independence, by no means characteristic of the classical quartet form as employed by Beethoven, is difficult to apply to Eliot's *Quartets*. In them it may be possible to distinguish several meanings existing simultaneously in the same word, but lacking a clear counterpart of the four instruments of a string quartet, the different meanings often melt into each other, and are always closely interrelated. Yet the analogy points to something very important.

The poetic equivalent of counterpoint, if that is where the analogy to music lies in the *Four Quartets,* consists in using words and phrases capable of bearing several meanings, of having several senses, or associations, at the same time. The *Quartets* are concerned with human experience seen from widely different aspects, but with the identity of the experience as much as with the difference of aspects. Not satisfied to apply the different aspects consecutively, Eliot seems to have attempted to apply them simultaneously, not by means of juxtaposition simply, but by making a word or image pass through

[35] *On Poetry and Poets,* pp. 32 f.

different contexts so that, retaining a different meaning from each context, it can produce a kind of synthesis when it occurs at the end of the poem.[36] On a less conscious and less systematized level this method has been employed by a great many poets without the aid of musical analogies,[37] but there are particular reasons why Eliot should have developed it into a deliberate poetic method. More than most other poets, at least contemporary ones, he is aware of the deep and fundamental dualism of existence, of the division of appearance and reality, between the temporal and the eternal, between the human and the divine, and it seems to be his primary concern, as poet and thinker, to reconcile these opposites, to see his private experience from both aspects, but only in order to bridge the gap, to arrive at a synthesis. To convey all this in poetry imposes a very heavy strain on language however poetic, and it would not be at all surprising to find Eliot using such a "contrapuntal" technique.

"Point of intersection" is by Eliot sometimes used to mean Incarnation, as was demonstrated in the preceding chapter, and on the metaphysical, religious level, the synthesis aimed at in Eliot's later poetry lies in the Incarnation of Christ. But he also uses "point of intersection" to mean the place where the music of a word arises. That is to say, in other words, that the contrapuntal method of the *Four Quartets* bears some analogy to the religious conception of Incarnation – perhaps at first sight a startling notion, but nevertheless suggesting the deepest level of meaning in the *Four Quartets*.

The word "quartet", then, may be taken to refer to the four "dimensions" of time – past, present, future and eternity – which, in the poems, are interrelated as the voices or instruments in a musical quartet. Moreover, this technical interrelation bears some analogy to the interrelation of the metaphysical and religious categories of the *Four Quartets*. In order to understand how Eliot conceives of this relation between the temporal and the eternal, between the human and the divine, we must turn to Dante.

[36] A similar view is expressed by Fussell, p. 240.

[37] This, of course, is in particular true of Shakespeare's late plays, from which Eliot may have learnt a great deal in this respect.

III

In the *Divine Comedy* Dante used a special allegorical method in order to express his idea of the relation between the temporal and the eternal. This method consists in regarding things and events as having four different meanings on different levels of interpretation, and as such it is a poetic method which comes close to the one Eliot has used in the *Four Quartets.* Dante's influence on Eliot, deeper and more important than that of any other single author, has already been emphasized in this study, and even if Eliot did not model the *Four Quartets* on the *Divine Comedy* consciously and deliberately, it is still relevant to trace the influence of Dante. This influence may have been unconscious, to some extent, or half-conscious, but without it the *Quartets* would surely have been something very different from what they are now. Eliot is certainly familiar, not only with the method itself as used by Dante, but with the underlying medieval conception of the world and its relation to God. Dante used this particular kind of allegory to express his fundamentally religious view of life, to picture history and human experience *sub specie aeternitatis,* and in adopting and adapting this kind of expression, Eliot subscribes to the same view of life, taking his stand against the secularized civilization of the present time. Allegory, to Dante, was both a matter of philosophical and theological interpretation of life and a matter of poetic technique. He used the only means open to him as a poet in which to express his deep feeling, his conviction of a Reality behind this world, of which this world offered itself as a vast analogy. And, in his time, the same is true of Eliot. In the *Four Quartets* he gives a vision of life perhaps closer to Dante's *Divine Comedy* in spirit and method than any other modern work of poetry, even though the difference in substance and approach is immense.

The possibility of regarding the *Four Quartets* as being written so as to suggest distinct meanings in the Dantean sense, has been hinted at by several critics. Helen Gardner, for example, distinguishes three different meanings in the *Quartets,* a literal, a moral and a mystic meaning.[38] For some reason disregarding the fourth, the

[38] Gardner, *The Art of T. S. Eliot,* pp. 163–184.

allegorical meaning of the *Divine Comedy,* she does not connect Eliot's idea of a literary quartet with Dante's four meanings. Other critics have emphasized the division into four separate meanings, but without any reference to Dante. Thus the four voices of the *Quartets* have been defined as "die intellektuelle, die ästhetische, die sittliche und die religiöse Stimme".[39] Sister M. Cleophas, finally, applies all four of Dante's categories to the *Quartets,* but without recognizing the musical analogy.[40]

The "fourness" implied in the word quartet may be found in the four "dimensions" of time in the *Four Quartets,* but it may also consist in a parallel to the four Dantean levels of meaning. In effect, the Dantean scheme is only a more precise way of relating the temporal – time past, time present and time future – to the eternal order. Whether Eliot has made deliberate use of the Dantean scheme in the *Quartets* or not, is unknown; nevertheless it is relevant to draw attention to Dante's allegorical method as a possible model for the *Quartets* and as a useful method of interpreting these poems.

The method of allegorical interpretation of the *Divine Comedy* has been expounded by Dante himself in his letter to Can Grande. The relevant passage reads:

> For the elucidation, therefore, of what we have to say, it must be understood that the meaning of this work is not of one kind only; rather the work may be described as "polysemous", that is, having several meanings; for the first meaning is that which is conveyed by the letter, and the next is that which is conveyed by what the letter signifies; the former of which is called literal, while the latter is called allegorical, or mystical. And for the better illustration of this method of exposition we may apply it to the following verses: "When Israel went out of Egypt, the house of Jacob from a people of strange language; Judah was his sanctuary, and Israel his dominion." For if we consider the letter

[39] Lübker, R., "Vier Quartette von T. S. Eliot. Versuch zu einer Einführung", *Die Neueren Sprachen,* 1954, p. 75; Lübker quotes from an article by G. Schäder in *Die Sammlung,* 1950. L. Frankenberg distinguishes the following four "voices": The Didactic Voice, the Lyric Voice, the Narrative Voice, and the Apocalyptic Voice. *Pleasure Dome: On Reading Modern Poetry,* Cambridge (Mass.), 1949, pp. 101 f.

[40] Cleophas, M., "Notes on Levels of Meaning in 'Four Quartets'", *Renascence: A Critical Journal of Letters,* Vol. 2, 1950, pp. 102–116.

alone, the thing signified to us is the going out of the children of Israel from Egypt in the time of Moses; if the allegory, our redemption through Christ is signified; if the moral sense, the conversion of the soul from the sorrow and misery of sin to a state of grace is signified; and if the anagogical, the passing of the sanctified soul from the bondage of the corruption of this world to the liberty of everlasting glory is signified. And although these mystical meanings are called by various names, they may one and all in a general sense be termed allegorical, in as much as they are different (*diversi*) from the literal or historical; for the word "allegory" is so called from the Greek *alleon*, which in Latin is *alienum* (strange) or *diversum* (different).[41]

In effect, Dante is saying here that the *Paradiso* at least should be considered an allegory in this special sense; and it is not too much to infer that Dante intended the whole poem to be regarded as an allegory in the same way. Now the word "allegorical" seems to have had a special meaning to the medieval mind. Medieval theologians, as J. A. Mazzeo points out, drew a sharp distinction between "profane or poetic allegory, human discourse in words enclosing an abstract meaning in the narrative they form, and sacred allegory, the spiritual sense of things and events in Scripture as well as the spiritual sense of the discourse of Scripture whether historical or parabolic. These spiritual senses are always of divine origin."[42]

Poetic allegory in this way was accepted by the Church as a legitimate mode of literary expression whatever the subject-matter might be; sacred allegory, on the other hand, was not regarded as a mode of expression but as a method of interpretation, restricted to Scripture and some other sacred texts. The poet works out his own scheme of varied meanings to be inferred from a story of his own invention, whereas the allegorical possibilities of Scriptural passages were not conceived by the original authors but appertain to the very things and events described. That is to say that the true author of sacred allegory is God Himself, and man is but an interpreter. Accordingly the allegory of poets remains profane irrespective of

[41] *Dantis Allagherii epistolae: The Letters of Dante*, transl. and ed. by P. Toynbee, Oxford, 1920, pp. 134 f. The quotation is from Letter X, 7. (Dante, *Tutte le Opere*, ed. by E. Moore, London, 1909, pp. 379 f.)

[42] Cf. Mazzeo, J. A., *Structure and Thought in the Paradiso*, Ithaca, New York, 1958, p. 35.

the subject treated, and Bunyan's *The Pilgrim's Progress*, for example, would have been regarded more as belonging to the category of profane allegory, built as it is on abstractions invented by the author, whereas the Book of Job is divine allegory. Consequently the poet, creating or inventing his own allegorical system, can choose any number of abstract meanings to put into his story, whereas the interpreter of Scriptural allegory is restricted to the number actually intended by God. Opinions differed as to the exact number of meanings attributed to Holy Scripture, but at the time of St. Thomas Aquinas and Dante four categories of interpretation seem to have been generally agreed upon, and Aquinas' definitions of these categories are approximately the same as those propounded in the letter to Can Grande.[43]

Dante's claim, in his letter to Can Grande, that as a poet he employed sacred allegory is to be inferred from his choice of an example from the Scriptures and in his strict adherence to the four categories employed by theologians. How far Dante was aware of trespassing upon the ground of theology proper, is difficult to tell, but he certainly held a much higher opinion of poetry as a source of spiritual truth than for instance Thomas Aquinas. Aquinas would not accept poetry as a means of expounding religious truth; to him it belonged to the realm of profane, though edifying fiction. Thus Dante regards himself as something more than an ordinary poet in the medieval sense; he did not invent the allegory of the *Divine Comedy*, the spiritual meanings of which are there in the same way as in Scripture, appertaining, in fact, to the very events described. Yet Dante cannot be said to be guilty of blasphemy, for, Mazzeo holds, he "does not claim to create reality; he is saying rather that he can see reality, at least in part, as God sees it."[44] The background of such a claim is the medieval conception of Nature as a book written by God and differing from Scripture only in the method of representation. In Scripture the spiritual meaning of life and history is set forth both in plain statements and in symbolic form – the

[43] See P. Mandonnet, *Dante le théologien*, Paris, 1935, p. 184, note.

[44] Mazzeo, p. 35. Dante's claim to reveal philosophical truth in the *Comedy* is equally bold; see Curtius, E. R., *Europäische Literatur und lateinisches Mittelalter*, Bern, 1948, pp. 226–230.

allegorical meanings; in Nature the same meaning is to be found, but only in symbolic form. Relying on his divine inspiration Dante claimed to be able to decipher the symbols of Nature – at least that part of Nature and life which was familiar to him and thus his allegory is of the same kind as that of the Scriptures.

It would of course be preposterous to suggest that, in writing the *Four Quartets,* Eliot claimed to look on life as Dante did in writing the *Divine Comedy.* Very likely he was not fully aware how far Dante's idea of poetry was opposed to that of the Church – the above summary of the contrasting views is based on the most recent Dante scholarship, the results of which were not available to Eliot at the time of his writing the *Quartets.* But with all humility and modesty Eliot still seems to maintain, in the *Quartets,* that the spiritual meanings implied in these poems are more than poetic inventions, more than a way of expressing immediate experience; that, in fact, they reveal a divine purpose in his own life. The *Four Quartets* and the *Divine Comedy* are thus alike in so far as they are spiritual autobiographies seeking to express the spiritual meaning of temporal life by a complex symbolic structure. The vast, almost encyclopaedic scope of the *Comedy* is entirely foreign to the *Quartets,* but the search for a higher meaning in the central facts of their private experiences is common to both Dante and Eliot.

This is by no means all that can be said about the matter. Two recent critics have gone further in two studies on Dante, published after the composition of the first *Quartet.* They use a terminology that may have been foreign to Eliot, at least in the elaborate form in which it will be used here. This may seem an inappropriate approach to the *Four Quartets,* but the essential facts involved were certainly known to Eliot from his own study of Dante and from his theological reading. The two works used here are an essay by Erich Auerbach called "Figura" (1938) and Johan Chydenius' dissertation, *The Typological Problem in Dante* (1958), which is a further development of Auerbach's ideas.[45] The word "figura" as used by Auerbach, and "type" as used by Chydenius, both appear to mean the same as

[45] Auerbach, E., "Figura", *Archivum Romanicum,* Vol. 22, 1938; Chydenius, J., *The Typological Problem in Dante. A Study in the History of Medieval Ideas,* Diss., Helsingfors, 1958.

"allegory" in Dante's special sense of that word; since "type" seems to be the most appropriate English word, it will be used here as a synonym for, and translation of Auerbach's "figura". Eliot uses neither of these words in writing on Dante, but his term "allegory" contains many of the relevant connotations, as in the following passage, where Eliot asks his reader to admit that allegory was

> really a mental habit, which when raised to the point of genius can make a great poet as well as a great mystic or saint. And it is the allegory which makes it possible for the reader who is not even a good Italian scholar to enjoy Dante. Speech varies, but our eyes are all the same. And allegory was not a local Italian custom, but a universal European method.[46]

Moreover, in the *Quartets* Eliot uses the words "figured" and "transfigured" in a way that shows their connection with the Latin word "figura". In "Burnt Norton" II, Eliot writes:

> The dance along the artery
> The circulation of the lymph
> Are figured in the drift of stars
> Ascend to summer in the tree
> We move above the moving tree
> In light upon the figured leaf

In this passage "figured" is used to express a relation between the temporal world and a timeless pattern. And in "Little Gidding" III, temporal life and history are said to vanish in order

> To become renewed, transfigured, in another pattern.

Later in the same poem Eliot adds that "history is a pattern/Of timeless moments", thus confirming that "transfiguration" implies a transition from the temporal to the timeless.

According to Chydenius' definition, typology means "the understanding of past events as types foretokening other, future events. The typical way of interpretation is especially characteristic of Holy Scripture, where it may be traced back to the prophets of the Old Testament."[47] An example from Tertullian shows how this notion of foretokening was conceived. In the Old Testament we read that

[46] *Selected Essays*, p. 243.

[47] Chydenius, p. 11.

it was Joshua and not Moses who eventually conducted the people of Israel into Palestine, the Land of Promise, and in the same way it is Jesus and not the Jewish law that conducts the "second people", *i. e.* the Christian Church, into the promised land of eternal bliss. The people of Israel is a "type" of the Church, Moses of the law, and Joshua of Jesus; in the last case the typical relation is confirmed by the similarity of the two names. Joshua in his relation to Israel can also be regarded as a symbol of Jesus in His relation to the Church. What distinguishes this special kind of symbolism from other kinds and necessitates a special term such as typology, is the fact that both the symbol and the thing symbolized are real, historical phenomena.[48] Joshua, the actual man, is a type of Jesus though living long before the antitype; he is a living prophecy, the fulfilment of which is the life and work of Jesus. But to say that Joshua, the type, came before Jesus, the antitype, is true only from the historical point of view. In patristic literature, and especially in St. Augustine, the idea of typical prefiguration also implies a timeless dimension: type and antitype are both manifest in the dimension of time, but behind both lies a divine and eternal idea or purpose. Thus in history Jesus comes after Joshua, but Christ the Word existed before the creation of the world.[49] This gives some idea of what "typology" really means – the advent of Joshua overlaid with and prefiguring the advent of Jesus, again overlaid with and expressing the Augustinian idea, ending with the Neo-Platonic or Gnostic notion of Logos.

Eliot must have encountered this idea of "typological" prefiguration in many different contexts. The idea is foreshadowed by the prophets of the Old Testament, suggested by Christ in the Gospels when He speaks of Himself as the fulfilment of the prophecies, and developed by St. Paul.[50] This relation between the Old and the New Testament is also emphasized in the liturgy of the Anglican Church, and is in this form well-known to Eliot. The full metaphysical elaboration of the idea came with St. Augustine, whom Eliot has studied carefully, and in another of his favourite authors, Pascal, the idea is prominent. Several chapters of the *Pensées* deal with the interpretation of

[48] Auerbach, pp. 450 f.

[49] Ibid., pp. 459 ff.; cf. St. Augustine's *Confessions*, Book XI, chapter 7.

[50] Chydenius, pp. 11–19; Auerbach, pp. 464–466.

things and events described in Scripture as types (*figures*) of other events or of spiritual qualities. Pascal is especially concerned with the spiritual meaning of temporal events. To him the Scriptures are a cipher with a double meaning (*Chifre à double sens*), one literal, the other spiritual.[51] It is the same method of interpretation as that expounded in Dante's letter to Can Grande, only that Dante goes a step further, dividing the spiritual meaning into three separate categories, of which the allegorical, referring to the life and death of Christ, comes nearest to typology, or allegory of this complex and specially theological kind.

The antitypes of most Biblical types are in some way related to Christ, and typical interpretation as well as allegorical, in the special sense of that word, aims at establishing a connection between the things and events interpreted and the mission of Christ. The life and work, suffering, death, and resurrection of Christ appear, to the mind of the "typologist", as a spiritual pattern applicable, in the first place to other events in sacred history, but also to the individual lives of men at any period of history. It is thus that the figures of the Incarnation and the Atonement in the *Four Quartets* should be interpreted. It was observed in the foregoing chapter that Eliot attributes a dual meaning to the idea of Incarnation; in the first place it represents the unique event of the Incarnation of Christ, but it also represents "the intersection of the timeless with time" at any moment in history. The second meaning has been conceived by some critics as akin to the romantic notion of the immanence of the divine in Nature and as such foreign to the Christian doctrine. Seen as types and antitypes, however, the two meanings are easily reconciled. "The moment in and out of time" in the last Section of "The Dry Salvages", for example, is said to imply Incarnation, and that is to say that certain moments in the life of man, when a timeless, eternal dimension seems to reveal itself in time, are, not only in some way analogous with the occasion when eternity descended into time in the Incarnation of Christ, but types of that unique antitype. Had Eliot conceived this relation only as one of symbol to thing symbolized, and had he used the dogma of the Incarnation only as an illustration or metaphor of certain aspects of experience, then the relation would

[51] *Les Pensées de Blaise Pascal*, ed. by A. Molinier, Paris, 1877, Vol. I, p. 245.

only be a subjective relation, created by the author himself and possibly accepted, as a metaphor, by his readers. If, on the other hand, the relation is to be regarded as typological, then it is an objective relation, inherent in the nature of things and created by God. In the first case it is a matter of poetic construction and invention, in the second, of discovery and revelation. Which interpretation is correct, cannot be finally decided on the evidence of the text of the *Quartets* only, but the typological interpretation does to some extent explain features of the poems that otherwise seem obscure or contradictory, and discloses something of the relevance of Dante's four categories of meaning.

However, Dante's allegorical method must not be mechanically applied to the *Quartets*. Strict and consistent allegorizing is hardly compatible with the "disconnected" logic and symbolism of modern poetry. The idea of a division into four separate levels of meaning does not imply that each level can be clearly distinguished in each separate passage of the *Divine Comedy*, and even less in the *Four Quartets*. Here the musical analogy of voices or instruments may once again be relevant. In a musical quartet one or several of the instruments may be silent for long passages, and in the same way one or several of the levels of meaning in the *Quartets* may be completely indistinguishable in particular passages. But more than that, it is essential to emphasize that any division into separate levels of meaning is only approximate or suggestive. For each level is related to other levels, and the interrelation is as important as the division.

Moreover, the different levels, or categories of meaning cannot be so precisely fixed in the *Four Quartets* as is sometimes possible in the *Divine Comedy*. The literal meaning of the *Quartets*, if it is possible to separate a literal meaning from the other levels of meaning, is far less obvious than that of the *Divine Comedy*. Eliot has completely dispensed with even the suggestion of a narrative element, an element so prominent in Dante, and in so doing he also shows the great difference of approach between medieval and modern poets, between himself and Dante. Nevertheless the *Quartets* must have some sort of literal meaning in the sense that they must be based on some facts, some actual experience, which may be subject to allegorizing in Dante's sense of that term. Thus the literal meaning of the *Quartets* may be said to consist of the basic experience underlying these poems – an experience which is sometimes immediately recognizable in the poems and which includes, not only Eliot's personal experience, but to some extent that of his ancestors and his country as well. The moral level of meaning in the *Quartets* can be more or less narrowly defined. Some critics have applied the three "theological" virtues of faith, hope and charity to the last three of the *Quartets*,[52] but if any particular virtue is to be applied to "East Coker", for example, it is not faith, but humility – as suggested by these lines from the Second Section of that poem:

> The only wisdom we can hope to acquire
> Is the wisdom of humility: humility is endless.

The moral meaning of the *Quartets* is concerned with the poet's attitude towards life and towards the problems he is considering, and not with an ethical doctrine.

The distinction between the allegorical and the anagogical or mystic meaning is sometimes more difficult to draw. The mystic meaning of the *Quartets* lies in the spiritual patterns of, for example, the *via negativa* and the ladder of love – features of the religious life (when expressed in ordinary language often closely resembling certain types of profane experience) which are not immediately associated with sacred history. In Dante's example quoted above the anagogical meaning is said to consist in "the passing of the sanctified soul from the bondage of the corruption of this world to the liberty of everlasting glory". The allegorical meaning of the *Quartets* lies in the relation of the psycho-spiritual patterns to definite aspects of the life and mission of Christ as, for instance, the Incarnation and the Atonement; in Dante's example the allegorical meaning is "our redemption through Christ".

In converting the typological method of interpreting Scripture into a structural method in the *Divine Comedy*, Dante stretched the idea of typical prefiguration beyond its originally theological sphere. As an illustration of this we may choose the figure of Beatrice in Dante's work. Critics have been inclined to see her *either* as a portrait of an earthly woman whom Dante had met, *or* as an allegory of certain

[52] Gardner, *The Art of T. S. Eliot*, pp. 163–184.

theological concepts. Auerbach, however, holds that she is both, and even more than that, the earthly, "historical" Beatrice is a type of the transfigured Beatrice of the *Comedy;* she is in effect a prefiguration of divine Revelation.[53] In fact, Eliot seems to subscribe to a similar interpretation in his second essay on Dante. It is quite clear to him that Beatrice is both an actual earthly woman or girl and a symbol of something spiritual, and in both aspects she belongs to Dante's experience. Eliot recognizes this as a literary structure peculiar to Dante: "The system of Dante's organization of sensibility – the contrast between higher and lower carnal love, the transition from Beatrice living to Beatrice dead, rising to the Cult of the Virgin, seems to me to be his own."[54]

What may well be a counterpart to the function of Beatrice in Dante's work is to be found in the *Four Quartets* in the complex symbol of the rose garden. As shown above, the rose garden is a recurrent theme throughout Eliot's poetic work, clearly representing, in one of its aspects, the experience of earthly love. The symbol undergoes a gradual transformation in Eliot's poetry and within the *Quartets*, and when it appears for the last time at the end of "Little Gidding", it is wholly spiritualized and transfigured. The actual experience underlying the symbol is the type, as it were, and the antitype or fulfilment is the spiritual meaning, which is divine love as experienced by the poet; both type and antitype are thus experientially real, but behind both lies what might be called the divine or eternal prototype.

Thus an image such as the rose garden in Eliot's poetry can be said to form a point of intersection, in which different planes of meaning cross each other. It will be remembered that the point of intersection is used by Eliot both in a verbal and a metaphysical,

[53] Auerbach, pp. 488 f.: "Beatrice ist Inkarnation, ist *figura* oder *idolo Christi* (ihre Augen spiegeln seine Doppelnatur, Purg. 31, 126) und also zugleich auch ein Mensch. Ihr Menschentum ist mit solchen Erklärungen natürlich keineswegs erschöpft; sie steht zu Dante in einer Beziehung, die sich durch dogmatische Betrachtungen nicht völlig ausdrücken lässt. Unsere Ausführungen sollen nur zeigen, dass die stets nützliche und unentbehrliche theologische Deutung uns durchaus nicht zwingt die geschichtliche Wirklichkeit Beatrices aufzugeben – im Gegenteil." It will be remembered that "figura" is Auerbach's word for "type".

[54] *Selected Essays*, p. 275.

religious sense, implying both the poetic method of expressing the synthesis of the temporal and the eternal and the synthesis itself in its unique manifestation in the Incarnation of Christ.[55] It also appears that the division into four "dimensions" of time in the *Quartets* partly overlaps with Dante's four categories of meaning. The relation between the literal and the spiritual meanings in Dante is a relation between the temporal and the eternal, and this relation is applicable to the *Four Quartets*. The further division of the spiritual meaning into three distinct levels also has its counterpart in the *Quartets,* but only occasionally, and on this point the interpretation of these poems must not be pressed too far.

With all its shortcomings the attempt that has here been made to explain one of the most significant aspects of the work of Dante, and its special relevance to the work of Eliot, has naturally been limited. It should be emphasized that any such attempt, however ambitious and elaborate, can be only partially successful. Dante, in writing the *Divine Comedy,* like Eliot in writing the *Four Quartets,* was trying to express something which taxes expression of any kind, and it is only natural that critics should fail to achieve that which the poets themselves could only approach. In the last analysis poetry such as the *Four Quartets* is beyond explanation and beyond paraphrase of any kind. All that can be done on the intellectual level is to try to prepare the reader of the *Quartets* for a full understanding and enjoyment of the poems by supplying such explanations and background information as seem relevant and communicable in a medium other than that of the poems themselves. As this and the foregoing chapters have shown, there is a great deal of such information to be supplied about the background of the *Four Quartets*. But since the reader cannot share exactly the same feelings that Eliot has attempted to express in the *Quartets,* he has to substitute such experiences of his own as seem to correspond most closely to those of the poet, and that interpretative procedure, necessary if we want to make the poems wholly intelligible as works of art, invites a variety of personal interpretations, necessarily more or less remote from the author's own intentions. There is no other alternative.

[55] Cf. Knox, G. A., "Quest for the Word in Eliot's *Four Quartets*", *ELH – A Journal of English Literary History,* Vol. 18, 1951, pp. 310–321.

CHAPTER V

"Burnt Norton"

I[1]

Neither "Burnt Norton" nor the other three *Quartets* contain any narrative elements corresponding to Dante's journey in the *Divine Comedy,* and yet they must contain something that can be called a "literal" meaning for the other, derived, meanings to be based on. According to Helen Gardner, the literal meaning of "Burnt Norton" is "simply that the poet has felt a moment of inexplicable joy, a moment of release".[2] This suggestion seems to indicate an essential aspect of "Burnt Norton", but is not exhaustive.

In the absence of any narrative element we may seek the literal meaning in the more comprehensive imagery of the poem, which at times extends through whole scenes. The poem contains two such major scenes – the rose garden in the First Section and the London underground in the Third Section. These scenes form a sharp contrast. In the first the speaker is walking in a sun-bathed garden, and the atmosphere is one of excitement, happiness and thankfulness. In the other the poet describes "a place of disaffection", of "distraction" and "Tumid apathy with no concentration". These two scenes as well as the images that occur in a more isolated way, do not receive their full meaning until they are seen as parts of the experience of one person, of the speaker. The literal meaning of "Burnt

[1] In the following study of the *Four Quartets,* it will be necessary to make several cross-references from one poem to another. The following abbreviations are used: BN for "Burnt Norton", EC for "East Coker", DS for "The Dry Salvages" and LG for "Little Gidding"; a numeral after an abbreviation refers to Section within the poem.

[2] Gardner, H., *The Art of T. S. Eliot,* London, 1949, p. 163.

Norton", it would then seem, consists of elements of immediate experience appertaining, in the poem to the putative speaker, and in actual life, it may be inferred, to Eliot himself. The core of this experience is no doubt the moment of inexplicable joy, of which Helen Gardner speaks, but the complete literal meaning includes all the memories evoked in the mind of the speaker during the course of his meditation.

The connection between the various elements of personal experience implied and expressed in "Burnt Norton" does not lie in any chronological or causal relation between them, but in the process of the speaker's association on the one hand, and in the more objective structure of the spiritual meanings on the other. "Burnt Norton" may thus be regarded as a sort of silent soliloquy, a meditation on subjects derived from the speaker's, or poet's, experience. The spiritual meanings are gradually integrated with the speaker's consciousness, but the poet and the reader – as distinct from and above the supposed speaker – are often ahead of the speaker, as it were, realizing before he does the hidden meanings of the fragments of human life subject to meditation. Those meanings that are implied in the scenes and events recalled in the mind of the speaker, though not immediately recognized by him, form the spiritual or allegorical levels of meaning in "Burnt Norton".

The first ten lines of the First Section read, at first sight, as a set of abstract propositions about the nature of time, and the ideas expressed in that passage seem to be derived from the wide and varied philosophical reading of the poet. These philosophical implications should not, of course, be neglected, but it is equally important to understand the relevance of these ideas to the mind – the *state* of mind – of the speaker. Time past, time present, time future and the eternal – these are the ideas with which the speaker is concerned. Time present is his actual situation and in particular the time of his visit to the garden. Time past is the memories from his earlier life evoked during that visit – memories of highly emotional intensity. And during his meditation in the garden, his present situation and his past become related to an eternal order and the future is seen in a new light.

At the core of the speaker's speculation lies the idea of the discrepancy between "what might have been" and "what has been", between potentiality and reality. From what is said later in the same Section about echoes and memory, it appears that the speaker is talking about his own past life, that he is comparing his present situation with his conception of what might have been, under different circumstances. Though regretting that his life has taken the form it has in some particular respect, he is forced to accept his present situation as the only real thing; everything else is but futile speculation. Moreover, he seems not only to regret the opportunities he has missed, but almost to blame himself for not doing what he could have done. In so far as the speaker may be identified with Eliot himself, the idea of what might have been no doubt has a real counterpart in his earlier life, but of this nothing is known, and nothing needs to be known. Though perhaps prompted by some definite personal experience of the poet's the introductory passage of "Burnt Norton" seems to be concerned with a much more general problem – the deeply human tendency to torment the mind with the memories of past failures, opportunities missed and possibilities never realized. To these universally human thoughts a person of Eliot's devout temperament is likely to add the idea of sin implying wrong deeds that can never be changed and good deeds left undone.[3] This idea, perhaps implied in "Burnt Norton", is developed in "Little Gidding" II.

The language of the speaker in "Burnt Norton" is largely detached, sometimes almost academic. He seems to consider his situation in terms of a theoretical problem: How is it that the past cannot be changed, cannot be redeemed? One solution to this problem seems to be implied in the first three lines of the poem which may be read as the expression of a mechanistic view of life and the world: past, present and future are contained in each other in the sense that every event or action is caused by preceding events and actions, and is itself in turn the cause of subsequent events and actions; life appears as an unbroken and unbreakable chain of causes and effects.

[3] The idea of "what might have been" is briefly discussed by W. Schenk, "The Experience and the Meaning. A Note on T. S. Eliot's 'Burnt Norton'", *Humanitas* (Manchester), Vol. 1, 1947. Some parallel passages in *The Family Reunion* are cited by R. Preston, *"Four Quartets" Rehearsed*, London, 1946, pp. 10 ff.

In the following two lines, however, the poet goes one step further:

> If all time is eternally present
> All time is unredeemable.

This idea of all time being eternally present is a paradox in a dual sense. Being part of time, the present moment can hardly be said to contain that of which it is a part, and adding the term "eternally" to the concept of time, the poet combines two concepts otherwise contrary to each other. It is impossible to resolve this paradox logically, but it should be noted that the idea of the Eternal Now was found to be equally paradoxical.[4] Eliot seems in fact to refer to that idea – whether to its modern or its ancient expressions, is irrelevant. As indicated above, the idea of the Eternal Now seems to exclude the idea of free-will and entail a rigid determinism. Accordingly, time is said to be "unredeemable"; the past cannot be changed, old mistakes and sins can never be atoned for.

These are only a few of the philosophical aspects of the introductory passage to "Burnt Norton". Other problems concerning the nature of time, currently discussed in the early nineteen-thirties, are also raised in that passage, and should be considered in the light of these current views. The main function, however, of the introductory passage seems to be to establish a special and contrasting mood and feeling, against which the rose garden episode emerges.

The only actual place mentioned in the First Section is the rose garden. Expressed in terms of Eliot's own experience such as, in a previous chapter, it was suggested to have been, the poet appears to have entered the garden of Burnt Norton, in the stillness of which he sank into profound meditation on his own past – a meditation suddenly interrupted by some sort of extraordinary experience, some illumination.[5] Revealing entirely new meanings in the past life of the poet, this experience makes him in a sense into a different person, inaugurates as it were a new phase in his spiritual life. The opening passage, then, represents the poet's or speaker's state of mind before that experience occurred – the "natural", unilluminated state of mind.

[4] Vide supra, p. 93.

[5] Vide supra, p. 42.

The experience in the rose garden thus involves a different attitude towards the speaker's past. He begins to see a meaning and a purpose in his own past life such as it has actually been, and henceforth he never relapses into his former futile speculation upon what might have been, but never was. This release from the obsession with what might have been, he experiences as a manifestation of grace, and his former state of mind represents the condition of the awakened but unrelieved soul. Thus in a general way, the first part of the First Section of "Burnt Norton" is centred on the theme of time and determination, of temporal existence, while the second part hints at something above and beyond the temporal sphere.

On a less abstract level the experience in the garden appears as a moment of intense happiness, of elevation and freedom from care, suggested by the image of the laughing children:

> for the leaves were full of children,
> Hidden excitedly, containing laughter.

This laughter is perhaps symbolic of the speaker's own mood – he feels himself free and irresponsible as a child, and his experience is timeless as that of a child. Referring later to the moment in the garden, Eliot calls it "the intense moment / Isolated, with no before and after" (EC: V).

However, the children in the garden no doubt stand for something more than the speaker's feelings at that particular moment. In so far as the speaker may be identified with the poet himself, the image of the children is likely to have a personal meaning to him. At the time of writing "Burnt Norton" Eliot was forty-seven years of age, and childless in spite of a long marriage. As a poet and critic he had achieved full recognition comparatively late, and his life does not seem to have been very happy up to that time, full of frustrations and crises. Then came the experience in the garden of Burnt Norton, showing him as it were a new pattern in life and relieving him of his self-reproaching concern with the past. It is of course impossible to say exactly what it was or what it meant to Eliot himself. Beyond any doubt, however, he understood it as an act of divine Grace, though that by no means implies that he regarded its meaning as necessarily confined to the sphere of religion. Hence it is but natural that the experience in the garden should engender, not only a new hope of the salvation of the soul, but a hope of future, purposeful life on this earth as well.

Seen against this background the image of the laughing children takes on a new significance. They represent something which has been denied to the poet himself, which for him belongs to the world of what might have been. But the children of future generations are to come, for they are the fruit of love. And love is the core of the experience in the rose garden. The importance of the image to the poem as a whole is emphasized by its recurring at the end of the last Section:

> There rises the hidden laughter
> Of children in the foliage

The abstract speculation of the opening lines is followed by a passage which leads on to the rose garden scene: "Footfalls echo in the memory . . ." This phrase, it will be remembered, may be read as an echo of St. Augustine's likening the memory of things past to "footsteps, left imprinted in our minds",[6] and Eliot's thought in the First Section of "Burnt Norton" has certain connections with that of St. Augustine in the relevant passage from his *Confessions*. Speculating on the nature of time, both are arrested by the function of memory, and as St. Augustine's thoughts go back to his own childhood, so the speaker in "Burnt Norton" reverts to some recollection of his earlier life.

The real difficulties of interpretation begin with the "passage" and "door" leading to the rose garden. The clear thought and expression of the opening lines give way to bewildering imagery and complex symbolism. The "passage we did not take" and the "door we never opened" obviously belong to the world of what might have been, signifying something never realized or fulfilled, though the counterparts of these images in the poet's experience remain unknown.

In a short passage dividing the First Section of "Burnt Norton" into two parts,

[6] *St. Augustine's Confessions*, Loeb ed., London, (1912) 1946, II, p. 249.

But to what purpose
Disturbing the dust on a bowl of rose-leaves
I do not know

the speaker then seems to pause for a moment before abandoning himself to his memories, reluctant to touch what had perhaps better be left in peace, doubtful whether anything is to be gained by reviving half-forgotten memories.

The succeeding thirty lines of the poem perhaps form the most difficult passage in the *Four Quartets,* but at the same time they seem to be of paramount significance.

Since "Burnt Norton" derives its title from a country house which Eliot is known to have visited, it is natural that the garden of the poem should owe something to the garden of this house. There are in fact several elements in the description of the garden which have their counterparts in the actual garden of Burnt Norton. The concrete pool, the box circle, the rose bushes and shrubberies, for example, are all to be found there. In view of these facts it seems reasonable to assume that the poem describes an actual experience the poet has had in that particular garden. What else could account for the title of the poem? But the scene in the poem also contains many elements familiar to the reader of Eliot's earlier poetry, elements which appear as reminiscences from the garden scenes in "Ash-Wednesday", *The Waste Land* and even earlier poems. This leaves us with two gardens, it seems, which is in fact suggested by the text of the poem:

Other echoes
Inhabit the garden. Shall we follow?
Quick, said the bird, find them, find them,
Round the corner. Through the first gate,
Into our first world . . .

In speaking of "other echoes" the poet obviously refers to the footfalls which "echo in the memory" and the words which "echo in the mind" of the one he addresses. It might perhaps be suggested that Eliot, while alone in the garden of Burnt Norton, came to think of some other garden in which he had had an important experience. In his mind the two gardens then blend and suddenly the earlier experience is recalled with such intensity that it seems to repeat itself, a kind of *déja vue* phenomenon, perhaps – the same and yet not quite the same, for now he sees the meaning of the first experience. This, then, would be an example of the "crystallization" of which Eliot speaks in the essay on Pascal,[7] and the amalgamation of the actual experience and the one recalled, of the garden of Burnt Norton and the one referred to in his earlier poetry, might well account for certain ambiguities in the present passage and for the wavering between past and present.

What kind of memories, then, did the experience in the garden evoke? The answer which the poem gives to this question is evasive. The dreamlike atmosphere of the whole scene and the vague identity of the characters appearing in it, suggest that the poet is reluctant to share his memories fully with the reader. Thus the elusiveness of the scene is no doubt deliberate. And yet the imagery reveals enough to give the poem meaning.

It has already been mentioned that the rose garden episode contains allusions to childhood. The "echoes" are to be found by going

> Round the corner. Through the first gate,
> Into our first world

It is "our" first world, not only the poet's, or speaker's, but childhood as such. This interpretation is substantiated by referring the garden of "Burnt Norton" to a special garden which a man of Eliot's generation and background is almost certain to be familiar with – the rose garden in *Alice's Adventures in Wonderland*. In fact, Eliot has himself acknowledged the significance of *Alice* for "Burnt Norton".[8] Not too much symbolic importance, however, should be attached to this allusion; its relevance is something rather simpler. Anyone who has read the story must have felt something of the peculiar fascination of that rose garden of which Alice first gets a glimpse, but cannot get into until towards the end of the story. It is the kind

[7] Vide supra, pp. 66 f.

[8] Martz, L. L., "The Wheel and the Point: Aspects of Imagery and Theme in Eliot's Later Poetry", *T. S. Eliot. A Selected Critique*, ed. by L. Unger, New York, 1948, p. 448.

of little image that impresses and lasts, as Eliot implies it to have done in his case; it is to this level that the allusion relates.

There are several elements in the description of this garden which recur in "Burnt Norton" – the small passage leading to the narrow gate which opens into "the loveliest garden you ever saw" with "those beds of bright flowers and those cool fountains".[9] It is of course difficult to tell what feelings the garden may have evoked in Eliot, but being so lovely and yet so hard to get into, it readily offers itself as a symbol of all that which appears mysterious and fascinating but out of reach.

The garden of "Burnt Norton" is not only the "first world" of childhood. It is inhabited by "other echoes" referred to as "they":

> There they were, dignified, invisible,
> Moving without pressure, over the dead leaves

Various interpretations have been offered as to the identity of these figures. The fact that they are invisible may be taken to indicate that they belong to the world of what might have been, and represent something never realized in the life of the speaker.[10] But they may also be invisible because they are present in the garden only as "echoes" from the past, felt but not seen.

> There they were as our guests, accepted and accepting.

They are accepted by the speaker, and he is accepted by them – implying some authority on their part, which is also emphasized by the epithet "dignified". It may perhaps be suggested that these invisible echoes are the speaker's own forebears watching him and his companion in the garden, accepting what they are doing and thus linking their life and experience with those of past generations. It should be mentioned that the word "dignified" appears once more in the *Quartets,* there immediately associated with the poet's forebears:

[9] Carroll, L., *Alice's Adventures in Wonderland,* London, 1866, pp. 8 f.

[10] Cf. C. A. Bodelsen's suggestion that "'they' are the children of the might-have-been, and that they symbolize what the protagonist has missed in life: what he would have found 'down the passage which he did not take'". *T. S. Eliot's Four Quartets,* Copenhagen, 1958, p. 41. (Bodelsen's study should be referred to more often in this book, but unfortunately the present author did not read it until after the completion of the manuscript.)

The association of man and woman
In daunsinge, signifying matrimonie –
A dignified and commodius sacrament.
(EC: I)

Any attempt, however, at a narrow identification of the characters appearing in the rose garden is against the tone of the whole scene. They are all "moving without pressure", are only half real. The ones referred to as "we", on the other hand, seem more definite. One is the speaker and the other somebody accompanying him.[11] From what may be gathered as to the nature of Eliot's experience at Burnt Norton, it is obvious that he was alone, and any other person appearing in the garden of the poem may be taken as a product of the poet's imagination, or a projection of his memories.

The climax of the garden episode is witnessed, or experienced, by the speaker and his companion together:

So we moved, and they, in a formal pattern,
Along the empty alley, into the box circle,
To look down into the drained pool.
Dry the pool, dry concrete, brown edged,
And the pool was filled with water out of sunlight,
And the lotos rose, quietly, quietly,
The surface glittered out of heart of light,
And they were behind us, reflected in the pool.

Beyond any doubt this passage reflects an experience of love. There is the contrast between the dry sterility of the empty pool and the life-giving "water out of sunlight", and there is this strange flower, the lotos, in the midst of an English garden; the sexual meaning of the rising lotos has been noted by several critics.[12] The setting of the scene suggests the same thing, roses being traditional symbols of love. And reverting, at the end of the poem, to the experience in the garden, the poet speaks of "desire", thus indicating an element of desire in the vision by the pool.

In the corresponding passage in *The Waste Land* the erotic implications are even more obvious. Preceded and followed by quota-

[11] Cf. Bodelsen, p. 43.

[12] Cf. Unger, L., "T. S. Eliot's Rose Garden", *T. S. Eliot. A Selected Critique*, p. 384; Smidt, K., *Poetry and Belief in the Work of T. S. Eliot*, Oslo, 1949, p. 167.

tions from *Tristan und Isolde*, the relevant lines express an experience similar to the one in the rose garden:

> "They called me the hyacinth girl."
> – Yet when we came back, late, from the Hyacinth garden,
> Your arms full, and your hair wet, I could not
> Speak, and my eyes failed, I was neither
> Living nor dead, and I knew nothing,
> Looking into the heart of light, the silence.
> *Oed' und leer das Meer.*

The last line breaks the ecstatic mood and suggests a feeling of disappointment. The same thing happens in the rose garden:

> Then a cloud passed, and the pool was empty.

Whatever the experience was, it was never fulfilled, and afterwards, recalling it and meditating on its meaning, the speaker asks himself what might have happened, "what might have been", if the experience had been fulfilled. In the next line the image of the children occurs – children, the fruit of love.

> Go, said the bird, for the leaves were full of children,
> Hidden excitedly

The garden episode thus seems to reflect an experience of love between man and woman, but it also suggests a more infantile excitement. Here one of Eliot's early poems in French seems to be relevant. In "Dans le Restaurant", published in 1918, a man relates an experience from his childhood:

> J'avais sept ans, elle était plus petite.
> Elle était toute mouillée, je lui ai donné des primevères.
> – – –
> Je la chatouillais, pour la faire rire.
> J'éprouvais un instant de puissance et de délire.[13]

The flowers, the laughter and the ecstatic mood are all elements which recur in "Burnt Norton", and also the abrupt, almost brutal interruption: in "Dans le Restaurant"the speaker is suddenly chased away.

[13] *Collected Poems 1909–1935*, p. 51.

The rose garden episode in "Burnt Norton" thus seems to include a number of recollections from the speaker's, or poet's, past. Its "literal" meaning consists of his special and personal experience of human love and ecstasy at certain decisive points in his own past and of the actual experience in the garden of Burnt Norton, by recollection including, but at the same time transcending, the previous ones.[14]

The rose garden scene contains literary reminiscences as well, and seen against its literary background, it receives a wider symbolic meaning. *Alice's Adventures in Wonderland* has already been discussed. Critics have also put forward several other garden scenes in modern poetry and fiction as sources of the garden in "Burnt Norton"; Kipling, D. H. Lawrence and Walter de la Mare, for example, have been mentioned.[15] But since the symbolism of roses and rose gardens belongs to old tradition in all European literature, it may be well to look for Eliot's sources within this tradition.

One of the sources of this tradition is Guillaume de Lorris' *The Romance of the Rose,* a work providing some striking parallels to "Burnt Norton". Eliot's familiarity with the *Romance* may be inferred from one of his essays,[16] and some critics have noticed the relevance of this medieval allegory of the rose to Eliot's rose symbolism.[17]

In *The Romance of the Rose* is described a wonderful garden

[14] There are further details in the description of the garden, which probably have a definite "literal" meaning. Conjectures concerning the origin of the thrush have been put forward by Preston (pp. 13 f.), S. Musgrove (*T. S. Eliot and Walt Whitman,* Wellington, 1952, p. 68) and J. C. Maxwell ("Reflections on *Four Quartets*", *Month,* N. S., Vol. 4, 1950, pp. 59 ff.). C. L. Barber has made some suggestions concerning the rôle of the laughing children ("Strange Gods at T. S. Eliot's *The Family Reunion*", *T. S. Eliot. A Selected Critique,* p. 440).

[15] Helen Gardner (p. 160) suggests that the setting of "Burnt Norton" derives from Kipling's story, "They" (in *Traffics and Discoveries,* London, 1904). This suggestion is further developed by Bodelsen, pp. 40 f. Louis Martz (p. 449) mentions a story by D. H. Lawrence called "The Shadow in the Rose Garden" (in *The Prussian Officer and Other Stories,* London, 1914). A reference to Walter de la Mare's poem, "The Looking Glass" (in *Collected Poems,* London, 1951, pp. 260 ff.) is to be found in George Williamson's *A Reader's Guide to T. S. Eliot,* New York, 1953, p. 212, n.

[16] *Selected Essays,* p. 242.

[17] Cf. Preston, p. 12.

encircled by a high wall. Behind that wall the hero of the poem can see the trees of the garden in which sweet birds are singing, but in order to get into the garden he has to pass a small gate:

> Tant que ung guichet bien barré
> Trovai petitet et estroit;
> Par autre leu l'en n'i entroit [18]

The gate is opened and he enters the garden. Walking among the flowerbeds, fountains and shrubberies of the garden, he is especially attracted by a blossoming rose tree, which he approaches intending to pick a rose bud.

Many elements in the description of the garden in *The Romance of the Rose* recur in "Burnt Norton". Trees, shrubberies, fountains, roses and singing birds, however, are all elements that may come readily to anyone describing a pleasant garden, and it is also quite natural to find a gate at the entrance of a walled garden. Accordingly, the significance of the *Romance* to "Burnt Norton" does not lie in the mere description of the garden but in the secondary, allegorical meanings put into the various things described. The *Romance* is the fullest medieval expression of the idea of courtly love and with it the symbolic connection between roses and love was, as it were, codified. With its profound and far-reaching influence on subsequent medieval writers it formed the basis of a literary tradition.[19] Of this Eliot is no doubt aware, and the use of roses symbolically in the way he does, certainly has the effect of directing the reader's attention towards the medieval conception of love. It is not so much the *Romance* itself, however, that is of importance to "Burnt Norton", but rather the literary and spiritual development it prompted, a development culminating in the work of Dante.

The conception of love in Dante's work undergoes a gradual transformation from the more profane courtly love of the *Vita Nuova* to the purely divine love at the end of the *Paradiso*. An outer indication of this transformation is to be found in the change of symbolic colours. The rose of the *Romance* is red,[20] and accordingly Beatrice,

[18] Guillaume de Lorris, *Le roman de la rose*, ed. by P. Marteau, Orléans, 1878, I, p. 34.

[19] Cf. Lewis, C. S., *The Allegory of Love*, Oxford, 1936, p. 157.

[20] Guillaume de Lorris, p. 110.

when Dante sees her for the first time, appears "vestita di nobilissimo colore, umile ed onesto, sanguigno . . ."[21] As a contrast to this red colour traditionally symbolic of human love, of the passion of the blood, the white rose appears at the end of the *Paradiso*:

> In forma dunque di candida rosa
> Mi si monstrava la milizia santa,
> Che nel suo sangue Cristo fece sposa.[22]

In "Ash-Wednesday" II, the symbol of the rose is clearly reminiscent of medieval allegory. No particular colour is there attributed to the rose, but the whole section of the poem goes in white: the white leopards, the white bones and, above all, the "Lady in a white gown"; it should be noted that white is the liturgical colour of the Virgin Mary.[23] In one of his early poems, on the other hand, Eliot speaks of flowers whose "petals are fanged and red".[24] The transition thus symbolized, from human love to divine love, has been noticed in Dante by Eliot himself,[25] and the corresponding transition in Eliot's own work is one of the most significant aspects of his development as a poet.[26] As regards "Burnt Norton", one of its spiritual meanings seems to be related to this idea of love.

The garden symbolism has also been used for devout purposes, often with an allusion to some Scriptural garden, to the Garden of Eden or the one in the "Song of Solomon". An example of such Christian symbolism is found in an emblem book by the English Jesuit Henry Hawkins, *Partheneia Sacra* (1633). The introductory picture, or emblem, of this book represents an enclosed garden showing the familiar features of the small door leading into the garden, trees, birds, a fountain and flowers – including the rose.[27] This garden, devoted to the Virgin Mary, is but one of many instances of devout allegories of rose gardens parallel to the profane allegory of

[21] Dante, *Tutte le Opere*, ed. by E. Moore, London, 1909, p. 1.

[22] Dante, *Paradiso, XXXI*, 1–3.

[23] Cf. Braun, J., "Die liturgischen Farben", *Die liturgische Gewandung im Occident und Orient*, Freiburg i. B., 1907, pp. 728 ff.

[24] "Circe's Palace", *Harvard Advocate*, Nov. 25, 1908.

[25] *Selected Essays*, p. 275.

[26] Cf. Smidt, K., pp. 146, 161.

[27] See Freeman, R., *English Emblem Books*, London, 1948, pp. 181 ff.

The Romance of the Rose. Another, more secular example from seventeenth century English literature is Marvell's poem, "The Garden", to a certain extent a variation on the theme of the Garden of Eden.[28] Though such examples can easily be multiplied, enough have probably been given to show that the rose garden of "Burnt Norton" is evidently related to a literary tradition, the religious aspects of which are as important as the more secular ones.

The rose garden episode also has definite, religious implications, which emerge when it is seen in its context. Christian categories of thought and experience are no doubt highly relevant to the poem, but they reveal themselves only by implication and allusion.

There is one line in the First Section that is taken over from *Murder in the Cathedral:*

> human kind
> Cannot bear very much reality.

In "Burnt Norton" these words follow immediately upon the bird's exhorting the speaker to leave the garden after the interruption of the ecstatic vision, and interpreted in the light of the corresponding passage in *Murder in the Cathedral,* they imply that the vision was a vision of Reality:

> This is one moment,
> But know that another
> Shall pierce you with a sudden painful joy
> When the figure of God's purpose is made complete.
> You shall forget these things, toiling in the household,
> You shall remember them, droning by the fire,
> When age and forgetfulness sweeten memory
> Only like a dream that has often been told
> And often been changed in the telling. They will seem unreal.
> Human kind cannot bear very much reality.[29]

Reality, in this speech of Becket's, thus involves "the figure of God's purpose", and it may perhaps be assumed that the poet's vision in the garden of Burnt Norton involved a realization of a divine purpose in his own life.

[28] *The Poems and Letters of Andrew Marvell,* ed. by H. M. Margoliouth, Oxford, 1927, Vol. I, p. 48.

[29] *Murder in the Cathedral,* 4th ed., p. 68 f.

The symbol of the lotos,

> And the lotos rose, quietly, quietly,

has also been interpreted as referring to a conception of Ultimate Reality. To Kristian Smidt it "appears to be a symbol of the complete Reality of which sensible things (the concrete pool) are only a part." [30] He also observes, however, that "its import may be phallic", and it appears that the lotos, in Hinduism as well as in certain Chinese religions, is used as an emblem of deities of fertility and love.[31] The lotos is a conspicuous symbol in the holy books and pictures of many Eastern religions, but appertaining as it often does to the supreme deity, its symbolic character is as difficult to define as the character of the deity itself. Nevertheless it may be possible to distinguish two more or less distinct spheres of associations connected with the lotos. One is the more popular, ritual meaning, which often involves mythological patterns of fertility and regeneration common to most religions. The other is the more esoteric and philosophical meaning, in which the lotos is associated with concepts like Ultimate Reality. Thus in "Burnt Norton" the symbol of the lotos appears appropriately in the description of an experience which involves recollections both of profane love and a kind of mystic ecstasy. In using one image to symbolize both aspects of the experience, Eliot indicates an essential relation between the two.

A more significant symbol expressing the same thing is of course the rose garden itself. It was noted above that in medieval tradition the rose garden was used to symbolize both profane and divine love, and in "Burnt Norton" both meanings seem to be equally important. It should also be noted that in this tradition, ranging from *The Romance of the Rose* and the medieval allegorical interpretations of Scriptural gardens to the seventeenth century English poets, it is often difficult to say whether the profane or the sacred elements are predominant. There is no clear line of division – as is natural in medieval allegory. That is to say that the garden is a symbol, not only of two distinct forms of love, but also of the transition from one

[30] Smidt, p. 167, note 3.

[31] See Glasenapp, H. von, *Der Hinduismus*, München, 1922, p. 140; *The Mythology of All Races*, ed. by L. H. Gray, Boston, 1916–32, Vol. VIII, p. 105.

form to the other. This aspect of the symbol is very important indeed to the understanding of "Burnt Norton", and so deserves some further attention.

Human love and the apprehension of the Divine seem, then, together to constitute the symbolic meaning of the garden in "Burnt Norton", though Eliot by no means considers these two things identical. In choosing one symbol to embrace them both, he seems to indicate what he considers an essential relation between the two. His idea of the Dantean transition from human to divine love has already been referred to, and a corresponding development has also been noticed within his own poetry. The moment of ecstasy, the central element in many of Eliot's garden episodes, lends itself readily to such twofold symbolism.

This essential relation between profane love and mystic illumination seems to be the very core of the meaning of the speaker's experience in the garden. But the experience was also a vision of Reality, of "the figure of God's purpose", and the relationship disclosed in that vision is to be seen as a divine purpose. Here a parallel to the Dantean categories of allegory may be appropriate. The difference between sacred and profane allegory was in the previous chapter found to be that in the first case the two terms – the allegory and the thing allegorized – were both "historical" realities, whereas in the other case the allegory was a mere invention by the poet. Applied to Eliot's rose garden, this distinction reveals something very important. In so far as the garden is made, by poetic imagination and invention, to represent certain ideas and emotions, it is a symbol or an allegory in the profane sense – a means of poetic expression simply. But the relation, within the symbol of the garden, of early experiences of profane love and the mystic illumination, seems more in the nature of sacred allegory, or even a "typological" relation. That is to say that the more ecstatic moments described in Eliot's early poetry and recollected in "Burnt Norton" may be meant to be interpreted as "types" prefiguring the illumination received in the garden of Burnt Norton. If profane love is interpreted as a type, then the antitype or fulfilment is the divine love momentarily seen in the vision in the garden. This typical relation would then correspond to the transfiguration of Beatrice in the work of Dante. On the evidence of the First Section of the first *Quartet*, this interpretation may perhaps seem unwarranted, but it is borne out by many subsequent passages.

There are symbols in the First Section which suggest a transition from the human to the Divine similar to that implied in the rose garden symbol. The image of eyes, or the idea of being looked at, is prominent in many of Eliot's early poems, and recurs in "Burnt Norton" in the enigmatic and beautiful lines,

> And the unseen eyebeam crossed, for the roses
> Had the look of flowers that are looked at.

The symbol of the eye appears most conspicuously in "The Hollow Men", there combined with a feeling of horror or shame ("Eyes I dare not meet in dreams"), but it can be observed as early as in "The Love Song of J. Alfred Prufrock". According to Kristian Smidt, the allegory of the "eye (or eyes) from being entirely human in 'The Love Song' become semi-divine in *The Hollow Men,* and finally completely divine in *The Family Reunion,* 'Burnt Norton' and elsewhere." [32] This again confirms the view that the actual experience in the garden of Burnt Norton, recalling the earlier experience, compelled Eliot to see that earlier experience in a new light.

A further example of the spiritual significance of the symbolism within the rose garden scene is to be found in the phrase,

> The surface glittered out of heart of light.

Being part of the description of the ecstatic moment itself, the line may be taken as a description of what the poet actually felt – visions of light are known to accompany many forms of ecstasy – but "the heart of light" is also a literary allusion. It is an inversion of "Heart of Darkness", the title of a story by Joseph Conrad which is also echoed in *The Waste Land* and in the epigraph to "The Hollow Men".[33] The title of Conrad's story stands for the depth of despair

[32] Smidt, p. 161. Cf. Gardner, p. 109, and the psychoanalytical interpretation of the eye symbol by Barber, p. 418.

[33] Cf. Matthiessen, F. O., *The Achievement of T. S. Eliot*, 2nd ed., Oxford, 1947, p. 195, and Unger, L., "Laforgue, Conrad and T. S. Eliot", *The Man in the Name*, Minneapolis, 1956; Conrad's story was published in *Youth and Two Other Stories*, London, 1902.

and spiritual darkness, and its inversion thus suggests its opposite – divine illumination. This meaning of the "heart of light" is emphasized by Raymond Preston, who finds the phrase reminiscent of Dante's "del cor dell' una delli luci nuove . . ."[34]

As a final example of the spiritual meaning of the symbolism of the rose garden scene, the image of the laughing children may be mentioned once more:

> Go, said the bird, for the leaves were full of children,
> Hidden excitedly, containing laughter.

A child's laughter accompanies the ecstatic moment in "Dans le Restaurant", and the image may well derive from some actual experience of the poet's, but it is also possible that Eliot meant the lines in "Burnt Norton" to be read as an allusion to the children in the heavenly rose in Dante's *Paradiso*:[35]

> Chè tutti questi son spiriti assolti
> Prima ch' avesser vere elezioni.
> Ben te ne puoi accorger per li volti,
> Ed anco per le voci puerili,
> Se tu li guardi bene e se gli ascolti.[36]

Some of the literary sources cited above may appear questionable, but it can hardly be doubted that the rose garden is meant to symbolize a vision of Reality or of the Divine and the prefiguration of this vision in the experiences of profane love. From what has previously been said in this study of Eliot's philosophical background, it may be inferred that Ultimate Reality and the Divine are concepts which in his mind imply the concept of eternity, and thus the

[34] Preston, p. 13, footnote; Dante, *Paradiso*, XII, 28.

[35] Suggested by E. R. Curtius, *Kritische Essays zur europäischen Literatur*, 2nd ed., Bern, 1954, p. 341.

[36] Dante, *Paradiso*, XXXII, 44–48. This reference does perhaps not exclude another one – to the legend of Parsifal. Wallace Fowlie suggests that as "in the Holy Grail legend, Parsifal is guided to the Grail Castle by the voices of children in the tree", so is the poet of "Burnt Norton" "to the secluded chapel of his mature faith (Little Gidding)". (*The Clown's Grail. A Study of Love in its Literary Expression*, London, 1948, p. 150.) Cf. also E. Simmons Greenhill, "The Child in the Tree. A Study of the Cosmological Tree in Christian Tradition", *Traditio*, Vol. 10, 1954, pp. 323–371.

experience in the rose garden may also be interpreted as a vision of eternity.

The First Section of "Burnt Norton"is thus constructed round two themes, that of time in the first part and that of eternity in the second. The relation between the temporal and the eternal was only momentarily apprehended in the vision in the garden, but in the later Sections of "Burnt Norton" and in the later three *Quartets*, the poet has attempted to integrate this momentary insight with his framework of philosophical and religious ideas. In "Burnt Norton" I the eternal and the divine appear as an overwhelming vision, and the meaning discovered is not yet differentiated. Hence no distinct spiritual levels of meaning in the Dantean sense can be discerned at this stage – not until the meaning of the vision becomes more articulate. But the fundamental distinction between the temporal and the eternal is emphasized from the very beginning of the first of the *Quartets*. It should be noted, however, that while the theme of time is explicitly stated in the first paragraph of the poem, the rose garden scene contains no such word as "eternity", "eternal", or "timeless". The explanation perhaps is that, for reasons of poetic composition, Eliot wished to hold back the explicit statement of the meaning of the experience in the garden until the conclusion of the poem, thus creating a kind of dramatic tension.

At the end of the First Section, the theme of time recurs:

> Time past and time future
> What might have been and what has been
> Point to one end, which is always present.

Here the last line gains new meaning. On its first appearance in the tenth line of the poem, it sums up the idea of the identity of all times and of potentiality and reality in the Eternal Now. Reintroducing this idea at the end of the garden scene, the poet also seems to indicate a step forward in the speaker's spiritual progress: having discovered a meaning in his own past, in "what has been", the speaker is relieved from his concern with "what might have been", and henceforth abandons futile speculation on possibilities never realized and instead applies himself to the exploration of the meaning of the present, which contains past and future.

II

The Second Section of "Burnt Norton" is a meditation in more general and impersonal terms on the significance of the particular and personal experience in the rose garden. The speaker has withdrawn, as it were; his thoughts and feelings, though prompted by and closely connected with the experience described in the First Section of the poem, are projected into images of universal application.

Though the passage as a whole is clear, the two opening lines are among the most obscure in the whole of Eliot's work, and before even a tentative interpretation of them can be offered, the general character of the subsequent imagery has to be considered.

The imagery of the first part of the Section is dominated by the idea of motion manifest in words like "dance", "circulation", "drift", "ascend", "move" and "moving". Circular movement is combined with movement upwards, forming something like an ascending and expanding spiral. The images almost produce an effect of dizziness, no doubt intended by the poet as a contrast to the stillness of the "still point" of the following passage. Comparing and almost identifying the world of the human body with the heavenly world, Eliot alludes to the old notion of the correspondence between microcosm and macrocosm. He particularly emphasizes the correspondence between the circular movement of the heavens, traditionally associated with the idea of time, and the movement of blood and lymph within the body, constituting the essence of temporal life. The desire of the blood is a manifestation of the same power which revives nature in summer and which makes the boarhound chase its prey to death; this juxtaposition of life and death, of "murder and create", noticeable as early as in "Prufrock", is one of Eliot's favourite poetic themes, suggesting on the one hand his anthropological studies of fertility rites involving human sacrifice, and on the other his concern with the problem of spiritual rebirth.

The close connection between the concepts of time and motion in classical philosophy and in science has been discussed above, and it seems very likely that Eliot had this connection in mind when writing "Burnt Norton". Thus the passage under consideration may be interpreted as a development of the theme of time as introduced at the very beginning of the poem. "The dance along the artery" and "the drift of stars" are both contained in the world of time, constituting an endless circular movement, leading nowhere, only repeating itself. The word "dance" anticipates the passage that follows in the same Section, and indicates that even in the temporal world of blood and passion the divine pattern may be traced.

The deeper spiritual meaning of the Second Section is to be found chiefly in its second part, but some of the symbols in the present passage also seem to hold meanings on different levels. The symbol of the tree, for example, may have certain Scriptural implications, as set forth in the following quotation from Wallace Fowlie:

> In the medieval tradition the tree can easily be explained on the four levels of interpretation: first, as the literal tree in the setting of Eliot's rose garden; secondly, as the allegorical tree of the Crucifixion from the top of which the Voice speaks and directs; thirdly, as the tropological tree whose life cycle is the moral divisioning of time; and fourthly, as the anagogical tree when, suddenly, at the end of the final poem, it is called the apple tree and alludes, as does the spitting out of the apple seed in Ash Wednesday, to the spiritual drama of man's fall and redemption. As the tree in the first garden was the gauge or barometer of man's obedience and love, so the tree in Eliot's poems is the symbol of time and eternity which are the two aspects of man's personal drama.[37]

Though based on Eliot's later poetry generally, this interpretation no doubt suggests an important aspect of the present passage. As an example of "typological" interpretation, however, the reference to the tree of the Crucifixion may be too specific to agree with the less specifically religious tone of "Burnt Norton". The relation between macrocosm and microcosm is not a typical relation, but something rather similar: earthly desire is "figured in the drift of stars" and "reconciled among the stars", but even the stars move within the dimension of time; the ultimate meaning of the "song" of the blood lies beyond any pattern within the cosmos, lies beyond time. The same idea, expressed in the same kind of imagery, is to be found already in *The Rock*:

[37] Fowlie, *The Clown's Grail*, p. 150.

The Eagle soars in the summit of Heaven,
The Hunter with his dogs pursues his circuit.
O perpetual revolution of configured stars,
O perpetual recurrence of determined seasons,
O world of spring and autumn, birth and dying!
The endless cycle of idea and action,
Endless invention, endless experiment,
Brings knowledge of motion, but not of stillness.[38]

Thus the imagery of the first part of the Second Section of "Burnt Norton" forms a consistent whole. The connection between the first two lines of that Section and the passage as a whole, is, however, very obscure.

Garlic and sapphires in the mud
Clot the bedded axle-tree.

Conjectures as to the meaning of these two lines abound, and with the aid of some of these conjectures one possible, though highly tentative interpretation will be suggested here.

Several critics maintain that the lines contain allusions to two separate poems by Mallarmé, to the phrase, "bavant boue et rubis" in "Le tombeau de Charles Baudelaire", and the phrase, "Tonnerre et rubis aux moyeux" in the sonnet, "M'introduire dans ton histoire".[39] The meaning of these allusions, if they really are allusions, is most obscure; mud and ruby and ruby and hubs, on the one hand, and sapphires, mud and axle-tree on the other.[40] The reference to Mallarmé is thus confusing rather than suggestive, but it is quite possible that Eliot intended to allude to Mallarmé; originally the two lines belonged, it will be remembered, to the poem, "Lines for an Old Man", in the manuscript dedicated to Mallarmé.

If Eliot had Mallarmé in mind, the substitution of sapphires for

[38] *Collected Poems 1909–1935*, p. 157.

[39] Cf. Matthiessen, p. 180.

[40] The "boue et rubis" in the poem on Baudelaire has been interpreted as a counterpart of the basic antithesis in Baudelaire's work between *spleen* and *idéal*, and may as such have some relevance to Eliot, though the antithesis in "Burnt Norton" seems to be between garlic and jewels rather than between jewels and mud. See Fowlie, W., *Mallarmé*, Chicago, 1953, p. 66; Davies, G., *Les poèmes commémoratifs de Mallarmé*, Paris, 1950, p. 167.

rubies must have some definite significance. Charlie Masters has drawn attention to the magic qualities traditionally attributed to the sapphire:

> its ability to turn the mind to aspiration toward higher things, its blue being a constant reminder of the blue of the heavens; also, a certain type of cloudy sapphire was known as Astrea, or the star stone, because of the six rays which emanate from it.[41]

Masters does not bring this magic meaning of the sapphire to bear on "Burnt Norton", but in view of the fact that the colour blue recurs in the Fourth Section of the poem, there referring to the Virgin Mary, it may be suggested that the sapphires stand for the higher spiritualized forms of love as contrasted with the cruder forms of profane love represented by the garlic as a symbol of fertility and vulgarity. It would perhaps be more accurate to say that garlic and sapphire are the seeds of different forms of love, seeds which are both planted in the mud, in the degradation of temporal existence. The "bedded axle-tree", finally, seems to anticipate the "still point" later in the same Section of the poem, both relating to the metaphor of the wheel. It would be futile, however, to add here to the number of uncertain, more or less fantastic conjectures offered by previous critics as to the exact meaning of these lines;[42] whatever the poet intended them to mean, he does not seem to have succeeded in conveying this meaning fully.

In the second part of "Burnt Norton" II, Eliot develops the central image of the wheel, the philosophical origins and implications of which have been discussed earlier in this study.

> At the still point of the turning world. Neither
>   flesh nor fleshless;
> Neither from nor towards;

[41] Masters, C., "Some Observations on 'Burnt Norton'", *American Prefaces*, Vol. 6, 1941, p. 213.

[42] Cf. Wheelwright, P., "Eliot's Philosophical Themes", *T. S. Eliot. A Study of His Writings by Several Hands*, ed. by B. Rajan, London, 1947, pp. 100 f.; Drew, E., *T. S. Eliot. The Design of His Poetry*, London, 1950, p. 190, footnote; Smith, G., *T. S. Eliot's Poetry and Plays*, Chicago, 1956, p. 257; Howarth, H., "Eliot, Beethoven, and J. W. N. Sullivan", *Comparative Literature*, Vol. 9, 1957, p. 329.

Against the whirling rotation of the cosmos pictured in the previous passage, Eliot here sets the still point of this "turning world", *i. e.* the centre or hub of the turning wheel of material existence. The turning world is traditionally the world of time, and accordingly the first part of "Burnt Norton" II is a development of the theme of time. The still point, however, is within the same tradition always associated with timelessness, with eternity, and accordingly Eliot affirms of the experience at the still point:

> And I cannot say, how long, for that is to place it in time.

The still point is not in time, but it is the point "where past and future are gathered". Here the poet seems to hint at the idea of the Eternal Now, already alluded to in the fourth line of the poem – "If all time is eternally present . . ." The idea of the still point thus involves timelessness, and the second part of "Burnt Norton" II is a development of the theme of eternity as introduced in the rose garden episode.

In his attempts to make the notion of the still point imaginable, Eliot resorts to a series of paradoxes. "Neither flesh nor fleshless", implying perhaps that though immaterial the still point may be apprehended by the senses, as in the rose garden; it thus suggests something of the ambivalent character of the experience in the garden, which was both of the flesh and of the spirit. "Neither from nor towards", "neither arrest nor movement" – these paradoxes seem to imply that, though void of the movement that constitutes time, the still point is not still in the sense of being motionless ("do not call it fixity") for that would mean death. This movement, which is not motion, Eliot calls the dance.

It has been suggested earlier in this study that the image of the dance in "Burnt Norton" may derive from the Plotinian metaphor of the dance of the blessed souls round the One, or from the Indian conception of the dance of Shiva, both of which are attempts to express the ineffable experience of the Divine. Whether Eliot consciously alluded to one or both of these sources, is impossible to tell; it seems clear, however, that he is concerned with the same category of experience as the Hindu or Plotinian mystic.

The image of the dance seems particularly appropriate in "Burnt

Norton" for other reasons as well, combining as it does the idea of movement with the idea of pattern. Dance is movement subject to artistic form:

> Only by the form, the pattern,
> Can words or music reach
> The stillness,

Eliot says in the last Section of "Burnt Norton", and in the same way movement reaches the stillness of the still point by the form or pattern of the dance. Thus time and eternity may be said to be reconciled in the dance.[43]

A further, contemporary source of Eliot's image of the dance has been suggested by several critics – Charles Williams' fantastic novel, *The Greater Trumps* (1932).[44] Eliot is indebted to Williams in many ways,[45] and it is quite possible that he had the following passage in mind when writing "Burnt Norton":

> . . . imagine that everything which exists takes part in the movement of a great dance – everything, the electrons, all growing and decaying things, all that seems alive, and all that doesn't seem alive, men and beasts, trees and stones, everything that changes, and there is nothing anywhere that does not change. That change – that's what we know of the immortal dance; the law in the nature of things – that's the measure of the dance . . . there is nothing at all anywhere but the dance. Imagine it – imagine it, see it all at once and in one![46]

In spite of the apparent verbal reminiscences in "Burnt Norton", too much importance should perhaps not be attributed to this parallel. Eliot and Williams may both have made use of a common source; Williams' description of the dance is in fact very close to some descriptions of the dance of Shiva. Here, as in so many other places in Eliot's work, it seems more appropriate to speak of a tradition of symbolic expression than of isolated sources.[47]

[43] Cf. Fussell, P., "The Gestic Symbolism of T. S. Eliot", *ELH – A Journal of English Literary History*, Vol. 22, 1955, pp. 207 f.

[44] First by Gardner, p. 161.

[45] See Evans, D. W., "T. S. Eliot, Charles Williams, and the Sense of the Occult", *Accent. A Quarterly of New Literature*, (Urb., Ill.), Vol. 14, 1954.

[46] Williams, C., *The Greater Trumps*, London, 1932, pp. 115 f.

[47] It has also been suggested that Eliot's image of the dance derives from a

What might be called "the experience at the still point" may well be a kind of mystic experience. Abandoning his attempts to express the experience in terms of abstract paradoxes, the poet reverts to the imagery of the rose garden scene, thus indicating that both passages describe the same moment of ecstasy – the one in the actual setting of the garden, the other as a more detached recollection of the moment itself apart from the circumstances under which it occurred. The phrases, "a white light still and moving" and "*Erhebung* without motion", for example, both occurring in the Second Section, correspond to "glittered out of heart of light" and "Moving without pressure" in the First. Eliot does not add anything essential to the first description of the illumination, he is only more articulate as regards the psychological aspects of the experience.

The experience in the rose garden also involved the discovery of a divine purpose in life, and in the Second Section Eliot seems to return to that aspect of it:

> both a new world
> And the old made explicit, understood
> In the completion of its partial ecstasy,
> The resolution of its partial horror.

The new world is probably the world of mystic illumination revealed to the poet, while the old world is the ordinary world including the poet's own earlier life. The "partial ecstasy" of the old world, the ecstasy of profane love, is understood, is recognized as having a meaning, in its completion in the mystic ecstasy. The resolution of the "partial horror" is damnation – the extreme contrast of the vision of the Divine:

> Yet the enchainment of past and future
> Woven in the weakness of the changing body,
> Protects mankind from heaven and damnation.

The "enchainment" of temporal life prevents man from realizing the heights and depths of spiritual life. This idea is more explicitly stated in a passage from Eliot's essay on Baudelaire:

poem by John Davies; see P. Wheelwright, *The Burning Fountain*, Indiana Univ. Press, 1954, pp. 361 ff. It should also be noted that the symbol of the dance is to be found in Dante, e.g. *Paradiso*, XII, 1–30.

> So far as we are human, what we do must be either evil or good; so far as we do evil or good, we are human; and it is better, in a paradoxical way, to do evil than to do nothing: at least, we exist. It is true to say that the glory of man is his capacity for salvation; it is also true to say that his glory is his capacity for damnation.[48]

Thus the divine purpose seen momentarily in the vision in the garden appears to involve the alternative of salvation and damnation as opposed, for example, to the mental state of the Dantean Limbo. That is to say that the "partial horror" and the "partial ecstasy" of temporal life prefigure the final state of the soul, being, in effect, "types" of "heaven and damnation."

The moment of ecstasy in the rose garden was followed by the reflection, "human kind / Cannot bear very much reality"; in the same way, the meditation in the Second Section on that moment is concluded by the statement that "flesh cannot endure" the realities of "heaven and damnation". If it is to be something more than a fleeting illumination, unendurable and unapplicable in daily life, the mystic experience has to be followed by spiritual discipline – this is the teaching of most mystics, Eastern and Western, a teaching developed in the next Section of "Burnt Norton".

Having developed the themes of time and eternity in the first two paragraphs of "Burnt Norton" II, in the concluding paragraph the poet sums up the insight gained:

> Time past and time future
> Allow but a little consciousness.
> To be conscious is not to be in time.

Here consciousness is no doubt the equivalent of direct apprehension of Reality and temporal life is, by implication, to be described by the traditional metaphor of sleep or dream as, for example, in the *Mandukya Upanishad* or in the philosophy of Heracleitus, to say nothing of the more modern views along the same lines. Though timeless, the vision of Reality can be remembered and interpreted only in time, remembered in time and yet transcending time. Eliot mentions two other such mystic or visionary moments,

> The moment in the arbour where the rain beat,

[48] *Selected Essays*, p. 429.

which seems to be identical with the experience described in "Dans le Restaurant",[49] and

> The moment in the draughty church at smokefall,

which, though never referred to earlier in Eliot's work, is probably another personal reminiscence. Through recollection of, and through meditation on the meaning of these moments, the soul may finally transcend the dimension of time:

> Only through time time is conquered.

III

In the Third Section of "Burnt Norton" the theme of time achieves its most sombre development. The phrase, "time before and time after" is repeated twice, lending to the whole passage a tone of hopelessness.

The scene of the first passage is vividly imagined and its literal meaning seems clear: it is one of the underground railways of London.[50] This subterranean scene appears even gloomier through the contrast with the rose garden scene. Situated in a remote and hilly landscape, the garden of Burnt Norton is surrounded by open air and wide prospects, while the tube train is a closed world surrounded by dust and darkness. As a citizen of London and a visitor to Burnt Norton, Eliot is personally involved in both scenes.

This is not the first time in Eliot's work that London stands for the futility and barrenness of modern civilization enclosed in the dimension of time. London is the scene of *The Waste Land* and of *The Rock,* where it is significantly called "the timekept City":

> I journeyed to London, to the timekept City [51]

> A Cry from the North, from the West and from the South
> Whence thousands travel daily to the timekept City; [52]

[49] "Les saules trempés, et des bourgeons sur les ronces – / C'est là, dans une averse, qu'on s'abrite." (*Collected Poems 1909–1935,* p. 51.)

[50] Cf. Matthiessen, p. 181; Gardner, pp. 161 f.; Bland, D. S., "Mr. Eliot on the Underground", *Modern Language Notes,* Vol. 68, 1953, pp. 27 f.

[51] *Collected Poems 1909–1935,* p. 157.

[52] Ibid., p. 166.

The London of "Burnt Norton" III is but another Waste Land, the inhabitants of which are empty and bare of soul and feeling. Commuting from station to station they partake in a movement which leads nowhere and has no goal, which is as different from the eternal dance as is time itself. The whole passage is dominated by a feeling of disgust. It describes "apathy" and "distraction" – but in images of an uncanny intensity:

Only a flicker
Over the strained time-ridden faces
Distracted from distraction by distraction
Filled with fancies and empty of meaning
Tumid apathy with no concentration
Men and bits of paper, whirled by the cold wind
That blows before and after time,
Wind in and out of unwholesome lungs
Time before and time after.
Eructation of unhealthy souls
Into the faded air, the torpid
Driven on the wind that sweeps the gloomy hills of London,

The emphasis of this scene is essentially negative. Its only meaning lies in the abasement of life it suggests – so far is the soul removed from the Divine as not even to feel its own deprivation. The spirit, the breath of eternity, is unknown in this modern Limbo where another wind is whirling – the "cold wind / That blows before and after time". It is "faded air" which like the wind of the Ecclesiastes "whirleth about continually", and not the wind of the Spirit which "bloweth where it listeth". Not even the light of momentary ecstasy is granted to the inhabitants of this twilight world. In contrast to the sun-bathed garden scene –

And the pool was filled with water out of sunlight

– the present scene is set

In a dim light: neither daylight
– – –
Nor darkness to purify the soul.

It is a world protected from the light of salvation and the darkness of damnation – or purification. It is the "twilight kingdom" of "The Hollow Men".

It is this darkness of the dark night of the soul that is the theme of the second part of "Burnt Norton" III. The corresponding passages in the First and Second Sections of the poem describe the moment of spontaneous illumination; but, brief and transient as this moment is, it is not sufficient for the religious life – something that Eliot emphasizes in his essay on Pascal. It has to be followed by the spiritual discipline described in the present passage. The mystic way to union with the Divine here indicated, is the same way that is taught by the Indian Yogi, the Neo-Platonic mystic and St. John of the Cross. It is the negative way which through elimination of everything temporal leads to union with God, the Eternal.

The order of the gradual descent into utter darkness here implied, derives from the teaching of St. John of the Cross. He distinguishes three separate stages of the dark night: the negation, first of the senses, then of the intellect and finally also of the spirit; or in Eliot's words:

> Desiccation of the world of sense,
> Evacuation of the world of fancy,
> Inoperancy of the world of spirit;
> This is the one way, and the other
> Is the same, not in movement
> But abstention from movement;

The last three lines also have a counterpart in St. John of the Cross. Raymond Preston has drawn attention to the following passage in *The Dark Night of the Soul:* "For upon this road to go down is to go up, and to go up, to go down, for he that humbles himself is exalted, and he that exalts himself is humbled."[53] The same idea is to be found in the Heracleitian Fragment which Eliot has used as an epigraph to "Burnt Norton": "The way up and the way down is one and the same."

The lines dealing with the negative way, forming a further development of the theme of eternity, are concluded by an echo of the theme of time:

> while the world moves
> In appetency, on its metalled ways
> Of time past and time future.

[53] Preston, p. 20. The quotation is to be found in *The Complete Works of St. John of the Cross*, transl. and ed. by E. A. Peers, London, 1934, I, p. 461.

"While" seems here to be a significant word: while the world moves on in its endless circle of desire and frustration, the devout soul has liberated itself from this circle and descended into the absolute darkness that precedes the reception of grace. No doubt the "metalled ways" have a very concrete literal meaning: they are the rails of the London tube conducting the trains and their passengers in the meaningless commutation which Eliot uses as a symbol of temporal existence.

In the first two Sections of "Burnt Norton" the theme of time appears at the very end of the Section as if to reinforce the feeling of frustration and resignation following upon the moment of illumination. In the Third Section, however, the theme recurs with a significant modification. The soul of the speaker has progressed through the dark night and abides in expectancy.

IV

The Fourth Section of "Burnt Norton" constitutes a pause in the development of the earlier Sections. Intellectual structure is replaced by lyric intensity. The ten lines express a unified emotion in a series of images derived from nature, and their effect is to heighten the feeling of expectancy predominant at the end of the foregoing passage – a feeling shared by speaker and reader alike.

The identity of the speaker becomes vaguer for each new Section. In the Second Section Eliot still writes, for example, "I can only say, *there* we have been: but I cannot say where." Thereafter the first person singular is not used any more in "Burnt Norton". The Third Section is wholly objective in the sense that the words are not spoken by any particular speaker, and the same applies to the final Section. In the Fourth, however, Eliot uses the first person plural: "Will the sunflower turn to us," etc. This pronoun seems to include, not only the speaker and the reader of the poem, but mankind. Though the identity of the speaker remains obscure throughout "Burnt Norton", it is obvious that the whole poem is to be regarded as a meditation of one mind. A meditation implies continuity – the continuity of a meditating mind – and in "Burnt Norton" this continuity is generalized and human rather than particular and personal. Persuading the reader to participate, as it were, in the same experience, the speaker thus sometimes identifies himself with the reader, which seems to be the case especially in the Fourth Section.

Tone and theme are indicated in the first line:

> Time and the bell have buried the day . . .

It is night, dark night. The day has been buried by time – the emptiness and expectancy of the soul is a state within the dimension of time but that dimension must be crossed, must be intersected by a ray of the eternal light. The "black cloud" that "carries the sun away" corresponds to the cloud which interrupted the vision of "water out of sunlight" in the beginning of the poem. Darkness and night prevail, and death, implied in the word "buried".

Passively yet anxiously waiting for renewed illumination, the soul demands whether light will ever return:

> Will the sunflower turn to us, will the clematis
> Stray down, bend to us . . .

The clematis is blue, and in "Ash-Wednesday" blue is the colour of the Virgin Mary: "Going in white and blue, in Mary's colour", and "in blue of larkspur, blue of Mary's colour". According to Raymond Preston, "the Virgin's Bower" is another name for the clematis.[54] In Eliot, as in Dante, Mary is a representative of pure, divine love, here another symbol of grace. As Preston has observed, "the images are handled with the utmost tact as symbols of divine gifts which may be bestowed – but it is not in our power to draw them towards us. The sunflower may 'turn to us' as if an image of the divine light; the clematis [. . .] may 'stray down, bend to us'."[55] But before the soul can receive the divine light it must pass, not only through darkness, but also through death:

> tendril and spray
> Clutch and cling?
> Chill
> Fingers of yew be curled
> Down on us?

[54] Preston, p. 20, note 2.
[55] Preston, p. 20.

To the yew-tree, traditionally a symbol of death, Eliot adds words like "chill" and "clutch and cling" suggesting the chill grip of death.[56]

The natural imagery of the whole passage seems to connect it with the fertility myths Eliot utilized in his early poetry. The process of spiritual rebirth is natural in the same sense that the rebirth of nature in spring is natural, but as a direct work of God it is also supernatural. These two aspects have, of course, been permanently associated in the parable of the corn of wheat. Already in *The Waste Land* the idea of death is invariably connected with the idea of resurrection.[57]

The image of the kingfisher at the end of the lyric may have some connection with two images in the rose garden scene – "water out of sunlight" and "The surface glittered out of heart of light":

After the kingfisher's wing
Has answered light to light

Eliot may have seen this bird flashing momentarily under the willows on the border of streams and lakes, its brilliant blue and white plumage catching the rays of the sun, its wings "answering light to light". In the evening a harbinger of night yet reflecting the light of the sun, the kingfisher is thus altogether appropriate to the end of the Fourth Section.[58]

The short lyric ends by the juxtaposition of the two symbols of the light and the still point, indicating the timelessness of the hoped for illumination:

the light is still
At the still point of the turning world.

[56] Some critics have here discovered an allusion to a passage in Tennyson's *In Memoriam*, which, if relevant, reinforces the tone of death. See Maxwell, D. E. S., *The Poetry of T. S. Eliot*, London, 1952, p. 166.

[57] Leonard Unger interprets "kingfisher" as an inversion of the "Fisher King" in *The Waste Land*. (*A Selected Critique*, p. 385.)

[58] Eliot perhaps also alludes to the story of the kingfishers as told by Ovid – a story which, like so many others of the metamorphoses, involves a kind of rebirth. See *Metamorphoses*, Book, XI, 730–745. (Loeb ed., Vol. II, p. 172.)

V

The Fifth Section of "Burnt Norton" resumes the antithetical structure of the first three Sections, opening with a new development of the theme of time:

> Words move, music moves
> Only in time;

This juxtaposition of poetry and music, suggesting the temporal character of these arts in contrast to the spatial arts of painting and sculpture, seems especially appropriate in a poem like the present, which claims to have adopted certain elements of musical composition. In speech, word follows upon word as note upon note in music, unrolled in time and then disappearing:

> Words, after speech, reach
> Into the silence. Only by the form, the pattern,
> Can words or music reach
> The stillness.

In order to overcome the temporal limitations of words and notes, the artist imposes upon the movement and flux of his material a structure which lends to the work of art something of the timeless stillness.

The preoccupation in the present passage with the nature and function of words, exactly parallels the search for a spiritual meaning in the previous Sections of "Burnt Norton". As a word or note lasts but for a moment in time, so does the mystic vision; and as words and notes achieve stillness and meaning only by the structure of a work of art, so the mystic vision achieves permanence and meaning only by being submitted to the order and structure of spiritual discipline. The interpretation of the mystic vision thus becomes a parallel of poetic composition, and it seems quite natural that the illumination received in the garden of Burnt Norton should lead the poet to explore the meaning of this experience by writing a poem on it – a poem of an elaborate structure, as philosophical and spiritual as it is poetic. It also seems quite natural that the problems of poetic composition should enter into the meditation of the speaker, in "Burnt Norton" as well as in the subsequent *Quartets*.

The perfect "stillness" of a work of art, however, is not the stillness of homogeneous duration, as in a sustained musical note:

> Not the stillness of the violin, while the note lasts,
> Not that only, but the co-existence,
> Or say that the end precedes the beginning,
> And the end and the beginning were always there
> Before the beginning and after the end.
> And all is always now.

Here aesthetics are merged with metaphysics; the timelessness of a work of art is seen as a counterpart of the Eternal Now. As the Chinese jar "Moves perpetually in its stillness", so the Eternal Now contains the timeless movement of the dance. Apprehending the stillness of a work of art is analogous to apprehending the still point of the turning world.

The dramatic tension created in the Fourth Section, does not achieve its resolution and fulfilment in a crescendo, as might perhaps have been expected. The calm and convinced statement of the nature of divine love in the concluding paragraph of "Burnt Norton" is barely indicated in the foregoing passage. Suddenly the reader finds himself at the end of the spiritual quest of the poem, almost without realizing what has happened. This end is reached with the mention of the Word, the Incarnation of the Divine, which appears at the conclusion of the speaker's meditation on the art of poetry, on the right use of words. The same structural logic, leading from words to the Word, is to be found already in *The Rock:*

> The endless cycle of idea and action,
> Endless invention, endless experiment,
> Brings knowledge of motion, but not of stillness;
> Knowledge of speech, but not of silence;
> Knowledge of words, and ignorance of the Word.[59]

Thus there is a clear distinction in Eliot's speculation between the words of men, subject to the instability and transience of time, and the Word of God, which originates in the timeless dimension. But words and the Word have one thing in common – they are both subject to misunderstanding, misconstruction and even perversity. The Word itself "is most attacked by voices of temptation". Of all the words of human language, the one expressing the Incarnation

[59] *Collected Poems 1909–1935*, p. 157.

of the Divine has most often been misunderstood, misconstructed and attacked. Feeling that all the words he is using in his poetry are "assailed" by "shrieking", "scolding, mocking, or merely chattering" voices, Eliot expresses his awareness of the danger and responsibility involved in the contemplation of the Word itself.

The Word also appears as the fulfilment of the moment in the rose garden. As a moment both in and out of time, at the point of intersection of the timeless with time, the moment in the rose garden appears as a reflection or a repetition of the Incarnation of Christ, such as Eliot conceives of this occasion. The moment of mystic insight is, in other words, a "type" of the Incarnation, of the Word. Composed round the antithesis of time and eternity, "Burnt Norton" achieves, quite consequently, its synthesis in the Word. Already St. Augustine, it will be remembered, had conceived of Christ as the synthesis of time and eternity.

It may perhaps seem unjustified to identify the Word in "Burnt Norton" with Christ. Except for the "voices of temptation" attacking the Word in the desert, there are no explicit references in the poem to Scriptural or other unambiguously Christian conceptions.[60] The conception of the Divine in "Burnt Norton" seems rather to indicate a variety of religions than the specifically Christian faith. Speaking of the Word, Eliot may well refer to the Logos of the various Hellenistic religious philosophies and he certainly also refers to the Logos of Heracleitus, which is cited in the first epigraph to "Burnt Norton". The conception of the Divine as Ultimate Reality appearing at the end of the rose garden episode, may be characterized as philosophical as much as religious, Oriental as much as Occidental. The still point of the turning world as a symbol of the Divine is primarily Neo-Platonic and Christian only by implication. Light is another symbol of the Absolute in "Burnt Norton" – as it was to the ancient worshippers of the sun; but the light of which Eliot speaks may also, and more probably, refer to Him who said, "I am the light of the world."

[60] The "disconsolate chimera" paralleled with the Word has been identified as the Chimera appearing in Flaubert's *La Tentation de saint Antoine*; see John Hayward's notes to the French translation of the *Quartets* by P. Leyris, Paris, 1950, p. 133.

This ambiguity as regards the religious implications of "Burnt Norton" is no doubt deliberate. It is not to be taken to imply, however, that Eliot should attach equal importance to the various religions to which he seems to allude. His personal conviction of the essential truth and authority of Christian revelation, manifest in his critical writings contemporary with "Burnt Norton", cannot be doubted. This conviction, however, seems relative rather than absolute, for he could hardly be a poet otherwise. Nevertheless withholding his personal beliefs in the first of the *Quartets,* Eliot probably does so partly because he is concerned with a kind of religious experience which comes before any division into separate religions and creeds. It is that awareness of the Divine, not as having special attributes – of being loving, or merciful, or forgiving – but void of such attributes, which seems fully consistent with the doctrine of the negative way taught in the poem.

The final paragraph of "Burnt Norton" is a summary of the insight gained, a resolution of the antithesis of time and eternity and also an almost "musical" recapitulation of the major themes and symbols of the poem.

> The detail of the pattern is movement,
> As in the figure of the ten stairs.

Derived from St. John of the Cross, the metaphor of the stairs expresses the soul's aspiration towards God, but it also expresses a kind of synthesis of stillness and movement. The movement implied in the climbing of the stairs is but a detail in the whole pattern of spiritual purification, and to the author of "Burnt Norton", the idea of pattern implies stillness. The antithesis of movement and stillness is further developed in the following lines, paraphrasing Aristotle's conception of the Unmoved Mover: [61]

> Desire itself is movement
> Not in itself desirable;
> Love is itself unmoving,
> Only the cause and end of movement,
> Timeless, and undesiring
> Except in the aspect of time

[61] Cf. Kristian Smidt, p. 140; Aristotle, *Metaphysics,* Book XII, 7.

Analogous with the antithesis of time and eternity are those of movement and stillness and of desire and love. Yet time is the moving image of the eternal dance, and in the same way desire is the image of love, is love "in the aspect of time". The rose garden is used to symbolize both profane love, desire, and divine love. The moment in the garden is neither pure desire nor pure love; it is only a beginning, a hint of a meaning. It represents a state intermediary between potentiality and reality, between "un-being and being."

The images following upon the more speculative passage on the distinction between desire and love, clearly indicate that here at the end of the poem Eliot reverts to its beginning, thus bringing the thematic and symbolical development to a conclusion. The shaft of sunlight, the moving dust, the children laughing in the foliage and the bird's call are all elements taken out of the rose garden episode. By this brief recapitulation of significant images, Eliot makes the moment in the garden stand visible to the reader again, and this time the reader is prepared to receive the full meaning of that moment. Thus what seems a mere repetition becomes a veritable conclusion. The five adverbs recalling the bird's exhortation,

Quick now, here, now, always –

form a striking example of Eliot's way of loading words, in themselves insignificant, with an accumulated meaning.[62] Referring to the moment of ecstasy, the line seems to say that such a moment appears suddenly here in everyday life, in the dimension of time, but also that the memory and meaning of it will always remain with him who had the experience; or perhaps that the moment of mystic ecstasy is always a potentiality to be realized at any moment of time.

To "conquer time" is one of the objects of the poet of "Burnt Norton", and how far he achieves this conquest may be gauged from the very last lines of the poem. While the First and Second Sections closed in resignation, the Third closed on a more hopeful note: while the world moves on in time, the soul may rise to the vision of eternity. Here at the very end of the poem, the theme of time recurs. "Time past and time future" and "time before and time after" are words which have tolled monotonously throughout the poem. Here

[62] Cf. Gardner, *The Art of T. S. Eliot*, p. 53.

this sombre "musical" theme is repeated, but in a different mode, modified by the laughter of the children:

> Ridiculous the waste sad time
> Stretching before and after

Time is conquered by eternity.

In this interpretation of "Burnt Norton" the "allegorical" or "typological" aspect of the poem has only been hinted at. The division of the spiritual meaning into three distinct categories is more easily discernable in the later *Quartets,* but the essential distinction in Dantean allegory between literal and spiritual meanings is fully applicable to "Burnt Norton" as well. Without suggesting anything about Eliot's intentions in writing "Burnt Norton", we may attempt to interpret the poem as a whole in Dantean terms, though the separate Sections at most only occasionally permit such an interpretation. The literal meaning is the actual experience in the rose garden and the memories evoked by that experience. The moral level of meaning is perhaps more difficult to define; broadly speaking it may well be the virtue of humility, as suggested by Helen Gardner,[63] if humility is taken to imply the state of undemanding expectancy of the soul waiting for the grace of illumination. The anagogical or mystic meaning is the transition from desire to love, from profane to divine ecstasy. The allegorical or typical meaning, finally, is indicated by the reference to the Word; the ultimate meaning of the manifestation of the timeless in time implied in the mystic vision, is the Incarnation of Christ.

[63] Ibid., p. 163.

CHAPTER VI

"Poetry in Wartime" The Contemporary Background of the Later Quartets

I

In "Burnt Norton" the idea of time and eternity is treated as a personal problem. Time past, time present and time future are all regarded as aspects of the life of one man, of the poet or speaker, and the timeless or eternal dimension as something that is apprehended at certain moments in his own life. In the later *Quartets*, however, the problem of time is considered in a wider perspective; the individual is seen in relation to society and history, and the problem of time is considered as the problem of the meaning of history. It is the aim of the present chapter to outline the background of this development of the idea of time from personal, psychological time to the time of history.

"Even 'Burnt Norton' might have remained by itself if it hadn't been for the war, because I had become very much absorbed in the problems of writing for the stage and might have gone straight on from 'The Family Reunion' to another play. The war destroyed that interest for a time."[1] These words by Eliot indicate the chief reason why, in 1939, after a lapse of four years, he once more turned to poetry as a means of expression. Stressing the unity rather than the difference between the first and the later *Quartets*, critics have on the whole neglected to study the factors which contributed towards the revival of Eliot's poetic creativeness, a study which is essential to the understanding of the later *Quartets*. The immediate back-

[1] Lehmann, J., "T. S. Eliot Talks About Himself and the Drive to Create", *The New York Times Book Review*, Nov. 29, 1953, p. 5.

ground of "East Coker", the second *Quartet,* is as Eliot himself points out, his reactions to the social and political situation of his country at the outbreak of the second world war.

Before analysing these reactions it may be well to consider briefly the chronology of Eliot's writings between "Burnt Norton" and "Little Gidding". Written in 1935, "Burnt Norton" was published at the beginning of 1936. After that Eliot seems to have devoted his creative powers exclusively to the writing of a new drama, *The Family Reunion,* which appeared at the beginning of 1939.[2] In the summer of the same year, he began the composition of "East Coker", published in the Easter number of *The New English Weekly* of 1940.[3] "The Dry Salvages" and "Little Gidding" were first published in the same periodical in February, 1941, and October, 1942. During the three years he spent in writing the last three *Quartets,* Eliot also wrote a number of short articles and essays for various periodicals, but he did not produce any major critical work between *The Idea of a Christian Society* (1939) and *Notes towards the Definition of Culture* (1948). He thus seems to have concentrated most of his strength and energy on the writing of the *Quartets* – as the last issue of *The Criterion* appeared in January, 1939, he was no longer distracted by the duties of an editor.

Eliot has confessed that, during the early days of the war, he felt very much "thrown in on himself".[4] The comparative slenderness of his literary output during the first years of the war may well be a reflection of this feeling of isolation, but the effect was a regeneration of his poetic faculties. This period of creativeness seems, quite naturally, to have inspired him with a certain confidence, and towards the end of the war his prose writings often speak in a hopeful tone. But the year preceding the composition of "East Coker" was to Eliot a year of disappointment and apprehension. It may be an exaggeration to speak of a personal crisis, but the national situa-

[2] Cf. Gallup, D., *T. S. Eliot. A Bibliography,* London, 1952, p. 27. The play was first produced in March, 1939; cf. Smith, G., *T. S. Eliot's Poetry and Plays,* Chicago, 1956, p. 196.

[3] Hayward, J., Notes to the French transl. of the *Quartets, Quatre Quatuors,* Paris, 1950, p. 156.

[4] Lehmann, loc. cit.

tion in England certainly affected him very deeply. His feelings were clearly revealed in his farewell, his "Last Words", to the readers of *The Criterion* in the last issue of that critical review, the editor of which Eliot had been since its foundation in 1922.

The reasons for the cessation of *The Criterion* were two, Eliot indicates in his "Last Words".[5] One was a "feeling of staleness" and "a suspicion that I ought to retire before I was aware that this feeling had communicated itself to the readers." The other was the international situation. It had been the aim of *The Criterion* "to provide in London a local forum of international thought", and to maintain close contacts with the literary life of the Continent, but the political development of the nineteen-thirties made such contacts increasingly difficult. Moreover, Eliot found it almost impossible to discover any manifestations of the "European mind" his periodical aimed to reflect and criticize. The Continent prepared for war and national and political prejudices threatened completely to obscure the cultural unity of the West.

In this situation *The Criterion* had either to confine itself to the English scene or to cease publication. The choice of the second alternative was due, however, not only to the original international aims of *The Criterion*, but to Eliot's general discontent with the state of affairs in England before the war. He did not hesitate to publish his critical views, but he did not consider *The Criterion* an appropriate forum: "For myself, a right political philosophy came more and more to imply a right theology – and right economics to depend upon right ethics: leading to emphases which somewhat stretched the original framework of a literary review." Aware of "the grave dangers to this country which might result from the lack of any vital political philosophy", he himself proposed an outline of such a philosophy in *The Idea of a Christian Society*, which appeared about six months after the last issue of *The Criterion*. This work, related to an ecclesiastical Utopia rather than to the actual political situation, gives a religious alternative to the secular ideologies that had precipitated Europe into war.

The more personal reason for Eliot's retirement as an editor,

[5] *The Criterion*, Vol. 18, 1938–1939, pp. 269–275.

seems to have been his own reaction to the contemporary situation: "In the present state of public affairs – which has induced in myself a depression of spirits so different from any other experience of fifty years as to be a new emotion – I no longer feel the enthusiasm necessary to make a literary review what it should be." This was his situation immediately before the war, the coming of which he clearly foresaw in the autumn of 1938 at a time when others preferred to cling to the illusion that peace was still possible. He not only foresaw the war, but seems to have regarded its coming almost as a logical consequence of the moral, political and cultural decline of the day. And he envisaged hardships for those who still strove to carry on the great tradition: "For this immediate future, perhaps for a long way ahead, the continuity of culture may have to be maintained by a very small number of people indeed." A year later Eliot's prophecy seemed to have come true. England was engaged in a desperate war and the future appeared very dark indeed. Darkness is also a prominent theme in "East Coker", reflecting the poet's pessimism and depression.

> O dark dark dark. They all go into the dark,
> The vacant interstellar spaces, the vacant into the vacant,
> The captains, merchant bankers, eminent men of letters,
> The generous patrons of art, the statesmen and the rulers,
> Distinguished civil servants, chairmen of many committees,
> Industrial lords and petty contractors, all go into the dark,
> And dark the Sun and Moon, and the Almanach de Gotha
> And the Stock Exchange Gazette, the Directory of Directors,
> And cold the sense and lost the motive of action.
> And we all go with them, into the silent funeral,
> Nobody's funeral, for there is no one to bury.
>
> (EC: III)

II

There are many allusions to the war in the later *Quartets,* but the pessimism and despair are perhaps most poignantly expressed in the following passage.

Thunder rolled by the rolling stars
Simulates triumphal cars
Deployed in constellated wars
Scorpion fights against the Sun
Until the Sun and Moon go down
Comets weep and Leonids fly
Hunt the heavens and the plains
Whirled in a vortex that shall bring
The world to that destructive fire
Which burns before the ice-cap reigns.
(EC: II)

Probably written during the winter of 1939–1940, these lines certainly have a definite "literal" meaning. There are the "triumphal cars" of the enemy, whose forces could be said, literally, to "hunt the heavens and the plains". The war is regarded as a war between good and evil, between light and darkness: the image of the repulsive and cruel Scorpion is set against the image of the Sun. They fight each other "until the Sun and Moon go down"; darkness prevailing against the light and the world burning itself to death – this is the end that the poet foresees.

The tone of anguish and despair persists in the last two *Quartets,* but there it is also counterbalanced by a more hopeful tone. Eliot stayed in London, suffered the air raids and other hardships of the time, but he also experienced a general strengthening of the morale of the country. An indication of this is to be found in a poem dated the ninth of June, 1940. Published in *Britain at War*, a book which in text and pictures alike is a manifestation of confident English patriotism, the poem, called "Defense of the Islands", is in effect an address to all the men and women fighting for the freedom of Britain.

Let these memorials of built stone – music's
enduring instrument, of many centuries of
patient cultivation of the earth, of English
verse

be joined with the memory of this defense of
the islands

and the memory of those appointed to the grey
ships – battleship, merchantman, trawler –

contributing their share to the ages' pavement
of British bone on the sea floor

and of those who, in man's newest form of gamble
with death, fight the power of darkness in air
and fire

and of those who have followed their forebears
to Flanders and France, those undefeated in de-
feat, unalterable in triumph, changing nothing
of their ancestors' ways but the weapons

and those again for whom the paths of glory are
the lanes and the streets of Britain:

to say, to the past and the future generations
of our kin and of our speech, that we took up
our positions, in obedience to instructions.[6]

The last lines, inspired by a Spartan loyalty, show the poet's attempt to find a meaning in the contemporary events by regarding them in a wider historical perspective – "to say, to the past and future generations of our kin and of our speech . . ." It is the same kind of purpose in life and in death that is expressed in the last lines of "The Dry Salvages":

We, content at the last
If our temporal reversion nourish
(Not too far from the yew-tree)
The life of significant soil.

Besides the *Quartets,* Eliot published only two poems during the war; one is "Defense of the Islands" and the other, also directly prompted by the war, is called "Poetry in Wartime". Published in 1942 in the same month as "Little Gidding", it seems to reflect certain experiences of Eliot's, gathered in writing the last three *Quartets*. The pathos of the previous poem is here replaced by detached reflection upon the experience of war as subject-matter of poetry. The last two strophes of "Poetry in Wartime" contain something like a definition of poetry:

[6] *Britain at War*, ed. by M. Wheeler, New York, 1941, p. 8.

War is not a life: it is a situation,
One which may neither be ignored nor accepted,
A problem to be met with ambush and stratagem,
Enveloped or scattered.

The enduring is no substitute for the transient,
Neither one for the other. But the abstract conception
Of private experience at its greatest intensity
Becoming universal, which we call "poetry",
May be affirmed in verse.[7]

Eliot's reactions to the war, and the elements of patriotism in his writings from the first years of the war, have been considered here in some detail, not only because the political development from passive depression to confident activity forms the background of and seems to be reflected in Eliot's poetry of that period, but also because the emphasis in the later *Quartets* on the connection between the individual and his people and country seems to be due, at least to some extent, to the experience of the war. "Burnt Norton" is a poem about the way of the individual soul to union with the Divine, and even if this theme remains conspicuous in the later *Quartets* as well, they are also poems about the relation of the individual to his forebears, to his native soil, to his national tradition, and to his Church.

The war seems to have made Eliot conscious of the immediate impact of history, an impact which is manifest in various ways in the later *Quartets*. It is perhaps most obvious in "Little Gidding", containing as it does an allusion to the air raids on London, and Eliot's realization that "history is now and England."

The sense of history reflected in the *Four Quartets* has no doubt developed out of the historical sense discussed in "Tradition and the Individual Talent", but during this development it has become something different. In the essay on tradition and in the poems contemporary with it, Eliot is concerned with the – chiefly aesthetic – apprehension of the past as living in the present and also with the discrepancy between certain aspects of the past and the present; in them he appears as the literary historian analysing and exemplifying the idea of a cultural tradition. The later *Quartets* also illustrate this

[7] Quoted from F. O. Matthiessen, *The Achievement of T. S. Eliot*, 2nd ed., Oxford, 1947, pp. 196 f.

early sense of history, but in them the aesthetic or psychological sense of history is superseded by the teleological problem: Has history a meaning? Is it guided by a divine intention and does it proceed towards a goal? These are questions which were, by implication, raised already in *The Waste Land,* but at that time Eliot's agnosticism made an affirmative answer impossible. When, however, in 1939 the outbreak of the war thrust before him the problem of the meaning of history, Eliot was better equipped to meet it. In the later *Quartets* the problem of history is seen *sub specie aeternitatis* and in the light of Christian revelation, and the central fact of history and its essential meaning is found to be the Incarnation of Christ.

As early as *The Rock,* however, Eliot had approached the question of a Christian philosophy of history. Under the influence of the war the ideas of that play seem to have been further developed and integrated with the psychological and spiritual structure of "Burnt Norton". In the later *Quartets* the problem of history is considered as an extension of the more personal problem of "Burnt Norton" – the meaning of the life of the individual. Accordingly, the categories of time and eternity, of movement and stillness, are extended to apply to the life of nations and civilizations as well as of individuals. In extending the scope of the later *Quartets,* however, Eliot still seems to have relied on his initial source of inspiration – the experience in the garden of Burnt Norton – and thus the continuity and unity of the *Four Quartets* remain unbroken.

III

The "depression of spirits" afflicting Eliot in 1939 turned out to be the kind of depression that so often precedes a spell of creative activity. Though in a sense perfectly objective, as it was related to and apparently caused by the actual national and international situation, Eliot's depression may also have been rooted in the inner rhythm of his creative activity. It may well have been an extension of a psychological pattern, well-known from his earlier life – a pattern described in the essay on Pascal and derived, it would seem at least to some extent, from his experiences in writing *The Waste Land.*

According to Eliot, physical exhaustion and mental depression may not only precede but be favourable to artistic creation and spiritual illumination.[8] Eliot's personal situation was perhaps more desperate in 1922, the year of *The Waste Land,* than in 1939, but his affirmation that this later depression was "so different from any other experience of fifty years as to be a new emotion" indicates the importance attached to it by himself. Though written before he had begun to work on "East Coker", the words "a new emotion" seem to reveal the initial impulse to the writing of the later *Quartets:* to a poet like Eliot an entirely new emotion naturally engenders a demand for expression of this emotion.

The means of expression best suited to the exploration of a new emotion seems, in Eliot's case, to be poetry. On the whole his plays may be regarded as developments and elaborations of ideas, feelings and images first set forth in poetic form. Moreover, there are certain experiences which cannot adequately be conveyed in drama and for which poetry alone is appropriate. Thus Eliot's statement that the war destroyed his interest in writing for the stage,[9] may not only refer to the conditions of theatres and their public during the war, but perhaps to a feeling that drama was an inadequate form for what he wanted to express.

That Eliot was much concerned with the problems of poetic expression may not only be inferred from the pronouncements quoted above, but is apparent from the text of the later *Quartets* themselves. Each venture in poetry, Eliot writes in "East Coker",

> Is a new beginning, a raid on the inarticulate
> With shabby equipment always deteriorating
> In the general mess of imprecision of feeling,
> Undisciplined squads of emotion.

And again in "Little Gidding" V:

> Every phrase and every sentence is an end and a beginning,
> Every poem an epitaph.

Hence it may be relevant to consider briefly some statements in Eliot's subsequent critical writings, which throw some light on the

[8] Vide supra, Chapter II, p. 66.

[9] Lehmann, loc. cit.

composition of the later *Quartets* and on the question why he turned from drama to poetry.

From "Burnt Norton" Eliot went straight on to the writing of *The Family Reunion,* and this play is in many ways to be regarded as an elaboration of themes and images from "Burnt Norton". Though by no means to be identified with Eliot himself, Harry, the main character of the play, has much in common with the speaker of "Burnt Norton", and the central theme of both the poem and the play is the idea of spiritual awakening and rebirth. Accordingly the rose garden imagery recurs in the play, as does much of the more abstract speculation on the nature of time. To Harry as well as to the speaker of "Burnt Norton" the spiritual awakening implies a new attitude towards their own past lives and the realization of a timeless dimension in time. In fact, it is not at all surprising to find the theme of "Burnt Norton" transposed into dramatic form. In the moment of spiritual awakening and change, accompanied by strong emotions and involving new reactions to the surrounding world, there is all the material for a dramatic conflict.

It is that moment itself of change and awakening, however, rather than the permanent results of the moment, that is dramatically effective. *The Family Reunion* ends with Harry's departure on a pilgrimage to unknown places in search of the unknown. Eliot's next play, *The Cocktail Party,* is constructed in the same way. The spectator witnesses the awakening and rebirth of Celia, but of her life after her conversion there is only the brief suggestion of hearsay evidence. *The Elder Statesman,* Eliot's latest play, also links up with the idea of spiritual rebirth involving the discovery of a higher pattern in what seemed a wholly secular life, though there is no attempt in the play to explain what that pattern is. In the later *Quartets,* however, he has attempted to go beyond the initial spiritual experience, beyond the moment of awakening, in order to explore more fully and introspectively a meaning which was completely apprehended only as an overwhelming vision during that moment.

The relation and the difference between "pure" and dramatic poetry are discussed in two of Eliot's late essays, in "Poetry and Drama" (1951) and "The Three Voices of Poetry" (1953). It is significant that while Eliot has a great deal to say about the genesis and composition of his plays, he has little to say about his poetry. Quoting the German poet Gottfried Benn, he speaks of the "creative germ" that is the origin of a pure or lyric poem; a poem "directly expressing the poet's own thoughts and sentiments".[10] He then goes on to develop the idea of such poetry as the verbal realization of such an inarticulate germ of emotional experience. Eliot distinguishes several stages in this creative process. To begin with, the poet may be concerned exclusively with the problem of expression for its own sake; then he may become interested in the reactions of others to the poem he has created, first those of a few friends, and finally also those of the unknown reading public:

> The final handing over, so to speak, of the poem to an unknown audience, for what that audience will make of it, seems to me the consummation of the process begun in solitude and without thought of the audience, the long process of gestation of the poem, because it marks the final separation of the poem from the author. Let the author, at this point, rest in peace.[11]

This appeal to readers and critics to take a poem for what it actually is instead of attempting to connect it with the private world of the poet, seems to confirm the assumption that the *Four Quartets* are based on deeply personal experiences. For although apparently speaking of poetry in general, or the particular variety of poetry which he calls "meditative verse", Eliot is probably thinking very much of the *Quartets*, which may be said to be of a more "meditative" character than anything else he has ever written. This shyness appears even more striking in contrast to the almost ironic candour with which he speaks of his problems in writing *The Family Reunion* and *The Cocktail Party*.[12] Intended from the very beginning for a wider audience, the plays are in a sense more objective and impersonal than are his poems, and hence the author is less reluctant to discuss them. Realizing the futility of attempting to explain the "creative germ" of the later *Quartets*, it is yet important to note and keep in mind the distinction Eliot draws between dramatic and "meditative" verse. This distinction perhaps helps us to understand

[10] "The Three Voices of Poetry", *On Poetry and Poets*, p. 97.

[11] Ibid., pp. 99 f.

[12] "Poetry and Drama", *On Poetry and Poets*, pp. 84 f.

why, in 1939, he abandoned drama for a time and turned to poetry instead. The *Quartets* definitely belong to the kind of poetry in which the poet is primarily meditating with himself, and only secondarily sharing his meditation with his audience. Of dramatic poetry, which can be definitely identified as being "in character", there is hardly a trace. These three kinds of poetry – first, the purely meditative; secondly, poetry addressed to an audience; and thirdly, poetry addressed indirectly to an audience through the minds and speech of imaginary characters – these kinds Eliot calls "the three voices" of poetry. According to his own definitions, the *Quartets* may be said to speak chiefly with the first voice and occasionally also with the second. This division, however, into separate voices is something different from the four voices or parts of the *Quartets,* from what Eliot calls the "contrapuntal arrangement of subject-matter." With the first three voices it is a question of difference of diction and articulation, but the four parts or voices of a quartet are all contained, as it were, in the "meditative" voice.

Implying an intellectual and spiritual structure imposed upon, or read into, history and the life of the individual, the pattern of these four voices in the *Quartets* serves the purpose of reconciling time with the moment of timeless vision, the course of history with an eternal pattern. Any attempt to achieve such a reconciliation in terms of Platonic, Neo-Platonic or Idealist philosophy, tends to entail denial of the temporal world. "Typology", however, in the sense in which this word is used above, means a reconciliation of the temporal and the eternal which denies neither of them but shows their interrelation. It is a method of relating temporal events to each other *sub specie aeternitatis,* of expressing, or explaining, what Eliot calls the "transfiguration" of the temporal world in a timeless pattern (LG: III). In using what may be called a typological structure in the *Four Quartets,* Eliot thus achieves the closest possible integration of theme and form, of subject-matter and structure.

In using this highly complicated intellectual structure, Eliot was perhaps aware that the traditionally poetic elements of the *Quartets* had to be considerably reduced. But the abstract categories are counterbalanced by the strong element of emotional experience embodied for example in the rose garden symbol. Elements of this symbol recur throughout the later *Quartets* as if to show the poet's need to revert to the initial illumination or inspiration that prompted the whole sequence of poems. The moment of change, of awakening and rebirth thus becomes, not a single event in the life of man, but a moment repeated over and over again, and each moment means a new beginning.

The study of the later *Quartets* that follows is chiefly confined to the two aspects of, first, the development of the theme of time and eternity, and, secondly, the "contrapuntal" or "typological" structure of the poems. Close commentary on each image and passage, such as was offered in the foregoing chapter, is not attempted here.

CHAPTER VII

The Later Quartets

I

"East Coker", the second of the *Quartets,* was thus written under circumstances very different from those relating to the writing of "Burnt Norton". Not completed until the Easter of 1940, it shows the impact of the war on Eliot's mind and feelings, but it also forms a direct continuation of the first of the *Quartets.* And once the structure and mode of expression used in "Burnt Norton" are grasped, the subsequent poems are by no means so difficult to understand, using as they do much the same language and imagery as "Burnt Norton" in order to develop ideas and feelings which in many cases are anticipated in that poem. Critics have discovered some allusions in "East Coker", literary or to actual places and events, but none of these allusions are particularly obscure or questionable, and long passages of the poem can be fully comprehended without detailed commentary. In view of these facts the following analysis is chiefly confined to the development of the idea of time and eternity.

"In my beginning is my end" – this opening phrase of "East Coker" is repeated or echoed throughout the poem, and recurs in the last line in inverted form: "In my end is my beginning." The fundamental problem raised in the poem is in fact inherent in the word "end": Does time and history proceed towards an end in the sense of a goal, a final purpose, or is "end" to be understood merely as a close, as death and annihilation? This theme Eliot had anticipated already in "Burnt Norton" and *The Family Reunion.* In "Burnt Norton" he hints at the resolution of the antithesis of beginning and end in the lines,

And the end and the beginning were always there
Before the beginning and after the end.
And all is always now.

(BN: V)

In *The Family Reunion* the words are used in much the same way as later in "East Coker". On the eve of his departure for a spiritual quest, Harry speaks of a moment of happiness, a feeling "as if I had come home", adding the words, "This is like an end". To this Agatha replies, "And a beginning".[1] The road of Harry's quest is not described in the play, but it is pursued in the later *Quartets*.

In my beginning is my end. In succession
Houses rise and fall, crumble, are extended,
Are removed, destroyed, restored, or in their place
Is an open field, or a factory, or a by-pass.
Old stone to new building, old timber to new fires,
Old fires to ashes, and ashes to the earth
Which is already flesh, fur and faeces,
Bone of man and beast, cornstalk and leaf.

The imagery of this opening passage suggests an idea of recurrence of social and biological life and history. "Houses rise and fall", in their fall providing space and material for new houses, and in the same way the bodies of men and beasts grow and die, become ashes and earth, the soil of plants that will nourish future generations. Houses may here be taken to imply everything built by man to survive him: kingdoms, institutions, customs and ways of feeling, of thought and of expression. Thus both the natural and social life of man is subject to growth and decay, and these changes seem to follow each other cyclically. This idea of a cyclic evolution is of course very old and widespread and it is wholly irrelevant to trace its actual sources in this particular case beyond what has been said in a previous chapter of this study. What is of significance here is the application of the idea to a particular context. Already the pronoun "my" in the first line of the poem – "In my beginning is my end" – indicates that the speaker, or poet, is personally involved in what is

[1] *The Family Reunion*, p. 105. Cf. Gardner, H., "Four Quartets: A Commentary", *T. S. Eliot. A Study of his Writings by Several Hands*, ed. by B. Rajan, London, 1947, p. 64.

subsequently said. And the title of the poem emphasizes the same thing: East Coker is the name of a Somerset village which was the homestead of the Eliot family before they emigrated to America in the seventeenth century.[2]

Eliot is said to have visited East Coker in August, 1937,[3] and he has himself confirmed that the imagery of the First Section of the poem is "taken from the village itself".[4] Thus the houses that "rise and fall" take on a new significance; they were the homes of his forebears and in their place is now "an open field, or a factory, or a by-pass". Returning to the village of his ancestors, the poet found no trace of their homes, and yet both they and their houses literally form the ground on which the present inhabitants of the village live and build. Emigrating to America, Eliot's ancestors interrupted this progress of generations springing from and returning to the same soil. Their departure formed a beginning on a larger scale, the end of which was achieved when one of their descendants crossed the Atlantic in the opposite direction, became a British subject as they had once been, and finally made a pilgrimage to the place from which they had once departed. In visiting East Coker, Eliot seems to have felt that he had come full circle, as it were, that he had completed a cyclic movement which was different from that of "houses" and generations only in covering a longer space of time – three hundred years. Thus the phrase, "in my beginning is my end" implies a home-coming to the place of departure of his forebears, a reversion to the sources and origins of the poet's family, as in "Burnt Norton" there is a reversion to the childhood and early life of the poet. In "East Coker" the perspective has widened from the individual's life to that of his forebears, the search for origins is pressed one step further backwards in time.

Eliot's return to East Coker, however, has implications beyond the history of his ancestors. The First Section of the poem contains

[2] See J. Hayward, notes to the French transl. of the *Quartets*, Paris, 1950, p. 134.

[3] See Grover Smith, *T. S. Eliot's Poetry and Plays*, Chicago, 1956, p. 264.

[4] Häusermann, H. W., "'East Coker' by T. S. Eliot", *English Studies*, Vol. 23, 1941, p. 109. The reminiscences from Friedrich Gerstäcker's story *Germelshausen*, confirmed in the same letter, seem to contribute very little to the understanding of "East Coker".

a passage in archaic spelling which has been identified as a quotation from *The Boke Named The Gouvernour* (1531) by Sir Thomas Elyot.[5] This namesake of the author of the *Four Quartets* is said to have been born in East Coker, and is, though distantly, related to the family of Thomas Stearns Eliot.[6] However, the significance of the reference to this contemporary of Henry VIII and of Sir Thomas More lies not merely in the personal connection between him and the present poet. As suggested by James Johnson Sweeney, who first identified the quotations from *The Gouvernour*, Eliot seems to feel a certain spiritual kinship with his sixteenth century namesake; their literary, political and ecclesiastical interests have a great deal in common. But comparing himself and his own time with his predecessor and his time – the Renaissance – Eliot is also aware of great differences, Sweeney maintains:

> Something is amiss with contemporary civilization, its mode of conduct or philosophy of life. The elder Elyot had tried through *The Boke named The Gouvernour* to suggest for his period a pattern of harmonious living and concord based on the Platonic ideals of the Renaissance. The younger man, faced by the darkness of the present moment [1941], feels a certain irony in the parallels which he recognizes between his own interests and those of his precursor. In spite of all the confidence in intellectual progress of Sir Thomas Elyot's time, it is evident, today, that the neo-classical, individualist approach of the Renaissance led to a mechanical view and a spiritual poverty and produced the cataclysm which has overwhelmed the present age.[7]

[5] Sweeney, J. J., "East Coker: A Reading", (1941), *T. S. Eliot. A Selected Critique*, ed. by L. Unger, New York, 1948, p. 397. Sweeney quotes the relevant passage from *The Governour* (Book I, Ch. XXI): "It is diligently to be noted that the associatinge of man and woman in daunsing, they bothe obseruinge one nombre and tyme in their meuynges, was not begonne without a speciall consideration, as well for the *necessarye coniunction* of those *two persones*, as for the intimation of sondry vertues, whiche be by them represented. And for as moche as *by the association of a man and a woman in daunsinge may be signified matrimonie*, I coulde in declarynge *the dignitie and commoditie of that sacrament* make intiere volumes [...] In euery daunse, of a moste auncient custome, there daunseth to gether a man and a woman, *holding eche other by the hande or the arme, whiche betokeneth concorde*."

[6] Hayward, p. 135; cf. the letter quoted by Häusermann.

[7] Sweeney, p. 398.

The Platonic ideals seem irrelevant in this context, and the point of the allusion would rather consist in the contrasting of two political periods. At the time of Sir Thomas Elyot, England was rising to world-wide power, but in 1940 her very existence was threatened. Thus the period in English history beginning with the Renaissance and going up to the second world war forms a progress from birth and growth to decline and death, from beginning to end. At the beginning of this cycle is the elder Thomas Elyot, and at the end, which in a circle coincides with the beginning, is the younger Thomas Eliot. As a poetic illustration of this point which is both a beginning and an end, Eliot has chosen the village of East Coker.

The quotation from *The Gouvernour* has other implications as well. In an open field where perhaps stood the house of one of his ancestors, the poet sees a ghostlike vision on a summer midnight. This vision seems more in the nature of poetic invention than of actual experience. The poet sees a group of country folk dancing round a bonfire and his comments on the dance derive from *The Gouvernour*:

> The association of man and woman
> In daunsinge, signifying matrimonie –
> A dignified and commodious sacrament.
> Two and two, necessarye coniunction,
> Holding eche other by the hand or the arm
> Whiche betokeneth concorde.

In "Burnt Norton" the dance was used as a symbol of timeless movement, of the reconciliation of movement and stillness. In "East Coker" I, however, the dance has a slightly different meaning. It implies ordered and regular movement, but not stillness. It is in effect a symbol of the cyclic movement of human life:

> Keeping time,
> Keeping the rhythm in their dancing
> As in their living in the living seasons
> The time of the seasons and the constellations
> The time of milking and the time of harvest
> The time of the coupling of man and woman
> And that of beasts. Feet rising and falling.
> Eating and drinking. Dung and death.

This is the world of time – an illustration of "the enchainment of past and future". The "feet rising and falling" seem to symbolize in a different context the same feeling of imprisonment in time as Agatha in *The Family Reunion* describes in the words:

> And then I was only my own feet walking
> Away, down a concrete corridor
> In a dead air. Only feet walking . . .[8]

In using the symbol of the dance here, Eliot no doubt intends the reader to remember the dance of "Burnt Norton", and to remember both these passages when he comes to the line in "East Coker" III,

> So the darkness shall be the light, and the stillness the dancing.

Though symbolic of the cyclic progress of life and history, the image of the dance in "East Coker" I, one feels, must stand in some relation to the symbolic use of the same image in "Burnt Norton". This feeling induced in the reader is no doubt intended by the poet as an anticipation of the subsequent spiritual interpretation within the poem of its First Section.

The idea of the cyclic movement of history in "East Coker" does not constitute a philosophy of history in the sense that Eliot regards the endless repetition of identical events as constituting a meaning. Neither does he, as some critics have suggested, advocate a theory of determinism. The beginning and end of the cycles described is "dung and death", but to Eliot death is not the ultimate answer and solution to the problem of life. Death is only the first step towards the solution. No end within time means a goal or a purpose. The meaning of time lies beyond the temporal dimension, and hence each end in time means either death or a new beginning.

The poet's attempt to break through the dimension of time and cyclic recurrence is indicated in the concluding lines of "East Coker" I. After the nocturnal vision in the open field the poet feels the coming of dawn; he becomes aware of the sea and the wind – symbols to be developed later in the *Quartets*. He is preparing for a new departure, a new beginning, but on a different level and in a different dimension.

[8] *The Family Reunion*, p. 107.

The Section of "East Coker" that follows shows the connection between the poem and Eliot's situation and state of mind at the beginning of the war. The theme is autumn, "late November", and aging, developed in a passage by the poet ironically characterized as a "study in a worn-out poetical fashion", and then in a more straightforward and prosaic style.

The remarkable passage which begins Section II describes a kind of disintegration of the established order of the seasons and a violent upheaval of the whole cosmic world. The Zodiac is at war, sun and moon "go down", comets and meteors "weep" and "fly". Everything is

> Whirled in a vortex that shall bring
> The world to that destructive fire
> Which burns before the ice-cap reigns.

This whirling vortex appears in sharp contrast to the dignified and ordered motion of the dance in the First Section and it is also a contrast to and denial of the cyclic patterns alluded to in that Section. Behind this apocalyptic vision lies the experience of the war, as suggested in the preceding chapter, and the actual war is enlarged into the image of the "constellated wars".[9]

The following, more prosaic passage gives further explanation of the "disturbance" of the autumnal peace. According to traditional conceptions the autumn of human life should be a period of peace and serenity, but instead Eliot, looking forward at the age of fifty-two to such serenity and peace, finds himself in a state of deep depression and anxiety. In the same way the society and civilization in which he lives should be expected, at the end of a development covering about four centuries, to have acquired something of the "wisdom of age", but instead it has thrown itself into a war which, in its early days, appeared more cruel and desperate than any before it. Thus no doubt the poet feels that the cyclic theory of life and history has broken down and been disproved. His return to the point of departure, to all that of which the name of East Coker is a symbol, is no real home-coming, no conclusion, no goal. Like Dante at the beginning of the *Inferno* he finds himself "in a dark wood",

[9] Cf. Bodelsen, C. A., *T. S. Eliot's Four Quartets*, Copenhagen, 1958, pp. 64 ff.

and the way out of darkness is not through another cycle in time, but through descent into still greater depths of darkness.

Such then appears the subject-matter of "East Coker". It is the life and history of Eliot and his forebears, of his country and its cultural tradition, and in particular the crisis that the events of 1939–1940 brought into Eliot's life and the lives of those among whom he lived. Referring to the categories of Dantean allegory, we may also call this the "literal" meaning of the poem. And in terms of Christian morality the Second Section seems to say that any confidence in "the knowledge derived from experience" is illusory and deceptive; the only real knowledge is that of divine revelation, and waiting for revelation the soul cannot hope to acquire any virtue but one:

> The only wisdom we can hope to acquire
> Is the wisdom of humility: humility is endless.

The two concluding lines of the Second Section,

> The houses are all gone under the sea,

and

> The dancers are all gone under the hill,

refer back to the imagery of the First Section. Both the houses and the dancers were pictured as integrated with the pattern of perpetual recurrence, but since that pattern appeared to be false, the houses are submerged and the dancers disappear. Instead of the beginning of a new cycle in time, the poet is faced by emptiness, destruction and darkness.

In the First Section of "East Coker" Eliot considers time past – the past of the Eliot family and the past of England – in contrast to time present, a period of crisis, which is the subject of further consideration in the Second Section. In the Third, the attention is directed towards the future. The poet speaks of "hope" and "waiting" and the phrase "shall be" occurs twice. The immediate future, however, is nothing but darkness:

> O dark dark dark. They all go into the dark,
> The vacant interstellar spaces, the vacant into the vacant,

It is the darkness which, the poet feared, would overcome England and the European civilization when the war was over, the fighting "Until the Sun and Moon go down" (EC: II). Thus the poet sees no hope for the future. The hope lies beyond the dimension of time in the pattern of timeless, divine meanings.

The whole Section is a sustained theme on the deep ground bass of the dark night of the soul, which as a whole owes much to the mystic teaching of the "negative way", especially the teaching of St. John of the Cross. Among the few literary reminiscences of the Section, there is an allusion to Milton's *Samson Agonistes,* which reinforces the tone of hopelessness and despair.[10]

The speaker's feeling of darkness and emptiness is set forth in three elaborate metaphors:

As, in a theatre,
The lights are extinguished, for the scene to be changed
- - -
Or when, under ether, the mind is conscious but conscious of nothing –

The middle metaphor is familiar to the reader of "Burnt Norton":

Or as, when an underground train, in the tube, stops too
long between stations
And the conversation rises and slowly fades into silence
And you see behind every face the mental emptiness deepen
Leaving only the growing terror of nothing to think about;

Here as well as in "Burnt Norton" III the scene from the underground train is used to illustrate the emptiness and twilight of temporal life, and in both poems it is followed by a different kind of darkness – "the darkness of God".

[10] O dark, dark, dark, amid the blaze of noon,
Irrecoverably dark, total eclipse
Without all hope of day!
O first created Beam, and thou great Word,
"Let there be light, and light was over all;"
Why am I thus bereav'd thy prime decree?
The sun to me is dark
And silent as the moon.
When she deserts the night,
Hid in her vacant interlunar cave.

Samson Agonistes, 80–89. *The Poetical Works of John Milton,* IV, London, 1801, pp. 367 f. Cf. Preston, R., *"Four Quartets" Rehearsed,* London, 1946, p. 29.

In "Burnt Norton" this "darkness of God" is described, in accordance with the teaching of St. John of the Cross, as a progressive elimination or negation, first of "the world of sense", then of "the world of fancy" and finally of "the world of spirit". A similar tripartition is found in the corresponding passage in "East Coker": "I said to my soul, be still, and wait without hope" . . . "wait without love" . . . "wait without thought". But at the end of this abnegation and this waiting comes the illumination:

> So the darkness shall be the light, and the stillness the dancing.
> Whisper of running streams, and winter lightning.
> The wild thyme unseen and the wild strawberry,
> The laughter in the garden, echoed ecstasy
> Not lost, but requiring, pointing to the agony
> Of death and birth.

Also in the description of this positive experience, some images from "Burnt Norton" recur. The conjunction of light, stillness and dancing, the "laughter in the garden" and the "echoed ecstasy" are all elements connected with the mystic vision in the rose garden. The other images, here appearing for the first time in Eliot's poetry, may be interpreted as symbols of similar experiences, as natural objects revealing something transcendental. Eliot's tendency to use such highly personal imagery in the passages of greatest emotional intensity indicates that, though apparently concerned with more general human issues, he is very much dependent upon his own particular and personal experience throughout the *Quartets*. The recurrence of images from "Burnt Norton" in "East Coker" is no doubt intended to contribute to the unity and continuity of these poems together, but it may also be a reflection of the poet's feeling of the interpenetration of past and present as expressed in the opening lines of "Burnt Norton". Each new experience is saturated with the memory of preceding experiences, which together colour and modify every future experience. In the same way the major images of the *Quartets* give, by repetition and recurrence, unity and continuity to the mind of the speaker, and by being modified through interrelation with other images, they reflect the development of the speaker's mind. Their recurrence in the speaker's meditation may in fact be regarded as a symbol of his faculty of memory, as an illustration of his consciousness of time, as giving substance to his intellectual speculation on the problem of time and history. Interwoven with images belonging to the speaker's personal memory, the experience of the dark night in "East Coker" III is thus to be regarded in the first place as the speaker's – or poet's – own experience even if it is intended to have, and to a certain extent has, a wider application.

The meaning of this experience of darkness is to be found, in terms of Dantean allegory, on the anagogical or mystical level of interpretation. The state of depression and crisis, personal and national, which forms the literal meaning of the poem, is here seen as an affliction imposed by God, a kind of visitation of the Almighty. As the end and death of one cycle originates each new cycle in the temporal sphere, so also the life of the soul is regenerated by suffering, by the spiritual death of the dark night. Each new beginning involves "the agony / Of death and birth".

In the Fourth Section of "East Coker" there are also some reminiscences of the imagery of "Burnt Norton":

> The fever sings in mental wires.
> If to be warmed, then I must freeze
> And quake in frigid purgatorial fires
> Of which the flame is roses, and the smoke is briars.

There are the roses and the fever that "sings in mental wires" recalling

> The trilling wire in the blood
> Sings below inveterate scars
> (BN: II)

Both the roses and the trilling wire are associated with the theme of love and desire in "Burnt Norton", but here these symbols are "transfigured" in a religious pattern. The symbols of human love and passion are related to the Passion of Christ. The allegorical or typical level of interpretation, barely hinted at in "Burnt Norton", is thus developed in the Fourth Section of "East Coker". As observed by many critics, the five stanzas of that Section are highly reminiscent, both in form and imagery, of the Metaphysical poetry of the seventeenth century. The elaborate conceits of the surgeon, patient, nurse and hospital are integrated into a complete allegory in the normal sense of this term. The patient is man and his surgeon Christ; the nurse is the Church and the hospital the world. The whole Section celebrates the Passion of Christ – indicated already in the first line by the epithet "wounded" – and it was written for the Good Friday of 1940.[11] Its function in "East Coker" and the *Four Quartets* as a whole seems to be to connect the idea of human suffering generally and more particularly the idea of the dark night of the soul with the Passion of Christ. Crucified, dead, buried and descended into Hell, Christ passed through the darkest of all nights, and this passage is the antitype and fulfilment of all the types of purgative suffering in the world. This is the meaning, on the typical or allegorical level, of the dark and apparently hopeless situation of the poet and his country which forms the literal meaning of "East Coker".

Another aspect of the same Section is that of sin and Redemption. The "ruined millionaire" is Adam after the fall and his curse is Original Sin. As man's knowledge of sin increases, he approaches salvation: "to be restored, our sickness must grow worse." As Redemption was achieved through the Passion and Resurrection of Christ, so, at the end of the dark night, man may hope for grace and illumination.

In the last Section of "East Coker" the poet turns again to his actual situation and the problem of giving it poetic expression:

> So here I am, in the middle way, having had twenty years –
> Twenty years largely wasted, the years of *l'entre deux guerres* –
> Trying to learn to use words, and every attempt
> Is a wholly new start,

The "middle way" is of course an allusion to the very first line of the *Inferno*, and is but another instance of the spirit of Dante pervading the *Quartets*, and in "trying to learn to use words", Eliot surely regards Dante as one of the great masters, as one of the "men whom one cannot hope / To emulate".

As in "Burnt Norton" V the antithesis of time and eternity, of motion and stillness, was reflected in the discussion of the art of poetry, so also the idea of cyclic time and new beginnings in "East

[11] Hayward, p. 138.

Coker" is reflected in the corresponding passage of this poem. What there is to be discovered and expressed in poetry, has already been discovered and expressed several times. The life-work of one poet has to be done over again by his successors. Each new effort in poetry means a new beginning which implies

> the fight to recover what has been lost
> And found and lost again and again: and now, under conditions
> That seem unpropitious. But perhaps neither gain nor loss.
> For us, there is only the trying. The rest is not our business.

Under the unpropitious circumstances of living in a largely secularized society engaged in war, Eliot tries to recover the Christian vision of the world, expressed by so many great authors before him, but apparently lost to modern man.

The last paragraph of the poem sums up the progress made in it, and shows the way in which "East Coker" is connected with "Burnt Norton", but also the way in which it goes beyond "Burnt Norton". "Home is where one starts from" – this idea seems applicable both to the experience of the author of "East Coker" visiting the native home of his forebears and to the experience of the author of "Burnt Norton" meditating on recollections of his childhood. There is a difference, however. The momentary illumination in the garden of Burnt Norton is not sufficient:

> Not the intense moment
> Isolated, with no before and after,
> But a lifetime burning in every moment
> And not the lifetime of one man only
> But of old stones that cannot be deciphered.

It is the moment of timeless vision that begins the spiritual quest of the whole sequence of *Quartets*, but to bear fruit that timeless moment has to be seen in the perspective of time and history, of the lifetime of the poet and of the history of his family and country. (The undecipherable stones are the tombstones of the churchyard of East Coker.)[12] The following lines express the same idea:

> There is a time for the evening under starlight,
> A time for the evening under lamplight
> (The evening with the photograph album).

[12] Hayward, p. 138.

The evening under starlight surely is life in the cosmic aspect of eternity; the other, in the more personal aspect of time, of human civilization and its memories of the past; and both are necessary. But, the poet goes on to say, Love, in the *Quartets* the essence of the Divine, is beyond time and space, and each new beginning in space and time must transcend its original sphere and move "into another intensity" – an intensity not of this world.

"East Coker" is not conclusive in the sense that "Burnt Norton" is. In writing "East Coker" Eliot had begun to contemplate a sequence of four poems, which eventually became the *Four Quartets*,[13] and the last three of them constitute one sustained effort which does not reach its conclusion until the end of "Little Gidding". The last lines of "East Coker" lead on to "The Dry Salvages", anticipating some of the major images of that poem – the waves and vast waters. The last sentence, "In my end is my beginning", an inversion of the opening sentence, foreshadows the message of the following poem: "Fare forward, voyagers."

II

"The Dry Salvages" in effect continues the meditative stream of "East Coker". The idea of human life and history as an unending series of new beginnings is developed in new and powerful metaphors, and the idea of the manifestation of the timeless in time achieves its fullest expression within the *Quartets* in the passage on Incarnation in the last Section. The poetic qualities of "The Dry Salvages" have been differently judged; Matthiessen sees in it "the most thrilling transition of the whole series [of the *Quartets*]"[14] while one writer rashly assures his readers in effect that as a poem "The Dry Salvages" fails.[15] Be that as it may, in "The Dry Salvages"

[13] Lehmann, loc. cit.

[14] Matthiessen, F. O., *The Achievement of T. S. Eliot*, 2nd ed. Oxf. Univ. Press, 1947, p. 186.

[15] Davie, D., "T. S. Eliot: The End of an Era", *Twentieth Century*, Vol. 159, 1956, pp. 350–362.

Eliot makes much clearer than elsewhere in the *Four Quartets* his ideas of time, history and eternity.

The first part of Section I forms a kind of overture, and introduces the image of the river, an image which, however, is not subsequently developed in the *Quartets*. On the literal level of interpretation the river has been identified as the Mississippi, the river of Eliot's childhood spent in St. Louis. Eliot's attachment to his childhood environment and the deep and lasting impression the Mississippi has made on him, can be noticed in some of his critical writings and other pronouncements,[16] and the lines in "The Dry Salvages" about the rhythm of the river which "was present in the nursery bedroom" and "In the rank ailanthus of the April dooryard", seem in the nature of personal recollections. But the river is also a symbol of much wider significance. "Untamed", "implacable", "reminder / Of what men choose to forget", the river seems to symbolize the dark forces in man and mankind, the untamed forces of nature apparently conquered by civilization but in fact "waiting, watching and waiting". But the river has also traditionally been used as a symbol of the onward and irrevocable movement of time, and retaining this symbolic meaning in "The Dry Salvages" it may be interpreted to symbolize the "inner" time of man and mankind, their sense of time and history, their halfconscious or unconscious memories of ages long past, of times when the river was not yet "tamed".

The idea and experience of time implied in the opening passage of "The Dry Salvages" may thus be regarded as an extension of the theme of time in "East Coker", which in turn was an extension of the same theme in "Burnt Norton". It is a development and extension of the idea, first from within the limits of the individual personality to his family and country, from the life of one man to the time of history, and then to the wider circle of mankind as a whole, and from there beyond the limits of what we call history, beyond recorded time. In this vast perspective the sense of direction in time vanishes, and the limited and explorable past of the individual and

[16] See "The Eliot Family and St. Louis", Appendix to an address delivered by Eliot at Washington University on June 9, 1953, prepared by the Department of English. *Washington University Studies*, N. S., Language and Literature, no. 23, St. Louis, 1953, pp. 27 ff.

the community in which he lives is merged in the unlimited and unknowable totality of the human race. Accordingly, the symbol of the river is naturally followed by the symbol of the sea.

> The river is within us, the sea is all about us.

The sea is clearly a symbol of time in this wider meaning. The "tolling bell" of the sea

> Measures time not our time, rung by the unhurried
> Ground swell, a time
> Older than the time of chronometers, older
> Than time counted by anxious worried women
> Lying awake, calculating the future,
> Trying to unweave, unwind, unravel
> And piece together the past and the future

As the symbol is developed later in the same poem, the sea is not only the time of a past infinitely removed, but it also implies an endless future. It is, that is to say, all time. It is temporal existence seen in the widest possible perspective; so wide, in fact, as to appear similar to eternity:

> And the ground swell, that is and was from the beginning.

But the sea does not stand for eternity in the sense of timelessness. That is an altogether different dimension, to be apprehended by those sailing the sea, but not related to the sea itself. The bell of the sea measures time, but it also speaks with the voice of annunciation, as appears from the Second Section of the poem.

Before pursuing the spiritual implications of the sea and the bell, it may be well to consider these symbols on the "literal" level of meaning. "The Dry Salvages" is connected with Eliot's personal background partly through the imagery derived from the Mississippi and St. Louis, as has just been pointed out, but the title of the poem indicates that the essential connection lies elsewhere. The name of The Dry Salvages is explained by Eliot himself in a note appended to the title. They are "a small group of rocks, with a beacon", off the coast of Massachusetts, a district with which Eliot is familiar since his undergraduate years at Harvard, when he was a fervent yachtsman.[17] As the last piece of land that the sailor sees

[17] Hayward, p. 139.

before setting out on the open sea, the Dry Salvages aptly symbolize the point of departure. Though derived from Eliot's own experience, these rocks and their beacon symbolize the landmarks of any voyager sailing on any sea at any time.

The imagery of the First Section is carried on into the next. To the image of the sea are added those of voyaging and sailors, and the sailor setting out on the sea of time is a metaphor of man on his voyage from birth to death – a metaphor as old as poetry itself, here through its entire and probably intentional lack of originality giving to the whole passage a wider and deeper human appeal. This voyaging is a movement which becomes one with the rhythm of the ground swell, with "the trailing / Consequence of further days and hours", and to the question where there is an end of all this, the only answer is, "There is no end, but addition". Here the poet returns to the problem of the meaning of history, of the progress of time, and the Second Section of "The Dry Salvages" contains the most explicit statements concerning this problem within the whole of the *Quartets*.

The idea of time symbolized by the sea retains something of the idea of cyclic recurrence introduced in "East Coker". In the First Section of "The Dry Salvages" Eliot speaks of "hints of earlier and other creation" tossed up by the sea, but this idea of recurrence is submerged in the waste of flux and change that is the time of the sea. And that time has no meaning, leads nowhere:

> We cannot think of a time that is oceanless
> Of an ocean not littered with wastage
> Or of a future that is not liable
> Like the past, to have no destination.

The same idea returns later in the same Section. The past is not a mere sequence, not even development; for the idea of development is

> a partial fallacy
> Encouraged by superficial notions of evolution,
> Which becomes, in the popular mind, a means of disowning the past.

Thus, though in Eliot's view history has no predestined end, not even in the sense of progressing towards higher forms of evolution, it is nevertheless not without some meaning, some warnings – hence the allusion to the fog-horn and the bell-buoy – a warning, and an "annunciation".

The complicated pattern of rhymes in the sestina beginning "The Dry Salvages" II strongly reinforces the emphasis on the word "annunciation" appearing as the last word in the first, third and sixth stanzas. First, there is the "calamitous annunciation", a reminder and warning of the perils of the life of the sailor. Then "the bell of the last annunciation", the harbinger of death. Finally, there is "the one Annunciation" of the coming of Christ. The one Annunciation is prefigured in the earlier ones; death is "the final addition" after which the sailor's voyage in time is completed, and the annunciation of death is the annunciation of the liberation of the soul from this mortal coil. It foreshadows that moment of intersection of time with the timeless which is death, as the one Annunciation foreshadows the unique intersection – the Incarnation of Christ. The words "bell" and "annunciation" are themselves examples of "points of intersection" in the musical sense of this term.[18] On the literal level of interpretation the bell of annunciation is the actual sea bell mentioned in "The Dry Salvages" I; in the Second Section it is given various symbolic meanings, one of which refers to the life of Christ. Thus the idea of annunciation serves to indicate the typical or allegorical level of meaning in "The Dry Salvages", at the same time anticipating the full statement of this meaning in the final Section of the poem, the subject of which is Incarnation.

The only meaning or purpose in life and history apprehended by those sailing on the sea of time, lies in the annunciations. Since their voyage has no end or destination in time, its meaning lies in another dimension momentarily revealed by the "clamour of the bell". In the second part of "The Dry Salvages" II, Eliot speaks of these revelations as the "moments of happiness" or "the sudden illumination" recalling the moment in the rose garden – "Sudden in a shaft of sunlight" (BN: V). That moment involved recollections of the past experience of the speaker, but through the presence in the garden of some others, perhaps the shadows of the speaker's forebears, that moment was linked with a wider past "of many generations":

[18] See *On Poetry and Poets*, p. 32. Cf. supra, p. 139.

I have said before
That the past experience revived in the meaning
Is not the experience of one life only
But of many generations – not forgetting
Something that is probably quite ineffable:
The backward look behind the assurance
Of recorded history, the backward half-look
Over the shoulder, towards the primitive terror.

It is the same idea that was expressed in the words:

Not the intense moment
Isolated, with no before and after,
But a lifetime burning in every moment
And not the lifetime of one man only
But of old stones that cannot be deciphered.
(EC: V)

All the moments of timeless insight mentioned in the *Quartets* appear as parallels to or reflections of the moment in the rose garden, and throughout the *Quartets* Eliot strives to bring the meaning apprehended in that moment to bear on the life of time past and time future. Here in "The Dry Salvages" it is connected with a past so far removed that it cannot be seen except for "the backward half-look / Over the shoulder, towards the primitive terror". And the primitive terror is the threat of the river, the river that is "untamed and intractable", "waiting, watching and waiting" (DS: I).

In the Third Section of "The Dry Salvages" the poet is chiefly concerned with the moral aspects of the voyage on the sea of time. It is irrelevant to attempt to limit the moral meaning of any of the *Quartets* to any specific virtue in the traditional sense. This meaning is rather a question of attitudes and of the motives of action. In "The Dry Salvages", as to some extent also in "East Coker", the chief virtue is the untiring effort required at each new venture out on the sea of time, implied in the exhortation, "Fare forward, voyagers!" And the motive of action should be, not the result, but the value inherent in right action as such:

And do not think of the fruit of action.

Spoken by Krishna admonishing Arjuna, these words are in fact a quotation from the *Bhagavad-Gita*: "To action alone hast thou a right and never at all to its fruit; let not the fruits of action be thy motive; neither let there be in thee any attachment to inaction." [19] This saying should be regarded in the light of the moral teaching of the *Gita* as a whole, the ethical message of which has been summarized by Sarvepalli Radhakrishnan in the following words:

> The *Gītā* is a comprehensive Yoga-śāstra (treatise on *yoga*), large, flexible, many-sided, which includes various phases of the self's development and ascent into the Divine. The different *yogas* are special applications of the inner discipline which leads to the liberation of the self and to a new understanding of the unity and meaning of mankind. This goal of union with God may be attained by *jñāna-yoga* (the way of knowledge), *bhakti-yoga* (the way of devotion), or *karma-yoga* (the way of action). Knowledge, devotion, and work are complementary both when we seek the goal and after we attain it.[20]

On the whole, the *Quartets* emphasize the ways of knowledge and devotion rather than the way of action, but in the Christian doctrine as well as in the *Gita*, good works form an essential complement to faith and love. And the way of action is also a means of liberation from the "enchainment" of time:

> And right action is freedom
> From past and future also.
> (DS: V)

The fare-forward theme in "The Dry Salvages" III seems to contain other allusions as well. S. Musgrove has interpreted Eliot's use of the theme as a "profound denial" of Walt Whitman's "progressive optimism" as expressed for example in "Song of the Open Road": [21]

> Of the progress of the souls of men and women along the grand
> roads of the universe, all other progress is the needed
> emblem and sustenance.
> Forever alive, forever forward,[22]

[19] *Bhagavad-Gita*, Ch. II, 47. *A Source Book in Indian Philosophy*, ed. by S. Radhakrishnan and C. A. Moore, Princeton, 1957, p. 110.

[20] Ibid., p. 102.

[21] Musgrove, S., *T. S. Eliot and Walt Whitman*, Wellington, 1952, pp. 54 f.

[22] Whitman, W., *Leaves of Grass*, New York, 1919, Vol. I, p. 188.

Eliot's "fare forward!" may also be set against Baudelaire's "En avant!" in the poem, "Le Voyage":

> L'un court, et l'autre se tapit
> Pour tromper l'ennemi vigilant et funeste,
> Le Temps! Il est, hélas! des coureurs sans répit,
>
> Comme le Juif errant et comme les apôtres,
> A qui rien ne suffit, ni wagon ni vaisseau,
> Pour fuir ce rétiaire infâme; il en est d'autres
> Qui savent le tuer sans quitter leur berceau.
>
> Lorsqu'enfin il mettra le pied sur notre échine,
> Nous pourrons espérer et crier: En avant! [23]

Again, the allusion is based on a contrast: While Baudelaire is concerned with the escape from time, "the enemy", Eliot is concerned with the redemption of time in the Pauline sense.[24]

The fare-forward theme may also have implications on the anagogical level of interpretation. In the following lines Eliot seems to say that each new departure in time is a departure from one's own self:

> Fare forward, you who think that you are voyaging;
> You are not those who saw the harbour
> Receding, or those who will disembark.

Correspondingly, during the mortal life of man, his soul undergoes a number of changes and deaths, all of which are prefigurations of final death and the rebirth into eternity. In its most specific form this kind of change is known, within the *Quartets*, as the psycho-spiritual experience of the dark night of the soul. However, the implication may be even wider. "Those who saw the harbour / Receding" may be interpreted as the men and women of past generations and the voyage as the endless progress of mankind and history.

The tone of the Third Section of "The Dry Salvages" may, generally speaking, be said to be in harmony with the Christian teaching of the *Quartets*, but the introduction of ideas derived from Hinduism and quotations from the *Bhagavad-Gita* presents certain pro-

[23] Baudelaire, Ch., *Les Fleurs du Mal*, ed. by A. v. Bever, Paris, 1917, p. 242.
[24] "Redeeming the time, because the days are evil." *Eph.*, V: 16.

blems. It is not in itself remarkable that Eliot should allude to Indian philosophy and religion – his special knowledge of the subject has been emphasized above – but it is perhaps surprising that he does so in a Section which is preceded by one dealing with the Annunciation and followed by one dealing with the Incarnation, both conceptions which, in Eliot's view, are of paramount significance to the Christian religion and which distinguish that religion from most others, including Hinduism and Buddhism.[25] Krishna, in the *Bhagavad-Gita,* is an incarnation of the supreme deity, but he is only one of many incarnations, some earlier and some later, whereas the Incarnation of Christ stands alone.

Though some critics maintain that Eliot's introduction of Krishna into "The Dry Salvages" is inappropriate and almost distracting, the allusion may instead be intended to reveal certain elements of Eliot's own beliefs which are nearer to Indian religious thought than might have been expected of a devout Anglican. In view of the fact that "The Dry Salvages", on the allegorical level of meaning, is concerned with the idea of the Incarnation and its prefiguration in the Annunciation, the reference to the *Gita* seems very appropriate, since that poem is also very much concerned with the idea of incarnation. This aspect of the *Gita* is cogently put in an introduction to that poem by Sarvepalli Radhakrishnan:

> The *Gītā* is interested in the process of redeeming the world, and so this aspect of Viṣṇu is emphasized. Kṛṣṇa represents the Viṣṇu aspect of the Supreme. The *Gītā* makes out that Kṛṣṇa is an incarnation (avataraṇa) or descent of the Divine into the human frame. If the Infinite God is manifested in finite existence throughout time, its special manifestation at one given moment and through the assumption of one single human nature by the Divine person is but the free fulfillment of that same movement by which the Divine plenitude freely fulfills itself and inclines toward the finite.[26]

Thus the difference between the doctrine of the *Gita* and the Christian doctrine lies, not in the idea of incarnation as such, which is common to both, but in the Christian emphasis on the special and

[25] Vide supra, p. 47.

[26] *A Source Book in Indian Philosophy*, p. 101.

singular nature of the Incarnation of Christ against the doctrine of repeated *avatars*.[27]

As a Christian Eliot is of course convinced of the special character of the Incarnation of Christ, but nevertheless it is noteworthy that the word "Incarnation" on its single appearance in the *Quartets* – in "The Dry Salvages" – appears without the definite article but with capital I. Thus the reader cannot feel quite sure whether Eliot is speaking of incarnation in a more general sense, or of the central event in sacred history. In the final Section of "The Dry Salvages" Eliot attempts a resolution of this apparent contradiction. In so far as he achieves a resolution, the excursus to the *Bhagavad-Gita* seems justified. There are further discrepancies, however, between Indian and Christian notions of time and history worth considering in the present context.

According to Scripture and traditionally Christian views, the Incarnation of Christ is not the only manifestation of the divine will in history; the Creation of the world and its annihilation after the Last Judgement are each, in this sense, unique. That is to say that, from the Christian point of view, the course of history has a definite goal in the second coming of Christ and the Last Judgement. But, in spite of this, Eliot affirms in "The Dry Salvages" II that we cannot think

> of a future that is not liable
> Like the past, to have no destination.

The apocalyptic aspect of time and history is thus completely absent in the *Four Quartets*. If the *Quartets* are intended to reveal a meaning in history, that meaning is not to be conceived as a goal or destination, but as something that can be apprehended at any moment of history, as a timeless and eternal pattern manifest in time.

This notion of history has much in common with certain Indian notions of the Wheel of Existence as a projection, albeit illusory, of the Divine, and from this point of view the reference to the *Gita* again seems appropriate. In effect, the Krishna passage is a modification of the Christian view of time and history as put forward elsewhere in the *Quartets* – a modification preparing the reader for

[27] *Bhagavad-Gita*, Ch. IV, 5–8. Cf. supra, p. 82.

the "message" of the final Section of "The Dry Salvages" that the meaning of history is not to be found within the dimension of past and future, but in the timeless patterns in time.

The lyric Fourth Section of "The Dry Salvages" is a prayer to the Virgin Mary as the patroness of sailors. The sailors no doubt stand for man and mankind, as in the earlier Sections of the poem, but their symbolic meaning may also be more particular. Written in 1941, this prayer "for all those who are in ships" and

> on behalf of
> Women who have seen their sons or husbands
> Setting forth, and not returning,

must have special significance as a prayer in wartime, and it shows the poet's feeling of solidarity with the people and nation. But it is also a prayer for "those / Whose business has to do with fish", and the fish is a well-known symbol of Him Who said, "Follow me, and I will make you fishers of men". This links the lyric with the allegorical or typical level of interpretation in the poem. The reference to the Virgin Mary also relates to this level of meaning, since it was she who, at the Annunciation, received the "hint half guessed" and the "gift half understood". And in the last line of the lyric, the tolling of the sea bell is identified as a "perpetual angelus" – a prayer said, at the sound of a bell, in commemoration of the Incarnation.

In the first, second and fourth of the *Quartets*, the Fifth Section contains a discussion of the art of poetry. "The Dry Salvages" V, however, apparently breaks this pattern – but only apparently.

The Section opens with a list of various occult practices:

> To communicate with Mars, converse with spirits,
> To report the behaviour of the sea monster,
> Describe the horoscope, haruspicate or scry,
> Observe disease in signatures, evoke
> Biography from the wrinkles of the palm
> And tragedy from fingers; release omens
> By sortilege, or tea leaves, riddle the inevitable
> With playing cards, fiddle with pentagrams
> Or barbituric acids, or dissect
> The recurrent image into pre-conscious terrors –
> To explore the womb, or tomb, or dreams;

All these things are reflections of "Men's curiosity" which "searches past and future / And clings to that dimension". Against this curiosity Eliot sets the apprehension of the "point of intersection of the timeless / With time". All the occult practices are attempts to divine the future by means of interpreting the features of time present as signs or symbols or omens. The poet of the *Four Quartets* is also concerned with the interpretation of signs and symbols, but not as omens of future events. He seeks the meanings of the signs, not in time, but in the timeless dimension, and to find this meaning is the object of the *Quartets*.

Interpreted in this way, the present passage confirms the assumption underlying this study of the *Quartets* that the structure and symbolism of the poems is something more than a means of communicating experience, that it is, in effect, a means of conveying a pattern of meanings inherent in the actual experience described. This is a symbolic relation which may be called a relation between sign and fulfilment, between literal meaning and spiritual meaning, or between type and antitype; in "The Dry Salvages" V, the two categories are called time and the timeless.

The apprehension of the "point of intersection" – the point where the eternal is realized in time – is said to be "an occupation for the saint", but to a certain extent it is also an occupation for the poet of the *Quartets*, as the imagery of the subsequent passage shows:

> For most of us, there is only the unattended
> Moment, the moment in and out of time,
> The distraction fit, lost in a shaft of sunlight,
> The wild thyme unseen, or the winter lightning
> Or the waterfall, or music heard so deeply
> That it is not heard at all, but you are the music
> While the music lasts.

Several of these images have appeared earlier in the *Quartets*. The "moment in and out of time" "lost in a shaft of sunlight", is the moment in the rose garden recalled in the phrase, "Sudden in a shaft of sunlight" (BN: V). "The wild thyme unseen" and "the winter lightning" derive from "East Coker" III, and the "music heard so deeply / That it is not heard at all" recalls the "unheard music hidden in the shrubbery" (BN: I) and also the passage on music in

"Burnt Norton" V. This recapitulation of symbols, suggesting a recollection in the speaker's mind of the experiences thus symbolized, leads up to the idea of Incarnation:

> These are only hints and guesses,
> Hints followed by guesses; and the rest
> Is prayer, observance, discipline, thought and action.
> The hint half guessed, the gift half understood, is Incarnation.

The timeless moments of the poet's experience are the signs to be interpreted; in them the eternal meaning is manifest in time. And this meaning is Incarnation – the Incarnation of Christ, but not that only. Here lies the resolution of the apparent contradiction between Indian and Christian conceptions of incarnation. As F. O. Matthiessen observed, Eliot's idea is entirely different from the "romantic heresies of Deification",[28] and yet Incarnation seems, in the present context of "The Dry Salvages", to refer to events that can be repeated, that are not singular or special. The resolution of the apparent paradox implied in this use of the term may be expressed thus: The Incarnation of Christ is a unique event, but constituting a "point of intersection of the timeless / With time", it stands in a definite relation to all other such points, which are the moments of ecstatic vision. This relation is that of types to antitype in the medieval, Dantean sense of these terms. As an antitype, the Incarnation stands alone, though it has its counterpart, from time to time, in the experience of the mystic.

In a sense the final Section of "The Dry Salvages" thus forms a conclusion to the preceding exploration of the ideas of time and eternity in the earlier *Quartets*. The full realization of the eternal meaning is an occupation for saints, but

> For most of us, this is the aim
> Never here to be realised;
> Who are only undefeated
> Because we have gone on trying;
> We, content at the last
> If our temporal reversion nourish
> (Not too far from the yew-tree)
> The life of significant soil.

[28] Matthiessen, p. 187.

With the last three lines, holding associations of death, home-coming to the soil and eternal life, comes the transition to "Little Gidding", the last of the *Four Quartets*, where these ideas receive their final development.

III

The last of the *Quartets* is related to a definite place, or rather to two places. One is, as in "Burnt Norton" and "East Coker", Eliot's own surroundings in London, and the other the chapel of Little Gidding – a small village in Huntingdonshire. The First Section of "Little Gidding" is the account of a visit to that chapel. Though using the more general pronoun "you", the poet obviously draws on his own experience in visiting Little Gidding. That experience, including a host of memories and historical associations, may be taken as the "literal" meaning of the poem.

The first paragraph is symbolic throughout, and yet it is also a picture of a winter's afternoon in the English countryside as effectively impressionistic as anything Eliot has written:

> Midwinter spring is its own season
> Sempiternal though sodden towards sundown,
> Suspended in time, between pole and tropic.
> When the short day is brightest, with frost and fire,
> The brief sun flames the ice, on pond and ditches,
> In windless cold that is the heart's heat,
> Reflecting in a watery mirror
> A glare that is blindness in the early afternoon.
> And glow more intense than blaze of branch, or brazier,
> Stirs the dumb spirit: no wind, but pentecostal fire
> In the dark time of the year. Between melting and freezing
> The soul's sap quivers. There is no earth smell
> Or smell of living thing. This is the spring time
> But not in time's covenant. Now the hedgerow
> Is blanched for an hour with transitory blossom
> Of snow, a bloom more sudden
> Than that of summer, neither budding nor fading,
> Not in the scheme of generation.
> Where is the summer, the unimaginable
> Zero summer?

The winter's afternoon here described is the actual time of the poet's visit to the chapel of Little Gidding, but it also seems to stand for the afternoon and winter of his own life. Eliot here reverts to a symbolism of seasons close to that previously used in the *Quartets*. The time of the visit to the garden of Burnt Norton was late summer; in "East Coker" it is "late November"; and here in the last of the *Quartets* it is winter. In "East Coker" the poet found the hoped for serenity in the autumn of his life replaced by an upsurge of emotions rightly belonging to spring and summer, but here in "Little Gidding" there is sharp but well-balanced contrast between winter and spring. This "midwinter spring", "not in time's covenant" and "not in the scheme of generation", is the forerunner of the "unimaginable / Zero summer". The psychological and spiritual implications seem clear. At a time when he might have expected sterility and drought, the aging poet feels "the soul's sap quiver" – the return of his creative powers – and this creativeness becomes to him a "type" of the divine creativeness manifest in the Nativity of Christ in the middle of winter. But the excitement implied in the soul's quivering is also related to the "Zero summer" – it is the fear, wonder and joy of the soul contemplating the "unimaginable" summer of eternal life that comes after winter and death.

The afternoon of the poet's visit to Little Gidding is also symbolic of the afternoon of his country. In the last of the *Quartets* the theme of history achieves its final development, and the name of Little Gidding itself holds several historical associations. It is the place where Nicolas Ferrar in 1626 founded an Anglican community organized on almost monastic principles and intended to provide the opportunity for a devout life of contemplation ("You are here to kneel") in the midst of the political and religious upheaval of the time. The place is also associated with King Charles I who visited it twice, the last time in secrecy at night, shortly after his final defeat ("If you came at night like a broken king"). As already mentioned, Richard Crashaw was also one of the visitors to Little Gidding, and George Herbert was deeply influenced by the religious ideas of Nicolas Ferrar.[29] Thus Little Gidding aptly symbolizes the particu-

[29] Vide supra, p. 60. Cf. Gardner, H., *The Art of T. S. Eliot*, London, 1949, pp. 176 ff., and Preston, p. 53, n.

lar period of English history referred to in the poem. Section III, for example, contains a number of references to the time of the Civil War:

> If I think, again, of this place,
> And of people, not wholly commendable,
> Of no immediate kin or kindness,
> But some of peculiar genius,
> All touched by a common genius,
> United in the strife which divided them;
> If I think of a king at nightfall,
> Of three men, and more, on the scaffold
> And a few who died forgotten
> In other places, here and abroad,
> And of one who died blind and quiet,
> Why should we celebrate
> These dead men more than the dying?
> It is not to ring the bell backward
> Nor is it an incantation
> To summon the spectre of a Rose.

There is the king, again, and an allusion to his execution and to the royal emblem of the Rose – the White Rose of the Stuarts.[30] There are the members of various political and religious parties and factions, "United in the strife which divided them", together with Milton, "who died blind and quiet".

It is not difficult to see the connection between that period of distress and war and the time when "Little Gidding" was written – 1941–42. Little Gidding seems to form an instance of the "significant soil" of which Eliot speaks in the last line of "The Dry Salvages", significant both as a historical symbol and as a symbol of a tendency in Eliot's own life and personality. Eliot has always shown a tendency to revert, in his thought and reading, to the seventeenth century, its poets and playwrights, its religious and political thinkers. It was that century which witnessed the formation of the Anglican Church to which Eliot was to turn and which nurtured many of the poets and preachers who have most deeply influenced his thought and his work. It is significant also that the political thought of that period raised the very problem that Eliot raises in his essay, *The Idea of a*

[30] See Stephenson, E. M., *T. S. Eliot and the Lay Reader*, 2nd ed. London, 1946, p. 91; Bradbury, J. M., "*Four Quartets*: The Structural Symbolism", *Sewanee Review*, Vol. 59, 1951, p. 268.

Christian Society – the problem of the place of the church in a secular society.

Thus the speaker's visit to Little Gidding in the midst of the war, becomes symbolic of his sense of continuity and tradition, his sense of history, but also of something else and much more important: his conviction that tradition and history, to have a real meaning, must partake of a timeless pattern. This is the theme of the First Section of "Little Gidding".

The second paragraph of the same Section resumes the theme of motion and travelling. In the previous *Quartets* motion was pictured either as circular or as progressing infinitely without a goal or destination, but here motion and travelling forward achieve dynamic purpose, not in the sense that an end or a goal is reached but because a timeless dimension is realized in time.

> And what you thought you came for
> Is only a shell, a husk of meaning
> From which the purpose breaks only when it is fulfilled
> If at all. Either you had no purpose
> Or the purpose is beyond the end you figured
> And is altered in fulfilment. There are other places
> Which also are the world's end, some at the sea jaws,
> Or over a dark lake, in a desert or a city –
> But this is the nearest, in place and time,
> Now and in England.

In prayer, the speaker goes on to say, and particularly in praying in the chapel at Little Gidding, he has experienced a moment of timeless vision similar to that in the garden of Burnt Norton. But the moment in the chapel is not only a repetition of the earlier one, it is also its fulfilment, and the experience in the garden "is altered in fulfilment" because it has become integrated with the historical and religious order of which Little Gidding is a symbol. Thus, here at the end of the First Section of "Little Gidding", the previous *Quartets* seem to realize their conclusion. The initial experience described in "Burnt Norton" has been explored and developed in its various aspects throughout the first three *Quartets*, and here it is repeated, but under completely different circumstances. Instead of the timeless moment "with no before and after" in the remote setting of the garden, the poet here connects the timeless moment with a historical tradition, and through that moment this tradition receives its meaning.

> Here, the intersection of the timeless moment
> Is England and nowhere. Never and always.

If this moment is a fulfilment of the moment in the garden, it is also altered in its fulfilment; that is to say that the meaning Eliot set out to explore appeared to be different from what he had expected at the outset. It is a meaning to be found within history, and yet it transcends history extending into the world of eternal life. This meaning, which "is beyond the end you figured", is indicated in the last two Sections of "Little Gidding".

The Second Section opens with three stanzas which, varying the Heracleitean idea of the chain of the four elements,[31] sum up the previous *Quartets* by recapitulation of significant images. There are the roses and the "Dust in the air suspended" from "Burnt Norton" I, the "wall, the wainscot and the mouse" from "East Coker" I, the images of water from "The Dry Salvages" and the "sanctuary and choir" reminiscent of the chapel at Little Gidding. This technique of recapitulating significant symbols is used already in the final Section of "Burnt Norton" and then in each of the subsequent *Quartets*. Each time the span of the speaker's recollections and the reader's associations becomes wider, and at the same time the whole set of poems is integrated into a unified symbolic structure.

However, these stanzas on the death of the elements have other implications as well. They immediately precede a scene in which the speaker is walking the streets of London just after an air raid, and some of the images in the stanzas suggest the destruction wrought by the bombs:

> Dust in the air suspended
> Marks the place where a story ended.
> Dust inbreathed was a house –
> – – –
> The parched eviscerate soil
> Gapes at the vanity of toil,
> Laughs without mirth.
> This is the death of earth.

[31] See Matthiessen, p. 190.

The scene that follows is enacted "In the uncertain hour before the morning" when the speaker encounters "some dead master", and the Section closes with the disappearance of this master "on the blowing of the horn" – the sounding of the "All Clear". The identity of the dead master seems deliberately obscured; it is not one but many, a "familiar compound ghost". The metre and tone of the passage suggest Dante, who probably forms the chief component in the "compound ghost", but there are also allusions to Virgil, Milton, Swift, Mallarmé and several others.[32]

The function of this episode seems to be partly to pay homage to all the poets of past ages, who belong to the literary tradition on which Eliot builds, and partly to bring to a conclusion all the previous passages dealing with the art of poetry. Since "Little Gidding" is concerned with connecting the private experience of the poet with a historical tradition, it seems appropriate that the expression of this experience should be connected with a literary tradition.

The theme of aging also recurs in the speech of the dead master. It is a gloomy picture he gives of old age, suggesting the fears of the aging poet himself. But like most of the themes of "Little Gidding", this one not only sums up the earlier developments of the theme of age but goes beyond them in pointing towards the final conclusion of the whole sequence of poems:

> From wrong to wrong the exasperated spirit
> Proceeds, unless restored by that refining fire
> Where you must move in measure, like a dancer.

The symbol of the dancer is familiar, but the symbol of fire is not fully developed until the end of "Little Gidding". Earlier in the present Section it is foreshadowed in "the flickering tongue" of "the dark dove" – the fire of the bomber – which also anticipates the tongues and dove of Section IV.

The Third Section of "Little Gidding" contains perhaps the poet's clearest account of his purpose in writing the *Four Quartets*:

[32] As usual, Grover Smith has discovered more allusions than any other critic: op. cit., pp. 285 ff.

This is the use of memory:
For liberation – not less of love but expanding
Of love beyond desire, and so liberation
From the future as well as the past.

This is a development and explanation of the idea of personal time – of memory as first introduced in "Burnt Norton" – and in speaking of the "use of memory" Eliot seems to refer to the motive and purpose of writing the *Quartets*. The use of memory is for "liberation / From the future as well as the past". That is to say that the recollections from the poet's earlier life realized in the experience in the garden and in the subsequent meditations of the *Quartets*, had the effect of liberating him from the "enchainment of past and future", and this effect was achieved by the "expanding / Of love beyond desire". In the ecstatic vision in the rose garden the recollections of desire, of the profane ecstasy, reflected in Eliot's earlier poems, received a meaning beyond their original temporal meaning, were recognized as having a divine purpose – as, in that sense, "types" of divine love.

The idea of personal time is also bound together with the idea of history. By the "expanding / Of love beyond desire" the individual achieves liberation from time, and "Thus", the poet goes on to say,

love of a country
Begins as attachment to our own field of action
And comes to find that action of little importance
Though never indifferent. History may be servitude,
History may be freedom. See, now they vanish,
The faces and places, with the self which, as it could, loved them,
To become renewed, transfigured, in another pattern.

The line of thought Eliot seems to be pursuing is that the sense of history, conceived as an extension of personal memory to include the past of the nation or even the race, may be a means of liberation. The "attachment to our own field of action" is expanded into and then beyond "love of a country". "History may be servitude" – if the temporal dimension of history is not transcended by the timeless dimension – but "History may be freedom" as well. The temporal content of memory and history must vanish, the "faces and places" referring, it seems, to the objects of desire and patriotic attachment, and also "the self which, as it could, loved them". In the line,

> To become renewed, transfigured, in another pattern,

Eliot indicates the end of the process of liberation from past and future. This is, in effect, a statement of the Dantean allegorical method used in the *Quartets*: the literal facts supplied by memory and history are renewed and transfigured in being interpreted on the various spiritual levels of meaning; and the pattern in which they are transfigured is a timeless pattern, for, as Eliot says in the last Section, "history is a pattern / Of timeless moments".

The transfiguration of human life and history in the timeless pattern must also involve a resolution of the antithesis of good and evil – this seems to be the meaning of the lines which follow, perhaps somewhat abruptly, upon the passage just considered:

> Sin is Behovely, but
> All shall be well, and
> All manner of thing shall be well.

This quotation from the *Revelations* of Julian of Norwich is the answer she received to the question how the existence of sin was to be reconciled with a good and righteous God.[33] The problem of sin and evil plays a subordinate part in the *Quartets*, and it is hardly to be expected that Eliot should really attack this problem here. But in quoting Dame Julian he indicates that in the divine order of things there is place even for that which to us appears as evil.

In the Fourth, lyric Section all the spiritual levels of meaning are set forth in symbols of great complexity. The "dark dove" of Section II is here transformed into the dove of the Holy Ghost appearing at the Baptism of Christ, and the "flickering tongue" of the aircraft's gun into the "cloven tongues like as of fire" which descended upon the Apostles on the day of Pentecost. The uniting element is fire, and the different aspects of fire relate to the different levels of meaning in "Little Gidding". The experience of

[33] See Gardner, H., "Four Quartets: A Commentary", pp. 75 f.

"midwinter spring" at the visit to the chapel of Little Gidding was said to be "pentecostal fire / In the dark time of the year", foreshadowing the allegorical or typical meaning of the poem which is the fire of the Holy Ghost, which again is love. The literal fire of destruction is also the fire of Hell, but, on the anagogical level, it may appear as the fire of purgation:

> unless restored by that refining fire
> Where you must move in measure, like a dancer.

The moral meaning, Helen Gardner has suggested, may be defined as Charity [34] – the human reflection of divine Love.

There is a deep tone of pain and despair in "Little Gidding" – a tone most fully heard in the Fourth Section. The poem refers to a time when London seemed to be abandoned to the element of destructive fire, when Hell seemed to be realized on earth. And the only hope of liberation from despair, the poet meditates, lies in regarding the affliction as a visitation of God, in the transfiguration of the fire of destruction into the fire of purgation:

> The only hope, or else despair
>   Lies in the choice of pyre or pyre –
>   To be redeemed from fire by fire.

Here, again, the poet raises the problem of evil, and the answer is the same as in the preceding Section:

> Who then devised the torment? Love.
> Love is the unfamiliar Name
> Behind the hands that wove
> The intolerable shirt of flame
> Which human power cannot remove.
>   We only live, only suspire
>   Consumed by either fire or fire.

What the lyric seems to say, then, is that the fire which made "the soul's sap quiver" in the aging poet and the destructive fire of the war may both be transformed into the fire of purgation and ascend to union with the flames of the Spirit as a manifestation of divine Love.

[34] Gardner, H., *The Art of T. S. Eliot*, p. 184.

The final Section of "Little Gidding" is not only a conclusion to that poem, but to the *Four Quartets* as a whole. It hardly contains a single line without an allusion to one of the earlier *Quartets*.

The Section opens with a reversion to the central idea of "East Coker":

> What we call the beginning is often the end
> And to make an end is to make a beginning.

This idea is then brought to bear on general problems of the art of poetry raised in the preceding *Quartets*. It is further connected with the theme of death and rebirth and finally it is led on to the conception of the timeless moment, the moment in the garden and that in the chapel. The symbolic and thematic development of the *Quartets* has come full circle, the poet is back where he started but the return is different from the outset because of the insight gained in the meantime:

> The moment of the rose and the moment of the yew-tree
> Are of equal duration. A people without history
> Is not redeemed from time, for history is a pattern
> Of timeless moments. So, while the light fails
> On a winter's afternoon, in a secluded chapel
> History is now and England.

The meaning of these lines may perhaps be expressed thus: The moment of mystic ecstasy occurring in temporal life and the moment of death (implied in the symbol of the yew-tree) are "of equal duration", i.e. beyond duration in the temporal sense, in the realm of timeless eternity. Since history, or rather the meaning of history, consists in a pattern of timeless moments, the absence of history, or of personal memories, does not redeem a people, or an individual, from time. The redemption of time lies, not in the negation or annihilation of time, but in the transfiguration of time in a timeless pattern. This transfiguration, however, must be achieved, for a people as well as for an individual, in time; the timeless must be apprehended in time, for "only through time time is conquered". So, while the moment in the garden seemed to be without past and future, the moment in the chapel of Little Gidding is related to time and history and to "significant soil". The timeless pattern of that moment is experienced as projected in time, and therefore the poet, in ending his long meditation on the idea of time and history in the *Quartets*, may say,

History is now and England.

The concluding paragraph of "Little Gidding" is preceded by a line quoted from the anonymous mystical treatise, *The Cloud of Unknowing*,

With the drawing of this Love and the voice of this Calling,

which together with the quotations from Julian of Norwich extend the spiritual tradition symbolized by the name of Little Gidding beyond the seventeenth century back to the early Christian mysticism in England.[35]

The last paragraph of the last of the *Four Quartets* is clearly devised as a "musical" finale, in which are gathered the symbols that have recurred throughout the whole sequence of poems. Here, on their final appearance, these symbols are no doubt intended to convey the whole range of meanings accumulated in them, and this wealth of meanings is in effect but another reflection of the deeply musical structure of the *Quartets*. The purely formal structure of a piece of music can often be analysed lucidly enough, but who can define the emotional effect it has? The same musical phrase, movement or composition may mean the very depth of anguish and despair to one hearer, and the height of joy to another, and still both may well be right in their interpretations. This is because music offers a good deal of freedom – what the sounds actually mean depends not a little on the hearer. But the poet is much more limited. The sounds he uses are words, and are hence tied, more or less, to particular connotations. In the *Four Quartets*, however, Eliot has attempted to use words as a musician uses sounds, so that they are sometimes capable of evoking, as we have seen, very varied interpretations. It is perhaps in this respect that the musical analogy implied in the use of the word "quartet" is most apt and most significant.

In the final paragraph of "Little Gidding" the technique of "mu-

[35] Gardner, H., "Four Quartets: A Commentary", p. 76.

sical" recapitulation is perhaps somewhat mechanically applied; it sometimes tends to become mere addition:

> We shall not cease from exploration
> And the end of all our exploring
> Will be to arrive where we started
> And know the place for the first time.
> Through the unknown, remembered gate
> When the last of earth left to discover
> Is that which was the beginning;
> At the source of the longest river
> The voice of the hidden waterfall
> And the children in the apple-tree
> Not known, because not looked for
> But heard, half-heard, in the stillness
> Between two waves of the sea.
> Quick now, here, now, always –

After a variation on the theme of beginning and end from "East Coker" comes the gate leading into the rose garden, to "the last of earth left to discover" which "was the beginning" – "our first world" (BN: I). The river and the waterfall both derive from "The Dry Salvages" (I and V), and the lines that follow echo "Burnt Norton" I and V and "The Dry Salvages" II.

In the very last lines of the poem, the images of the fire and the rose recur together with the only new image in the whole paragraph – "the crowned knot of fire". This image, though perhaps derived from mystical literature,[36] seems to be prompted by the preceding images; closely bound together as these images are, they may be said in effect to crown the whole work. All the preceding images of the paragraph are in some way symbolic of the timeless, mystic vision, and together they point to the Divine Reality which is also Fire and Love and which is the ground and guarantee of the final promise and prediction:

> And all shall be well and
> All manner of thing shall be well
> When the tongues of flame are in-folded
> Into the crowned knot of fire
> And the fire and the rose are one.

[36] Drew, E., *T. S. Eliot. The Design of His Poetry*, London, 1950, p. 239, n.

Thus the elaborate recapitulation of images and symbols is clearly intended, not only to bring the sequence to an artistically satisfactory close, but also to be, as it were, a benediction, a reaffirmation.

It has already been remarked that this conclusion owes a great deal to the conclusion of Dante's *Paradiso*. Eliot surely had no intention to rival Dante in writing these lines, but he seems to have aimed at a similar effect of elevation and at the same time of finality. The conclusion is a conclusion not only to "Little Gidding" and the whole sequence of the *Quartets* but, since some of the images revert to his earliest poems, a conclusion to Eliot's poetic work as a whole. Moreover, though written eighteen years ago, "Little Gidding" is the most recent poem published by Eliot and perhaps also his last.

If "Little Gidding", and the *Four Quartets* as a whole, fail to achieve the final effect the poet seems to have intended, the failure is certainly not one of poetic technique, or even of inspiration, but a failure of poetry as a medium of communication. Even the most complex poetic structure seems to fail fully to convey the meaning Eliot has tried to convey in the *Four Quartets* – a meaning not only beyond the scope of poetry but perhaps beyond communication in any medium. That Eliot himself is well aware of the limitations of poetry as a vehicle of religious truth, is evident from the meditations on the art of poetry contained in the *Quartets*. Nevertheless in completing the sequence in spite of all doubts and difficulties, Eliot reveals the depth and power of his inspiration and of the motives for persevering in the struggle to realize this inspiration. The psychological motive Eliot has indicated in describing the unwritten poem as "a burden which he [the poet] must bring to birth in order to obtain relief".[37] The moral motive may perhaps be expressed by a phrase borrowed from "East Coker": "For us there is only the trying. The rest is not our business."

[37] *On Poetry and Poets*, p. 98.

Bibliography

In this bibliography are included only such works as are quoted or otherwise referred to in the present study. It might perhaps have been convenient to have the works and articles on Eliot listed separately, but since observations on Eliot are to be found in a great number of works otherwise devoted to entirely different subjects, a division into a section of criticism and a general section has seemed impracticable.

The list of works by Eliot is confined to the editions consulted. For further particulars, see Donald Gallup's *T. S. Eliot. A Bibliography*, London, 1952.

I: *Works by Eliot* (in order of publication)

"Song", *Harvard Advocate*, June 3, 1907.

"Before Morning", *Harvard Advocate*, Nov. 13, 1908.

"Circe's Palace", *Harvard Advocate*, Nov. 25, 1908.

"Nocturne", *Harvard Advocate*, Nov. 12, 1909.

"Humoresque", *Harvard Advocate*, Jan. 12, 1910.

"The Development of Leibniz's Monadism", *The Monist*, Vol. 26, 1916, pp. 534–556.

"Leibniz's Monads and Bradley's Finite Centres", *The Monist*, Vol. 16, 1916, pp. 566–576.

The Sacred Wood. Essays on Poetry and Criticism, London, 1920.

For Lancelot Andrewes. Essays on Style and Order, London, 1928.

"The Latin Tradition". (Review of E. K. Rand's *Founders of the Middle Ages*), *Times Literary Supplement*, March 14, 1929.

Introduction to G. Wilson Knight's *The Wheel of Fire*, Oxf. Univ. Press, 1930.

The Use of Poetry and the Use of Criticism. Studies in the Relation of Criticism to Poetry in England, London, 1933.

After Strange Gods. A Primer of Modern Heresy, London, 1934.

The Rock. A Pageant Play, London, 1934.

"Literature and the Modern World" (1935), repr. in *The Literature of the United States*, ed. by W. Blair, T. Hornberger and R. Stewart, Chicago, 1949.

Collected Poems 1909–1935, London, 1936.

"An Anglican Platonist: The Conversion of Elmer More". (Review of More's *Pages from an Oxford Diary*), *Times Literary Supplement*, Oct. 30, 1937.

Introductory essay in *Revelation*, ed. by J. Baillie and H. Martin, New York, 1937, pp. 1–39.
Murder in the Cathedral, 4th ed., London, 1938.
"Last Words", *The Criterion*, Vol. 18, 1938–1939.
The Family Reunion, London, 1939.
The Idea of a Christian Society, London, 1939.
"Defense of the Islands", in *Britain at War*, ed. by M. Wheeler, New York, 1941, p. 8.
Four Quartets, London, 1944.
Letter to J. C. Pope, *American Literature*, Vol. 18, 1946–47, pp. 319–320.
"On Henry James", in *The Question of Henry James. A Collection of Critical Essays*, ed. by F. W. Dupee, London, 1947, pp. 123–133.
Notes towards the Definition of Culture, London, 1948.
A Sermon Preached in Magdalene College Chapel, Cambridge, 1948.
The Cocktail Party, London, 1950.
Quatre Quatuors, transl. by P. Leyris, notes by J. Hayward, Paris, 1950.
Selected Essays, 3rd enlarged ed., London, 1951.
"Brief über Ernst Robert Curtius", *Freundesgabe für Ernst Robert Curtius zum 14. April 1956*, Bern, 1956, pp. 25–27.
On Poetry and Poets, London, 1957.
Introduction to Paul Valéry's *The Art of Poetry*, (Bollingen Series XLV: *The Collected Works of Paul Valéry*, ed. by J. Mathews, Vol. 7), New York, 1958.
The Elder Statesman, London, 1959.

II: *Other Works Cited*

ALEXANDER, S., *Space, Time, and Deity*, I–II, London, 1920.
–, *Spinoza and Time*, London, 1921. (The 4th "Arthur Davis Memorial Lecture", the Jewish Historical Society, London.)
[ANON.], *On the Four Quartets of T. S. Eliot*, London, 1953.
[ARISTOTLE], *The Works of Aristotle*, ed. by W. D. Ross, Vol. VIII: *Metaphysica*, Oxf. Univ. Press, (1908) 1940.
AUERBACH, ERICH, "Figura", *Archivum Romanicum* (Firenze), Vol. 22, 1938.
ST. AUGUSTINE, *Confessions*, with an English transl. by W. Watts (1631), I–II, London, (1912) 1946. (The Loeb Classical Library.)
–, *On the Holy Trinity*, in *A Select Library of the Nicene and Post-Nicene Fathers of the Christian Church*. 1st Series, Vol. III, Grand Rapids, Michigan, 1956.
BABBITT, IRVING, *The Dhammapada*, Transl. from the Pāli with an Essay on Buddha and the Occident, Oxf. Univ. Press, 1936.
–, *Rousseau and Romanticism*, Boston/New York, 1919.
BARBER, C. L., "Strange Gods at T. S. Eliot's *The Family Reunion*", *T. S. Eliot. A Selected Critique*, ed. by L. Unger, New York, 1948.

BAUDELAIRE, CHARLES, *Les fleurs du mal*, ed. by A. van Bever, Paris, 1917.

–, *Le spleen de Paris*, ed. by A. van Bever, 3rd ed., Paris, 1915.

BEER, ERNST, *Thomas Stearns Eliot und der Antiliberalismus des XX. Jahrhunderts*, Wien, 1953. (Wiener Beiträge zur englischen Philologie, Bd. 61.)

BELL, C., "How Pleasant to Know Mr Eliot", *T. S. Eliot. A Symposium from C. Aiken et al.*, ed. by R. March and Tambimuttu, London, 1948.

BERGMAN, PÄR, *Något om bakgrunden till simultanismen i den moderna litteraturen*, (unpubl. thesis, Univ. of Uppsala), 1959.

BERGSON, HENRI, *Creative Evolution*, London, 1911, new ed. 1919.

–, *Durée et simultanéité à propos de la théorie d'Einstein*, Paris, 1922.

–, *Essai sur les données immédiates de la conscience*, (Diss.), Paris, 1889. (Transl.: *Time and Free Will. An Essay on the Immediate Data of Consciousness*, London, 1910.)

–, *An Introduction to Metaphysics*, London, 1913.

–, *Matter and Memory*, London, 1911.

[BLAKE, WILLIAM], *The Poetical Works of William Blake*, ed. by J. Sampson, Oxford, 1905.

BLAND, D. S., "Mr. Eliot on the Underground", *Modern Language Notes*, Vol. 68, 1953.

BODELSEN, C. A., *T. S. Eliot's Four Quartets. A Commentary*, Copenhagen, 1958.

BOETHIUS, *The Consolation of Philosophy*, with the English transl. of "I. T." (1609), London, (1918) 1946. (The Loeb Classical Library.)

BOHNSACK, FRITZ, *Zeit und Ewigkeit im Spätwerk T. S. Eliots. Versuch einer Deutung*, (unpubl. diss.), Hamburg, 1951.

BRABANT, FRANK HERBERT, *Time and Eternity in Christian Thought*, London, 1937.

BRADBURY, J. M., "*Four Quartets*: The Structural Symbolism", *Sewanee Review*, Vol. 59, 1951.

BRADLEY, FRANCIS HERBERT, *Appearance and Reality. A Metaphysical Essay*, London, 1893.

BRAUN, J., *Die liturgische Gewandung im Occident und Orient. Nach Ursprung und Entwicklung, Verwendung und Symbolik*, Freiburg i. B., 1907.

BRENT, W., *Discourse upon the Nature of Eternity, the Condition of a Separated Soul, According to the Grounds of Reason and Principles of the Christian Religion*, London, 1655.

BROAD, C. D., "Mr. Dunne's Theory of Time in An Experiment with Time", (1935), repr. in *Religion, Philosophy and Psychical Research. Selected essays*, London, 1953.

–, *Scientific Thought*, London, 1923.

BROOKS, C., "The Waste Land: An Analysis", *T. S. Eliot. A Study of his Writings by Several Hands*, ed. by B. Rajan, London, 1947.

BROWN, C. S., *Music and Literature. A Comparison of the Arts*, Athens, Georgia, 1949.

BROWN, J. H., *Eternity: is it a Biblical Idea? A Suggestion on the "Larger Hope" Question*, London, 1926.

BROWNE, SIR THOMAS, *Religio Medici*, ed. by J.-J. Denonain, Cambridge, 1953.
BROWNING, ROBERT, *The Ring and the Book*, Oxf. Univ. Press, 1912.
BUCHAN, J., *The Gap in the Curtain*, London, 1932.
BURNET, J., *Greek Philosophy*, I (*Thales to Plato*), London, 1914.
BUTZ, H. E., *The Relation of T. S. Eliot to the Christian Tradition*, (unpubl. thesis, Univ. of Ann Arbor), 1953.
CALLAHAN, J. F., *Four Views of Time in Ancient Philosophy*, Cambridge (Mass.), 1948.
CARROLL, LEWIS, *Alice's Adventures in Wonderland*, London, 1866.
CHYDENIUS, JOHAN, *The Typological Problem in Dante. A Study in the History of Medieval Ideas*, (Diss.), Helsingfors, 1958. (Societas Scientiarum Fennica. Commentationes Humanarum Litterarum XXV. 1.)
CLEOPHAS, M., "Notes on Levels of Meaning in 'Four Quartets'", *Renascence: A Critical Journal of Letters*, Vol. 2, 1950.
CONRAD, JOSEPH, *Youth: a Narrative, and Two Other Stories*, London, 1902.
COOMARASWAMY, ANANDA K., *The Dance of Śiva. Fourteen Indian Essays*, London, 1924.
–, "Primordial Images", *PMLA*, Vol. 61, 1946.
–, *Time and Eternity*, Ascona, 1947. (=Artibus Asiae, Suppl. VIII.)
CULLMAN, OSCAR, *Christus und die Zeit. Die urchristliche Zeit- und Geschichtsauffassung*, Zürich, 1946.
CURTIUS, ERNST ROBERT, *Europäische Literatur und lateinisches Mittelalter*, Bern, 1948.
–, *Kritische Essays zur europäischen Literatur*, 2nd enlarged ed., Bern, 1954.
[–], *Freundesgabe für Ernst Robert Curtius zum 14. April 1956*, Bern, 1956.
[DANTE], *Dantis Allagherii epistolae: The Letters of Dante*, transl. and ed. by P. Toynbee, Oxford, 1920.
–, *Tutte le opere*, ed. by E. Moore, London, 1909.
DAVENPORT, S. F., *Immanence and Incarnation*, Cambridge, 1925.
DAVIE, DONALD, "T. S. Eliot: The End of an Era", *Twentieth Century*, Vol. 159, 1956.
DAVIES, G., *Les poèmes commémoratifs de Mallarmé. Essai d'exégèse raisonnée*, (Diss.) Paris, 1950.
DE LA MARE, WALTER, *Collected Poems*, London, 1951.
DIBELIUS, MARTIN, *Der Brief des Jakobus*, 8th ed., Göttingen, 1956, (W. Meyer, *Kommentar über das Neue Testament*, 15. Abt.)
DIELS, HERMANN, *Die Fragmente der Vorsokratiker*, Berlin, 1903.
[DONNE, JOHN], *The Poems of John Donne*, ed. by H. Grierson, Oxf. Univ. Press, 1949.
DONNER, W., "Marcel Proust och den litterära traditionen i Frankrike", *Finsk Tidskrift*, Vol. 105, 1928.
DREW, E., *T. S. Eliot. The Design of his Poetry*, London, 1950.
DUNNE, J. W., *An Experiment with Time*, London, 1927.
–, *The Serial Universe*, London, 1934.

DURRELL, LAWRENCE, *Key to Modern Poetry*, London, 1952.

EDDINGTON, A. S., *Space, Time and Gravitation: An Outline of the General Relativity Theory*, Cambridge, 1920.

[ELIOT, T. S.], *T. S. Eliot. A Bibliography*, by Donald Gallup, London, 1952.

–, "The Eliot Family and St. Louis", (Appendix to an address delivered by Eliot at Washington University), *Washington University Studies*, N. S., Language and Literature, no. 23, St. Louis, 1953.

–, *T. S. Eliot. A Selected Critique*, ed. by L. Unger, New York, 1948.

–, *T. S. Eliot. A Study of his Writings by Several Hands*, ed. by B. Rajan, London, 1947.

–, *T. S. Eliot. A Symposium for his Seventieth Birthday*, ed. by N. Braybrooke, London, 1958.

–, *T. S. Eliot. A Symposium from C. Aiken et al.*, ed. by R. March and Tambimuttu, London, 1948.

EVANS, DAVID W., "T. S. Eliot, Charles Williams, and the Sense of the Occult", *Accent. A Quarterly of New Literature*, Vol. 14, 1954.

FLAMMARION, CAMILLE, *Death and its Mystery*, I–III, London, 1922–1923.

FOSTER, G. W., "The Archetypal Imagery of T. S. Eliot", *PMLA*, Vol. 60, 1945.

FOWLIE, WALLACE, *The Clown's Grail. A Study of Love in its Literary Expression*, London, 1948.

–, *Mallarmé*, Chicago, 1953.

FRANKENBERG, LLOYD, *Pleasure Dome: On Reading Modern Poetry*, Cambridge (Mass.), 1949.

FRAZER, JAMES GEORGE, *The Golden Bough. A Study in Magic and Religion*, I: 1–2, 3rd ed., London, (1911) 1932.

FREEMAN, R., *English Emblem Books*, London, 1948.

FUNATO, HIDEO, "T. S. Eliot's Idea of Time", *Rikkyo Review*, No. 16, 1955.

FUSSELL, B. H., "Structural Methods in *Four Quartets*", *ELH – A Journal of English Literary History*, Vol. 22, 1955.

FUSSELL, PAUL, "The Gestic Symbolism of T. S. Eliot", *ELH – A Journal of English Literary History*, Vol. 22, 1955.

GALLUP, DONALD, See [Eliot, T. S.].

GARDNER, HELEN, *The Art of T. S. Eliot*, London, 1949.

–, "Four Quartets: A Commentary", *T. S. Eliot. A Study of his Writings by Several Hands*, ed. by B. Rajan, London, 1947.

GENT, WERNER, *Die Philosophie des Raumes und der Zeit. Historische, kritische und analytische Untersuchungen*, Bonn, 1926.

–, *Die Raum–Zeit–Philosophie des 19. Jahrhunderts*, Bonn, 1930.

GILSON, E., *Dante et la philosophie*, Paris, 1939. (Etudes de philosophie médiévale, 28.)

GLASENAPP, H. VON, *Der Hinduismus. Religion und Gesellschaft im heutigen Indien*, München, 1922.

GLASSER, RICHARD, *Studien zur Geschichte des französischen Zeitbegriffs*, München, 1936. (Münchener Romanistische Arbeiten, V.)

Goldsbrough, G. F., *Recent Discussions on "Time"*, London, 1927.
Greenhill, E. Simmons, "The Child in the Tree. A Study of the Cosmological Tree in Christian Tradition", *Traditio*, Vol. 10, 1954.
Guillaume de Lorris, *Le roman de la rose*, I, ed. by P. Marteau, Orléans, 1878.
Gunn, J. Alexander, *The Problem of Time. An Historical & Critical Study*, London, 1929.
Hall, Donald, "The Art of Poetry I: T. S. Eliot" (Interview with Eliot), *Paris Review*, No. 21, 1959.
Häusermann, H. W., "'East Coker' by T. S. Eliot", *English Studies*, Vol. 23, 1941.
[Hayward, J.], (Notes to the English transl. of the *Quartets*:) *Quatre Quatuors*, Paris, 1950.
Heidegger, Martin, "Sein und Zeit", *Jahrbuch für Philosophie und phänomenologische Forschung*, Vol. 7, 1927.
Heracleitus, *On the Universe*, with an English transl. by W. H. S. Jones, London, (1931) 1943. (The Loeb Classical Library.)
–, See also Diels, H.
[Herbert, George], *The Works of George Herbert*, ed. by F. E. Hutchinson, Oxford, 1941.
Hodgson, John, *The Time-Journey of Dr. Barton: An Engineering and Sociological Forecast*, London, 1929.
Howarth, Herbert, "Eliot, Beethoven, and J. W. N. Sullivan", *Comparative Literature*, Vol. 9, 1957.
Hügel, Friedrich von, *Eternal Life. A Study of its Implications and Applications*, Edinburgh, 1912.
Hulme, T. E., *Speculations. Essays on Humanism and the Philosophy of Art*, ed. by H. Read, London, (1924) 1936.
Huxley, A., *Point Counter Point*, London, (1928) 1947. (Collected Works, 4.)
Hyde, A. G., *George Herbert and His Times*, London, 1906.
Inge, William Ralph, "Is the Time Series Reversible?", *Proceedings of the Aristotelian Society*, Vol. 21, London, 1920–1921.
–, *The Philosophy of Plotinus*, I–II, London, 1918.
–, *The Platonic Tradition in English Religious Thought*, London, 1926.
James, Henry, *The Sense of the Past*, together with James' own notes for the novel ed. by Percy Lubbock, London, 1917.
[–], *The Question of Henry James. A Collection of Critical Essays*, ed. by F. W. Dupee, London, 1947.
James, William, *Collected Essays and Reviews*, London, 1920.
Johansen, S., *Le symbolisme. Etudes sur le style des symbolistes français*, Copenhagen, 1945.
[John of the Cross], *The Complete Works of St. John of the Cross*, I–III, transl. and ed. by E. Allison Peers, London, 1934–1935.
Joyce, J., *Ulysses*, (1922), New York, 1934.
Jung, C. G., *Modern Man in Search of a Soul*, New York, 1933.
Kenner, Hugh, "Eliot's Moral Dialectic", *Hudson Review*, Vol. 2, 1949–50.

Kipling, R., *Traffics and Discoveries*, London, 1904.

Knight, W. F. Jackson, "T. S. Eliot as a Classical Scholar", *T. S. Eliot. A Symposium for his Seventieth Birthday*, ed. by N. Braybrooke, London, 1958.

Knox, George A., "Quest for the Word in Eliot's *Four Quartets*", *ELH – A Journal of English Literary History*, Vol. 18, 1951.

Laboulle, M.-J.-J., "T. S. Eliot and Some French Poets", *Revue de Littérature Comparée*, Vol. 16, 1936.

Langslet, Lars Roar, "Tidsopplevelsen i Eliots 'Four Quartets'", *Kirke og Kultur* (Oslo), Vol. 61, 1956.

Lawrence, D. H., *The Prussian Officer and Other Stories*, London, 1914.

Lebois, A., "T. S. Eliot, les Imagistes et Jean de Boschère", *Revue de Littérature Comparée*, Vol. 26, 1952.

Lehmann, J., "T. S. Eliot Talks About Himself and the Drive to Create", *The New York Times Book Review*, Vol. 58, no. 48, Nov. 29, 1953.

Leisegang, Hans, *Die Begriffe der Zeit und Ewigkeit im späteren Platonismus*, Münster i. W., 1913. (Beiträge zur Geschichte der Philosophie des Mittelalters, Bd. XIII. Heft 4.)

Leone, H., "The Vedantic Absolute", *Mind*, Vol. 21, 1912.

Levý, J., "Synthesis of Antitheses in the Poetry of T. S. Eliot", *Essays in Criticism*, Vol. 2, 1952.

Lewis, C. S., *The Allegory of Love. A Study in Medieval Tradition*, Oxford, 1936.

Lewis, Wyndham, *Time and Western Man*, London, 1927.

Lövgren, Sven, *The Genesis of Modernism. Seurat, Gaugain, van Gogh and French Symbolism in the 1880's*, (Diss. Uppsala), Stockholm, 1959.

Lübker, R., "Vier Quartette von T. S. Eliot. Versuch zu einer Einführung", *Die Neueren Sprachen*, N. F., 1954.

MacCallum, R., *Imitation & Design and Other Essays*, ed. by W. Blissett, Toronto, 1953.

MacCarthy, H. E., "T. S. Eliot and Buddhism", *Philosophy East and West*, (Univ. of Hawaii), Vol. 2, no. 1.

MacKenzie, J. S., "Time and the Absolute", *Mind*, Vol. 36, 1927.

Mallarmé, S., *Poésies*, 51st ed., Paris, 1937.

Mandonnet, P., *Dante le théologien. Introduction à l'intelligence de la vie, des oeuvres et de l'art de Dante Alighieri*, Paris, 1935.

Martin, P. W., *Experiment in Depth. A Study of the Work of Jung, Eliot and Toynbee*, London, 1955.

Martz, L. L., "The Wheel and the Point: Aspects of Imagery and Theme in Eliot's Later Poetry", *T. S. Eliot. A Selected Critique*, ed. by L. Unger, New York, 1948.

[Marvell, Andrew], *The Poems and Letters of Andrew Marvell*, I–II, ed. by H. M. Margoliouth, Oxford, 1927.

Masters, C., "Some Observations on 'Burnt Norton'", *American Prefaces*, Vol. 6, 1941.

Matthiessen, F. O., *American Renaissance. Art and Expression in the Age of Emerson and Whitman*, Oxf. Univ. Press, 1941.
–, *The Achievement of T. S. Eliot. An Essay on the Nature of Poetry*, 2nd ed., rev. & enl., Oxf. Univ. Press, 1947.
Mauron, Charles, "On Reading Einstein", *Criterion*, Vol. 10, 1930. (Transl. by Eliot.)
Maxwell, D. E. S., *The Poetry of T. S. Eliot*, London, 1952.
Maxwell, J. C., "Reflections on *Four Quartets*", *Month*, N. S., Vol. 4, 1950.
Mazzeo, Joseph Anthony, *Structure and Thought in the "Paradiso"*, Ithaca, New York, 1958.
Mendilow, A. A., *Time and the Novel*, London, 1952.
Meyerhoff, Hans, *Time in Literature*, Berkeley/Los Angeles, 1955.
[Milton], *The Poetical Works of John Milton*, IV, London, 1801.
More, Paul Elmer, *The Greek Tradition. From the Death of Socrates to the Council of Chalcedon*, Princeton, 1917–1931:
Introduction: *Platonism*, 1917.
Vol. I: *The Religion of Plato*, (1921) 1928.
Vol. II: *Hellenistic Philosophies*, 1923.
Vol. III: *The Christ of the New Testament*, 1924.
Vol. IV: *Christ the Word*, 1927.
Complementary Vol.: *The Catholic Faith*, 1931.
–, *Shelburne Essays*, I–XI Series, Boston/New York, 1904–1922.
Morrissette, Bruce A., "T. S. Eliot and Guillaume Apollinaire", *Comparative Literature*, Vol. 5, 1953.
Murray, Rosalind, *Time and the Timeless*, London, 1942.
Musgrove, S., *T. S. Eliot and Walt Whitman*, Wellington, New Zealand, 1952.
The Mythology of All Races, ed. by L. H. Gray, Boston, 1916–1932.
Newbolt, Henry, *A New Study of English Poetry*, London, 1917, repr. 1919.
–, "Poetry and Time", *Proceedings of the British Academy*, 1917–1918, London, 1918.
Ouspensky, P. D., *A New Model of the Universe: Principles of the Psychological Method in its Application to Problems of Science, Religion and Art*, London, 1931.
–, *Tertium Organum. The Third Canon of Thought: A Key to the Enigmas of the World*, Rochester, N. Y., 1920.
Ovid, *Metamorphoses*, I–II, London, (1916) 1946. (The Loeb Classical Library.)
Oxford Companion to Music, See Scholes, P. A.
[Pascal], *Les Pensées de Blaise Pascal*, I–II, ed. by A Molinier, Paris, 1877–1879.
[Plato], *Plato with an English Translation*, VII, by R. G. Bury, London, (1929) 1942. (The Loeb Classical Library.)
Plotinus, *The Enneads*, transl. by Stephen MacKenna, 2nd ed. rev. by B. S. Page, London, 1956.
Pope, J. C., "Prufrock and Raskolnikov Again: A Letter from Eliot", *American Literature*, Vol. 18, 1946–47.

POULET, GEORGES, *Studies in Human Time*, (transl.), Baltimore, 1956.
[POUND, EZRA], *The Letters of Ezra Pound 1907–1941*, ed. by D. D. Paige, London, 1951.
PRAZ, M., "T. S. Eliot and Dante", *T. S. Eliot. A Selected Critique*, ed. by L. Unger, New York, 1948.
PRESTON, RAYMOND, *"Four Quartets" Rehearsed. A Commentary on T. S. Eliot's Cycle of Poems*, London, 1946.
PROCLUS DIADOCHUS, *In Platonis Timaeum Commentaria*, I–III, ed. by E. Diehl, Leipzig, 1903–1906.
PROUST, M., *A la recherche du temps perdu*, Paris, 1913–1928.
–, *Remembrances of Things Past*, transl. by C. K. Scott Moncrieff and S. Hudson, London, 1922–1931.
RADHAKRISHNAN, S., See *A Source Book in Indian Philosophy.*
RAJAN, B., "The Unity of the Quartets", *T. S. Eliot. A Study of his Writings by Several Hands*, ed. by B. Rajan, London, 1947.
Revelation, by G. Aulén, K. Barth, T. S. Eliot et al., ed. by J. Baillie and H. Martin, New York, 1937.
RICHARDS, I. A., *Principles of Literary Criticism*, 2nd ed., London, (1926) 1949.
ROBBINS, R. H., *The T. S. Eliot Myth*, New York, 1951.
ROYCE, JOSIAH, *The World and the Individual*, II, New York, 1901.
RUSSELL, BERTRAND, *The A.B.C. of Relativity*, London, 1925.
–, *History of Western Philosophy and its Connection with Political and Social Circumstances from the Earliest Times to the Present Day*, London, 1946.
–, "The Philosophy of Bergson", *The Monist*, Vol. 22, 1912.
SCHAYER, STANISLAW, *Contributions to the Problem of Time in Indian Philosophy*, Krakow, 1938. (Krakau, Akad. umiejętn., Komisja oriental., Prace, N:o 31.)
SCHEFTELOWITZ, J., *Die Zeit als Schicksalsgottheit in der Indischen und Iranischen Religion. Kāla und Zruvan*, Stuttgart, 1929. (Beiträge zur indischen Sprachwissenschaft und Religionsgeschichte, H. 4.)
SCHENK, W., "The Experience and the Meaning. A Note on T. S. Eliot's 'Burnt Norton'", *Humanitas* (Manchester), Vol. 1, 1947.
SCHOLES, P. A., *The Oxford Companion to Music*, 5th ed., Oxf. Univ. Press, 1944.
SCOTT, N. A., *Rehearsals of Discomposure. Alienation and Reconciliation in Modern Literature: Franz Kafka, Ignazio Silone, D. H. Lawrence, T. S. Eliot*, London, 1952.
[SHELLEY], *The Complete Poetical Works of Percy Bysshe Shelley*, ed. by Thomas Hutchinson, Oxf. Univ. Press, 1907.
SMIDT, KRISTIAN, *Poetry and Belief in the Work of T. S. Eliot*, (Diss.), Oslo, 1949. (Skrifter utgitt av Det Norske Videnskaps-Akademi i Oslo II. Hist.-Filos. Klasse. 1949. No. I.)
–, "Point of View in T. S. Eliot's Poetry", *Orbis Litterarum*, Vol. 14, 1959.
SMITH, GROVER, *T. S. Eliot's Poetry and Plays. A Study in Sources and Meaning*, Chicago, 1956.

A Source Book in Indian Philosophy, ed. by S. Radhakrishnan and C. A. Moore, Princeton, 1957.

Stace, W. T., *Time and Eternity. An Essay in the Philosophy of Religion*, Princeton, 1952.

Stein, Gertrude, *Composition as Explanation*, London, 1926.

Stephenson, E. M., *T. S. Eliot and the Lay Reader*, 2nd ed., London, 1946.

Stocks, J. L., *Time, Cause and Eternity*, London, 1938.

Strich, Fritz, *Der Dichter und die Zeit. Eine Sammlung von Reden und Vorträgen*, Bern, 1947.

Strömsdörfer, Ilse, *Der Begriff der Zeit bei T. S. Eliot*, (unpubl. diss.), München, 1957.

Sweeney, J. J., "East Coker: A Reading", *T. S. Eliot. A Selected Critique*, ed. by L. Unger, New York, 1948.

Symons, Arthur, *The Symbolist Movement in Literature*, London, 1899.

Taupin, René, *L'Influence du symbolisme français sur la poésie américaine (de 1910 à 1920)*, (Diss.), Paris, 1929.

Typing, W., *Discourse of Eternity*, Oxford, 1633.

Unger, Leonard, *The Man in the Name. Essays on the Experience of Poetry*, Minneapolis, 1956.

–, "T. S. Eliot's Rose Garden", *T. S. Eliot. A Selected Critique*, ed. by L. Unger, New York, 1948.

[Vaughan], *The Works of Henry Vaughan*, ed. by L. C. Martin, 2nd ed., Oxford, 1957.

Wagner, Robert D., "The Meaning of Eliot's Rose-Garden", *PMLA*, Vol. 69, 1954.

Walton, I., *The Life of Mr. George Herbert*, London, 1670.

Weigand, Elsie, "Rilke and Eliot: The Articulation of the Mystic Experience", *Germanic Review*, Vol. 30, 1955.

Weinhold, K., *Glücksrad und Lebensrad*, Berlin, 1892. (Philosophische und historische Abhandlungen der königlichen Akademie der Wissenschaften zu Berlin, 1892.)

Weitz, M., "T. S. Eliot: Time as a Mode of Salvation", *Sewanee Review*, Vol. 60, 1952.

Wellek, R. & Warren, A., *Theory of Literature*, New York, 1949.

Wheelwright, P., *The Burning Fountain. A Study in the Language of Symbolism*, Indiana Univ. Press, 1954.

–, "Eliot's Philosophical Themes", *T. S. Eliot. A Study of his Writings by Several Hands*, ed. by B. Rajan, London, 1947.

White, E. L., *The Eternal Journey*, London, 1930.

Whitehead, A. N., *The Concept of Nature*, Cambridge, 1920.

Whitman, W., *Leaves of Grass*, I–III, ed. by R. M. Bucke, Th. B. Harned, and H. L. Traubel, New York/London, s. d. (1919).

Wilder, T., *The Cabala*, London, (1926) 1928.

Williams, Charles, *The Greater Trumps*, London, 1932.

Williamson, George, *A Reader's Guide to T. S. Eliot. A Poem-by-Poem Analysis*, New York, 1953.
Wilson, Frank, *Six Essays on the Development of T. S. Eliot*, London, 1948.
Wood, Frank, "Rilke and Eliot: Tradition and Poetry", *Germanic Review*, Vol. 27, 1952.
Wordsworth, J. C., "Time as Succession", *Mind*, Vol. 26, 1917.
Zimmer, Heinrich, *Myths and Symbols in Indian Art and Civilization*, ed. by J. Campbell, New York, 1946. (Bollingen Series VI.)

Index of Names

REFERENCES INCLUDE THE FOOTNOTES